WALK LIKE A MOUNTAIN
THE HANDBOOK OF BUDDHIST WALKING PRACTICE

Innen Ray Parchelo

WALK LIKE A MOUNTAIN
The Handbook of Buddhist Walking Practice
Innen Ray Parchelo

Text © Innen Ray Parchelo, 2012
All rights reserved

Book design: Karma Yönten Gyatso

Cover photo: Walking Buddha © Pitsanu Kraichana
Henro-pilgrim, p. 122: © Radu Razvan
All other pictures © Innen Ray Parchelo

Published by
The Sumeru Press Inc.
PO Box 2089, Richmond Hill, ON
Canada L4E 1A3

LIBRARY AND ARCHIVES CANADA CATALOGUING IN PUBLICATION

Parchelo, Innen Ray, 1949-
Walk like a mountain: the handbook of Buddhist walking practice /
Innen Ray Parchelo.

Includes bibliographical references.
ISBN 978-1-896559-17-9 paperback
ISBN 978-1-896559-18-6 e-book

1. Meditation–Buddhism. 2. Walking–Religious aspects–Buddhism. I. Title.

BQ5612.P37 2012   294.3'4435   C2012-907731-3

 For more information about The Sumeru Press
visit us at *www.sumeru-books.com*

Table of Contents

7   **FOREWORD**

9   **INTRODUCTION**

12   **PREFACE**
      Why Leave Your Abode?

      Chapter 1
24   **STIRRINGS FOR THE ROAD**
      Walking – the Hidden Life of the Buddha
      Walking Practice as Metaphor
      Walking as a 'Yoga'
      Walking as a Contemplative Practice

      Chapter 2
41   **IMAGININGS**
      Walking as Practice: Sitting, Walking; Walking, Sitting
      Walking with Jizo
      Dharma Masters Go On Foot
      Non-Buddhist Advice

      Chapter 3
61   **THRESHOLD – FOOT AND STEPS**
      Walking with the Whole Body

Chapter 4

77 **THRESHOLD: PREPARATIONS**
    Equipment, Sticks and Poles
    Purification and Dedication
    Winter Walking
    Companion Dogs
    Documentation: Cameras and Journals
    Disability Considerations

Chapter 5

101 **JOURNEY 1: FIRST STEPS**
    First Walking Practices
    Walking Practice # 1: Kinhin
    Alternate Contemplative Walking
    Leading a Formal Walking Practice

Chapter 6

117 **JOURNEY 2: CROSSING**
    Walking and Working
    Walking Practice # 2: Walking as Daily Life
    Walking Practice # 3: Alms Rounds

Chapter 7

131 **THRESHOLD 2: TURNING BACK**
    The Turning Point
    Walking Practice # 4: Circumambulation: Going Around in Circles
    Walking Practice # 5: The Sound of Walking – Walking Nembutsu
    Contemporary Practice: Mundy's Prayer Walking

Chapter 8

144   JOURNEY 3: THE LONG ROAD BACK

    The Road Back

    Walking Practice # 6: Pilgrimage

    Walking Practice # 7: Kaihogyo

Chapter 9

160   JOURNEY 4: NEW WALKING

    The End in Sight

    Walking Practice # 8: Walking a Symbolic Landscape

    Walking Practice # 9: Into the Labyrinth

    The Manda-Labyrinth

    Walking Practice # 10: "Sauntering" with Thoreau

    Walking Practice # 11: Walking for Change

Chapter 10

185   RETURNING HOME

    The Narrow Beach

    What Has Been Learned

    Re-entering Our Dwelling – Imagining The Next Crossing

198   AFTERWORD

    The Society

    The Scholarly Tome

    Walker's Supports

202   A WALKER'S BIBLIOGRAPHY

FOREWORD

In one of my reflections for a past newsletter, I wrote:

> I walked outside to do chores shortly after sunrise today. The sun was shining. The fragrance of smoke from our wood stove punctuated the coolness of the air. Dry leaves crunched under foot. The sound of geese flying south was a pleasant accompaniment to a glorious morning. As I lingered for a few minutes taking it all in, the Native American greeting to the sun and mountains, along with the salutation to the Buddhas in the Ten Directions arose in my mind. I mouthed the words quietly. This simple informal action transformed a mundane enjoyable pause in my routine into a sacred observance. It was an act of true mindfulness, a moment of veneration of the Buddha nature that resides all around us, a joyful expression of spirit. The Buddhist Path is a path of clarity and tranquillity through its many practices. It may satisfy the intellect, as well as guide us morally and ethically.

All around we are touched by and in touch with sentient beings who reside in the Buddha realms with us. This is important. Buddhism as a whole, and Tendai-shu in particular, communicate with the natural world of trees and grasses, small and large animals, streams and hills, seas and deserts. This is not a form of sentimentalism; it is a recognition that there is no distinction of spirit between the corporeal form we take as humans and the trout negotiating a stream's eddy. How can we connect with each other as humans and not extend our gaze to our environment?

Meditation in motion out-of-doors offers fertile ground for myriad contemplations and includes esoteric practice, devotion and veneration of nature. The body, along with the faculties of speech and mind is yet another channel by which to experience and manifest the Dharma. By engaging all three simultaneously, the effect is synergistic, each reinforcing the other. Practitioners often find that one channel seems more beneficial than another, but practising all three simultaneously will yield a balanced development.

In the pages of *Walk Like A Mountain*, Innen has provided us with more than encouragement and more than simple instructions or technique. This is a 'handbook' as he has intended to share with us, his fellow journeyers. It is like a trail companion that reminds us of the possibility of the trail and, at the same time, the promise of the Buddha-way. Our path is one of re-discovering our True Nature, and that brings us the greatest joy possible. However, while we are called to the Path, we need to remember that each step on the way is itself the path. Because it is all these things and more, do not lose sight that it is equally a path overflowing with simple pleasures. Linger just a tad and soak in the joy of the moment, you will be fulfilling the promise of the Buddhist Path.

I recommend we each set our feet on our chosen Path, and hope Innen's notes for the journey will bring us to the trail's end and the clear and tranquil path that takes us there.

Rev. Monshin Paul Naamon
Secretary General
Tendai-shu North America District
East Chatham, New York

INTRODUCTION

Walkers are also ruminators. Not that we chew grass, our cud is usually some random thought or narrative that floats around like the kicked-up dust from the road. Some years ago, during one of my walks down whatever country road happened to be close to home, I began to ruminate over what seemed like a minor mystery in my understanding of the Buddha-way.

I recognize that the Buddha-way is not the narrative that floats around many walkers' minds, but it does mine, mostly because of the personal and professional interests that have occupied me for a long time. Personally, I have studied, practised and taught the Buddha-way within several traditions since I was an older teen, more than forty years ago. Theravada, the two flavours of Zen and most recently Tendai and Pure Land, have been the vehicles carrying me towards the other shore. This has culminated in my ordination as the first Tendai priest in Canada and my continued development of Tendai in Canada, primarily through the Red Maple Sangha I founded in 2002.

Like a true Gemini, I jump between two parallel and often intersecting paths. In addition to my Dharma-path, I have been a social worker and community developer for thirty-plus years, almost exclusively in the rural communities of Eastern Ontario where I have found my homes and walking trails. Over that time I have watched with delight and some concern as Buddhist practice, especially *vipassana*-style mindfulness, emerged as an important modality in the securing of mental health. Since the appearance of the earliest treatment model, called Mindfulness-based Stress Reduction (MBSR), movement practices like walking have come to occupy a regular, if minor, position in the inventory of mindfulness skills.

About the cud, my mystery: very simply put, we know the Buddha got up from his seat under the Bodhi tree and stepped into religious history. He walked across North India and established a monastic order that walked with him. His birth story distinguishes him by his three steps. As a mature and troubled adult, when he left his palace he walked into the forest and walked for decades with a group of fellow renunciants. His early symbol was his foot-print (*padakan*). And on and on. The question that rolled around in my walking thoughts and led to this book has to do with the apparent relegation of walking as practice, as cultural image and as aspect of religious history to a minor role or even to be dismissed as unimportant. When I tried to imagine the Buddha's time, or that of Jesus or Moses or any other religious leader, when I imagined them walking for days and months as they shared their teaching, it seemed without question that some major teaching and practice would have happened along the way. It seemed without question that this walking experience would have played a key role in the cultivation of contemplative life. And so I wondered why it wasn't explored in great detail in subsequent literature or teaching.

Initially, I imagined a *magnum opus*, a wise and scholarly tome that examined images of foot, walk and path in the most obscure Indian and Chinese texts, that traced the teaching tradition across all schools. That may one day be written. However, in the end, the practical side, the walker, won out. Hence this book, which is not the scholarly tome but a handbook. It takes you on a journey; it shows you how to transform the ordinary act of walking into a beautiful and energized contemplative act.

I think it was my friend Greg Krech who tells his story of walking a trail in his Vermont neighbourhood. He recalls walking up the trail and grumbling at how rough and untended the trail was. He slipped into blame and resentment at the poor quality of the path. Once at the top, he recognized how collapsed his mind-state had become and approached the descent with a perspective open to gratitude. Walking the same trail he saw all the evidence of hundreds of personhours which had cleared branches, restored the ground and protected precious plants. In his haste and selfish-mind he had missed all the evidence of other hands.

Now that I have completed my journey, may I acknowledge the many hands involved in clearing the way for this project. Once more, I thank my parents and my walking-mentor, Ray Lowes, for introducing me to the trail so early in my life. I thank my precious friend and educator, Dr. Nalini Devdas, who opened my Dharma-eye and has always insisted on thoroughness and persistence in writing and study. I thank my sensei, Rev. Monshin Paul Naamon, Secretary General of the Tendai-shu North America District, who helped me learn many of the walking practices described in this book and in so many other ways. I thank all the writer-practitioners of the trail who have helped me to understand the source material of the book. I owe special thanks to Thomas Tweed for his notion of religions as "crossing and dwelling", to China Miéville for his imagined world of in-between/un-seen spaces. I thank my publisher, John Negru who planted the seed of this book and helped make it a reality. I thank my wife, Judy

LeClair who encouraged me to write and bore my absence and solitude with such understanding and patience. I thank my beloved four-legged trail-companion, Joshu-daiosho who brought me back to the trail so many times. I thank all my human trail-companions, those who have walked with me, short trail, long trail, winter, summer, all over the world. I bow to all my fellow walkers and un-official *henro*-pilgrims who have kept up the drumbeat of steps on the Earth. They remind me of *dogyo ninin,* we never walk alone. Last, but hardly least, I bow and offer thanks to Jizo-bosatsu, the Bodhisattva of the road. Even before I knew his name, he guided me along every trail, calling me forward, urging me to risk another step. To him, my constant road companion, I offer up whatever merit may arise from this book and every step taken along the way. *Om namu jizo busa.*

PREFACE
DWELLING

> When the spring stirs my blood
> With the instinct to travel,
> I can get enough gravel
> On the Old Marlborough Road.
>
> What is it, what is it
> But a direction out there,
> And the bare possibility
> Of going somewhere?
>
> If with fancy unfurled
> You may leave your abode,
> You may go round the world
> By the Old Marlborough Road
>
> From *The Old Marlborough Road*,
> Henry Thoreau, *Walking*

WHY LEAVE YOUR ABODE?

Its hard for me to separate walking from other practice forms, since it became fused to my practice regimen very early on. Walking had been a time of reflection for me from my early teens, well before my introduction to Buddhadharma. There seemed to be something in the steady rhythm of a walking pace that supported those times I reserved for contemplating the big questions of life for the first time.

Like the 19th century American philosopher-walker, Henry David Thoreau, I felt it important to combine reflection and walking. In his essay called *Walking*, he notes: "...moreover, you must walk like a camel, which is said to be the only beast which ruminates when walking" (*Walking*, p. 7). And like Thoreau, as much as a city teenager could, I sought relief from the roads and highways. I very often waited until dusk or after dark, when I could visit the many quiet ponds, parks and canal-trails near my home. Again, like Thoreau, I understood the difference between the urban thoroughfares fronted by shops, and those other, more desirable spaces where the commercial grid dissolved into foot-paths and river-banks. He proposed:

> "When we walk, we naturally go to the fields and woods; what would become of us, if we walked only in a garden or mall.... Roads are made for horses and men of business. I do not travel in them much, comparatively, because I am not in a hurry to get to any tavern or grocery or livery-stable or depot to which they lead. I am a good horse to travel, but not from choice a roadster." (*Walking*, p. 8, 12)

An early contemplative walking experience occurred while I was falling into what was to become my life-long thrall with Buddhadharma. In my first-year studies, where I began to explore Indian meditative history and practice, I was living in the part of Ottawa which nestled along the famous Rideau Canal. Adjacent to the Canal, which winds for about eight kilometres from the Ottawa River, to my then-school Carleton University, was a small pond. Late one Saturday evening, restless from too much essay-writing, I left my apartment to walk the quiet streets, towards the canal. After some 30-40 minutes, I found my self on the upper bank of a small pond, and there, with the nearly full moon, the warm early fall air and echoes of the Bhagavad Gita and Shakyamuni's quest, I too sat down. I probably imagined some trans-temporal link between my teen-age reflections and those more epic contemplations. Like those masters to whose lives I aspired, I began to find the harmony between sitting and walking practice.

In my early twenties, following my formal undergraduate university training, I began exploring organized Dharma practice in earnest. As it was for many contemporary Westerners, it was Zen I took to be real Buddhism. And, like so many, I took sitting practice, *zazen*, preferably staring at blank walls, to be the only valid practice. Throwing myself into formal Dharma practice, first through Rinzai Zen style and later Soto Zen style, I learned the most common walking practice, *kinhin*. The two schools have their own distinct versions of walking, one fast, the other slow, each an expression of the broader distinctions of the two schools. I didn't know or appreciate those differences and adopted the Soto style, a slower, measured pace, one which seemed familiar, so much like my pre-Buddhist walks. As I was taught as a good zen practitioner, I made walking an auxiliary practice, always subordinate to *zazen*. It was fine, I believed, if I wanted to go for walks, but that bore no relationship to the time on the mat. Living by then in a dirt-road rural location, I was offered countless opportunities for unstructured and undirected wandering. However, I always felt a certain tension between kicking stones down the road, exploring fields without much purpose, not unlike Thoreau a century earlier, and the Spartan discipline of wall and *zafu*. Walking, I knew, should be second best, or at least a minor distraction.

In an odd way I may have been called to walking. My father was a chemical engineer who left his lab at the Steel Company of Canada in Hamilton, Ontario, to join the group of scientists and researchers brought together to grow the agency that is now Statistics Canada. His lab-partner and close friend, a certain Ray Lowes, remained behind for a successful career at that Hamilton plant. My father brought his friend and I together with his name, although he was most commonly just known as 'Lowes'. Lowes and his wife, Jane, visited us from time to time in Ottawa. This often took us 'up the Valley,' as we say in Renfrew, for a hiking and camping trip to Algonquin Park. For us, Lowes meant the woods and walking.

Back in Southern Ontario, Lowes continued walking in the woods. He fell in love with a certain collection of walks which ran past his home on the Southern Niagara Escarpment, winding northward past Hamilton, Milton and Caledon. In 1960 he outlined his vision for an expanded and connected set of trails which would extend from just outside Buffalo, New York, up to Tobermory, at the edge of Lake Huron, some 800 km to the north. Shortly thereafter, along with three other founders, Lowes began to organize the trail. The nine Regional Clubs which oversee the trail were established. In 1967, Canada's Centennial Year, a cairn at Tobermory, the northern terminus of the Bruce Trail was unveiled. Seven years of determination, support, vision and hard work were realized when the Bruce Trail was officially opened. The Bruce Trail (http://brucetrail.org/) is now the oldest and longest continuous footpath in Canada. The Bruce Trail Conservancy has grown steadily since then, purchasing vulnerable natural treasures and ensuring their sustainability for future generations of walkers.

Over the next decades and phases of my life and practice affiliations, I continued to walk for practice, pleasure and adventure. In the country, walking was an accepted and expected mode of transport. Going to the grocery store in the village was a walking chore. Visiting friends often involved walking to and about their properties or walking to a swimming spot. More and more, I explored walking practice itself, practicing with walks into the woods where I would sometimes do my *zazen*. Although I didn't know it, I was investigating the step and breath counting, the silent recitation and mindfulness of the natural world that I would learn later as traditional walking practices.

As my world became larger, I learned that not everyone valued walking as I did. In fact, on one occasion, I came to understand that it was viewed as peculiar and even suspicious. One Christmas, I traveled by van with a couple of buddies down the East Coast of the US, headed for respective families in Virginia and Florida. At the end of one long day on the road, we stopped for an overnight with friends in Maryland. Their home was in one of those sprawling 1980's suburban developments, which had been laid out in a former farmer's field, now paved over and re-constructed with winding utilitarian sidewalk-free roadways which only served to connect neighbourhoods. Commerce was neatly tucked away in a carefully concealed mall. All original natural details had been erased in preference for someone's idea of a natural landscape – one which omitted trees.

On our dusk arrival and after ten or so hours on the road, my friend, John, and I decided it would be a pleasant distraction to take a walk. We set off from the house and, with no particular goal in mind, made our way around the development. Within about twenty minutes a police cruiser pulled up beside us and asked us our business. We explained we were out for a walk. The officer seemed completely non-plussed by the idea of people moving around the neighbourhood without the aid of a motorized vehicle. He left us alone, but not without a warning that this whole walking thing might be risky to us or unwelcome to the neighbours.

My next introduction to Buddhist walking was in Sri Lanka, a few years later, where I was participating in an international exchange program, Canadian Crossroads International. I was placed within the huge extended family known as *Sarvodaya Shramadana* (The Awakening of All through the Gift of Shared Labour). This "village reawakening" movement had hundreds of sites all over the island, each deeply embedded in village life. The *Sarvodaya* movement, the brainchild of Buddhist and neo-Ghandian school teacher Ari Ariyaratne, sought (and still seeks) to transform villages all over Sri Lanka through an interfaith philosophy summarized by the slogan "we build the road, the road builds us." Their trademark activity was organizing road-building work-bees. Hundreds of villagers would come together, to share their labour and participate in the creation of entirely new roads. Men, women and children, of all ages, each took some role in hauling stone, clearing jungle, or feeding the crews.

My home-site, in a kind of regional outpost, near the central jungle-fringed city of Kegalla, brought me into an close collective living arrangement with thirty or so local village youth, all of whom, like most Sri Lankans, were Theravadin Buddhists. We frequently moved around between villages and projects by either an old Land Rover, diesel-seasoned local buses, or, of course, lots of walking. Anytime we needed to go down the valley to the larger village of Randeniya, it was an hour-long walk to the nearest "bus halt." Wherever one might want to go, be it the bustling city life of Colombo, the tourist beaches along the south coast or the mountain tea-estates, one should expect a substantial pedestrian stage to the journey.

One morning at the centre, while I was doing *zazen* in my room (a re-purposed cement storage building), I became aware of one of the teenage trainees peeking in my paneless window. It seemed odd to me that sitting should interest another Buddhist. What could be more natural than doing sitting practice at wake-up? Later, my friend explained that in Sri Lankan Buddhism only a rare and senior monk might do extended meditation. Most people would do a brief three minute contemplation, but nothing as formal as *zazen*. The young men spying on me were wondering what sort of person I was to be doing this.

Later, my friend, Tilak, asked me if I might like to spend some time in another *Sarvodaya* location which was a Buddhist monastery in the hills. The clergy, I came to understand, were very much integrated into the *Sarvodaya* activities. I leapt at the chance, and within a week was transported to a monastery a few hours away and settled into my small, simple quarters, like a lay dorm. I was the only layperson and had only a little to do with the monks, since no one spoke English, and I think it was not proper for a layperson, even the esteemed "suddhu-aya" (older white brother), to mix with monks.

It was here that I witnessed another walking practice up close, although not very personally. Each day the monks would line up, bowls in hand, and file down the mountain road to another village for their daily alms round (which we will explore later as Walking Practice # 3). I was never invited but did come to understand the centrality of that walking practice for them. This was more or less the only way they secured food for themselves, so walking was woven into both the contemplative and daily living routines of their lives. That same thing happened, and has happened for centuries, in monasteries all over Sri Lanka and most other Buddhist nations. It would be years before I came to know the meaning of the alms-round for bringing Dharma to the villagers.

My months in Sri Lanka also introduced me to another type of walking which is also a very common religious practice, one which appears in most world religions: pilgrimage (which we will later meet as Walking Practice # 6). This practice sets the practitioner on a walking journey which physically, emotionally and symbolically repeats the steps of some ancient figure or visits the site of some milestone religious event or artifact. In my case, it was several visits to the treasures of the golden age of Sri Lankan Buddhism. In Anuradhapurra and Polonnaruwa, I walked through the one-square-kilometre city ruins of what was one of the largest cities of the 4th century BCE. The city became part of the new Buddhist expansion only two centuries after the Buddha's own life. Its boulevards, religious buildings and monastic residences are home to many extraordinary architectural treasures. Later in my trip, in the South of Sri Lanka, I walked through the gardens, stepped through the giant lion's claw threshold and climbed the stone staircase to the top of Sigiriya, the Lion's Rock,. This gigantic volcanic rock rises over 1,200 feet above a flat plain and has been a royal retreat with a surprising gallery of Buddhist paintings and, more usually, a Buddhist monastery. It too dates from the earliest days of Buddhism in Sri Lanka. Unlike the desert plains of Anuradhapura, the breathtaking vista from atop the Lion's Rock provides the kind of sobering perspective on the world which gives one pause. At that time, I was not sufficiently knowledgeable about pilgrimage to benefit from all the practice has to offer. Nonetheless, it still took the form of a pilgrimage, in the sense of leaving me with life-shaping memories and inspiration and, more than thirty years later, continues to connect me with my chosen faith.

These experiences signified two parallel abode-leaving transitions – my leaving my family home and entering young adulthood, and my leaving the vagueness of my late teen spiritual musings for the more formal Buddha-way. Both were equally important in forming my spiritual identity. From my naivete and lack of worldliness, I had almost no sense of how important this abode-leaving would be. Further, it seemed coincidental that walking should be so much a part of these leavings. As with many pilgrimage experiences, it is only through reflection over the years following that understanding and meaning emerge. Leaving one's abode is itself an act of faith, part of that mix of conviction, despair and hope which drives our search for new meaning.

UNFOLDING THE MAP

Like any good walk, this book covers a variety of both new and familiar terrain. It offers gentle strolls, steep climbs, shady nooks and expansive vistas. It won't wear you out nor will it (I sincerely hope) fail to challenge you. Like any good book or walk, this one is a journey. It starts where we are and points to a destination without revealing all of its adventures too soon. It's a book to be read and a book to accompany you on whatever walks you take.

Any walking reader will already have a similar slim bookshelf with titles about walking. It may feature one of the many pilgrimage diaries, like Dempster's *Neon Pilgrim*, or Tony Kevin's *Walking the Camino*. There will be a selection of technical books, perhaps some edition of Colin Fletcher's *The Complete Walker* or titles that begin: *Hiking the...*, or *Nordic Walking for...*, or *The....Walker*. The reflective walkers will have Basho's *Narrow Road to the North*, Thoreau's *Walden or My Life in the Woods*, and probably his *Walking*. The spiritually-oriented will have Halzer's *Warrior Walking* or Kortge's *The Spirited Walker*. For the religious, there may be a copy of Bunyan's *Pilgrims Progress*, Steven's thorough *The Marathon Monks of Mount Hiei* or Thich Nhat Hahn's multi-media collection, *Walking Meditation*. Every one a great companion.

This book is a unique resident for your bookshelf or backpack. This is the first book to deal with the many forms of Buddhist and other contemplative walking practices in a comprehensive way. It is the first to address the interests and needs of Buddhists and other spiritually-minded walkers in actually using traditional and more recent Buddhist and Buddhist-friendly foot practices as part of their contemplative journey. Its written with these people in mind. You're likely one of them if:

- you already have some regular Buddhist practice and may have had some introduction to *kinhin* walking;
- you have some form of meditation practice, Buddhist or otherwise, and need something to provide some variety between or as an alternative to sitting;
- you are curious about reflective practices, especially Buddhist, but find the prospect of sitting quietly for very long to be a bit daunting;
- you have participated in a pilgrimage or other contemplative walk and want to expand on that experience;
- you regularly enjoy walking and feel the need to give it a more structured reflective dimension;

- you have participated in socially-conscientious or fund-raising walks.

People are drawn to walking for many more reasons. Rather than the reasons above, yours might include walking for fitness and/or weight loss, competitive and race walking, trophy or 'bucket list' walking (that is, to collect trails as achievements), and walking for human or animal companionship. There are merits and benefits to each on this second list, however, in this book, we are concerned with the first list and have little to contribute to that second collection of interests.

SCANNING THE TERRAIN

Through all of this, I discovered there are many books about walking. Some call it walking, some call it hiking, the more common North American term, others trekking, which one sees more often in Europe. There are those that locate trails of interest and detail highlights one might pass en route. There are instructional guides which explain types of packs, boots, poles and so on. There are memoirs of "great trails I have done." There are manuals that extol the health benefits of walking as exercise. There are training guides that prepare one for competitive walking. There are books on walking Tai Chi, walking yoga, warrior walking, Nordic walking and walking chi kung. City, country, forest, mountain, pilgrimage, tourist, on and on.

As mentioned above, this is the first book to address the interests and needs of Buddhists and other spiritually-minded walkers in actually using traditional and more recent Buddhist and Buddhist-friendly foot practices as part of their contemplative journey. Our concern here is understanding and using those traditional and newer Buddhist foot practices within a personal contemplative training regimen.

There has been some debate about a proper term to describe the kind of walking I mean here. Some readers have objected to psycho-spiritual, some to the term spiritual, some are uncomfortable with the term religious. My intention has been to appeal to both the professional and lay psychotherapy reader, especially those using mindfulness methods, and to readers with more of a concern for religious issues, largely but not exclusively Buddhist. The term which has gained greatest resonance with me has come to be contemplation. This seems to encompass multiple styles of meditative practice, therapeutic mindfulness, and a wide inter-faith perspective. For that reason I will stick with contemplation/contemplative when referring to these kinds of walking practices.

In many Buddhist practice environments, walking is often either ignored as a practice mode or treated as an optional practice, more as a relief from sustained sitting practice. Here, we assume a great value for walking and concentrate on the how-to aspect of walking practice. In fact, we will come to understand walking practices as a fully legitimate and comprehensive set of practices. We will come to appreciate their value as a complement to more familiar sitting methods to fulfill the Buddha-way. As Zen Patriarch Yin Kuang explains:

> Since sentient beings are of different spiritual capacities and inclinations, many levels of teaching and numerous, methods were devised in order to reach everyone. Traditionally, the sutras speak of 84,000 (i.e. an infinite number depending on the circumstances, the times and the target audience.) All these methods are expedients - different medicines for different individuals with different illnesses at different times - but all are intrinsically perfect and complete. Within each method, the success or failure of an individual's cultivation depends on the depth of practice and understanding, that is, on his mind.
> *Pure-Land Zen*, ed. Forrest Smith, p. 7

PHASES OF OUR JOURNEY

Parables, stories and metaphors of travel and journey are part of the fabric of our culture. As I write this, the radio music in the background is singing the praises of "the broken road which leads me back to you," just one example of such stories of life as life on the road. In chapter seven of the Lotus Sutra, which is sometimes called The Apparitional City, we are told of a leader who responds to the distress of those around him by leading them on a journey, promising them the greatest treasure at the conclusion. It is in this chapter that we are introduced to the teaching of skillful means (*upaya*) whereby a great teacher constructs their teaching according to what is most resonant for those in need. In this case, the leader chooses a journey as his skillful means.

This book is about journeys, and takes the form of a journey. Every journey, no matter the length, purpose or mode of travel is a transition, a rite of passage, a transition ritual. In its simplest form it has three phases: separation or home-leaving; *limin* or pivot-point; and re-connection/re-collection. Separation or departure is recognizable as our leaving the family-hearth, making a break, however large with patterns and past. Often it is a home-leaving. Most importantly, this separation is purposeful. We are not driven onto the road, we deliberately step onto it with reasons and aspirations unique to ourselves. At some point we reach the *limin*, we become liminal. This liminality has an ambiguity, as Turner explains: "liminality is not only transition but also potentiality, not only 'going to be', but also 'what may be'." (*Image*, Turner, p. 3). Anyone who has walked a labyrinth understands that something shifts at the centre, what was approaching is now leaving, seeking has been satisfied. The ancient Romans used to place the two-headed god, Janus, in their doorways for this same reason. Being on the threshold or *limin*, Janus looked ahead, down the road, and back into the familiar, literally, the family hearth. The final phase is the re-entry, re-crossing the threshold back into the home we left. It is a re-connection, and yet, because of what we have become on the journey, we recollect how we are different.

Within the journey on which we are embarking are three parallel journeys. The first is the unfolding journey of walking in Buddhist history and practice. We'll join Shakyamuni, Bodhidharma, Jizo-bosatsu and countless others who unfolded the Dharma step by step. The second journey is our own journey of practicing walking. We explore how we can introduce foot-body-mind practices into the collection of practices which guide our own spiritual lives. We each will have a unique path to walk and that too will fork and meander as our practice-lives evolve. Finally, there is my own journey with walking, a pilgrimage that approaches fifty years. I hope to share how I've made my way along this wonderful Dharma-path, how I learned what Thich Nhat Hahn tells us – "peace is every step."

Walk Like A Mountain is divided into three parts:

Part I: Preparations
- Every journey demands preparation – destinations to name, maps to collect, baggage to secure. In this part, Chapters One to Four, we consider the Buddha-way as a foot path, we imagine where we might go and we anticipate the journey from the perspective of the threshold.

Part II: Journey
- Building on the metaphor of crossing and dwelling, we examine practices that are journey-like in form. In Chapters Five to Eight

we introduce the first seven of our set of walking practices, each of which appears in the form of a journey.

Part III: In-between Spaces
- Introducing a second metaphor for walking practice, that of inhabiting in-between spaces, we meet a set of practices which take that form. In Chapters Nine and Ten we consider an additional four practices, with emphasis on newer practices which lead us beyond traditional Buddhist practices.

The main chapters of our journey-book will use a journey form which is marked by the chapter title. In each chapter we reflect on the meaning of that phase of the journey. We identify a set of ten-plus foot practices, which combine Buddhist and modern affiliated practices. We'll examine the origins and place of walking in Buddhist history, the forms of these distinct practices, describing the form and weighing the value of each. We'll present simple step-by-step (so to speak) directions to make these strong elements of your practice.

We'll start off, as any Dharma practice instruction usually does, with a consideration of physical postures, body, foot and hand, and the importance of breath. We make some notes on accompanying equipment, not from the perspective of a 'buyers' guide', but more to enrich the practice dimension of these practices. Finally, since not all Dharma practitioners are able-bodied, we look into how those with physical disabilities can modify foot practices for their use.

You are encouraged to consider ways to direct your own practice to include foot practices. You can follow along the map of our journey. Alternately, if you have some appreciation for the general form of the practices (chapter 2), you can explore each of the ten forms (chapters 5-9) in whatever order you prefer. Chapters 5 through 9 divide the types of walking practice (which actually incorporate more than ten discreet forms). We begin in Chapter 5 with indoor forms, what most people are familiar with, introducing along the way the style of 'Tai Chi walking' which fewer people know. In Chapter 6 we meet *takuhatsu* or alms-round walks and some considerations of movement as a part of general monastic life. In Chapter 7, we try out some combined practices, where we walk and perform other practices, such as circumambulation, *nembutsu* or bowing. In Chapter 8, we look at the major long walking practices, including both the world-wide phenomenon of pilgrimage and the imposing *kaihogyo* practice developed by Japanese Tendai.

In Chapter 9, we consider practices where walking takes on a symbolic form. In particular, we explore how the Pure Land schools envision their practice as a journey and how *mandala* practices are based on a journey metaphor. We close Chapter 9 by looking at two more recent methods, a primarily European model, labyrinth walking, especially the newer approaches to this practice, and, second, what Thoreau referred to in his writing as 'sauntering'. The final new method emerges from 20th century social activism and Engaged Buddhist activities, that is, using walks for social change.

If you have been sitting before, you will find that your motionless experience can help to unfold the possibilities of foot practices. If walking is more of your first entrée into Buddhist practice, recognize that it is not a complete alternative to sitting forms. No matter how much walking you do, some experience with sitting practices is necessary to ground yourself in Buddhist practice. Later in your practice, as part of the teacher-student training decision process, you may choose, as I have, to focus in part or entirely on a foot practice. For the novice, it would be foolhardy to avoid the 'refining fire' of thorough and disciplined sitting methods.

I further encourage you to approach each practice on its own merits, whether you have some experience or none. Practice each form as a new practice, one which invites you into a new way of meeting your body and mind experiences. As with any practice, it is foolish to judge the practice on a superficial exposure. You will need several months, even years, of regular practice to cultivate the forms and learn what it has to offer.

However you approach or practice, embrace the journey. Dharma practitioners have made it their proving ground for centuries. As they say on the Shikoku, that Japanese pilgrimage which encircles Shikoku Island for 1930 km, *dogyo ninin*, "a practice of two together," that none of us ever walks alone. We always have the company of centuries of walking Buddhists, of countless Buddhas and Bodhisattvas, all of whom urge us forward, urge us to use the road to penetrate the Way.

CHAPTER ONE
STIRRINGS FOR THE ROAD

The green mountains lack none of their proper virtues; hence, they are constantly at rest and constantly walking. We must devote ourselves to a detailed study of this virtue of walking. Since the walking of the mountains should be like that of people, one ought not doubt that the mountains walk simply because they may not appear to stride like humans.

To doubt the walking of the mountains means that one does not yet know one's own walking. It is not that one does not walk but that one does not yet know, has not made clear, this walking. Those who would know their own walking must also know the walking of the green mountains.

Mountains and Waters Sutra, Dogen, transl. Bielefeldt, Stanford University

WALKING – THE HIDDEN LIFE OF THE BUDDHA

In the north of Sri Lanka, in the desert regions of Polonnaruwa, at a place named Gal Vihara, there is a magnificent and isolated trio of larger-than-life statues carved out of local stone. Representing "the vogue...of carving colossal images of the Buddha on the vertical faces of rocks" (*The Art of the Ancient Sinhalese*, Nirvatana, p. 22) which occurred in the 12th century CE, figures are scattered about a barren landscape. The scale (one stands 42 feet tall) transforms the viewer into Lilliputian dimensions, barely up to the Buddha's kneecap. Not unlike examples of Buddha statuary which began in India a few centuries after the Parinirvana, and appear all over Asia, and now in the West, the Gal Vihara Shakyamunis are represented in each of three classic postures.

One is the reclining pose, with the Buddha on one side, with his head resting on his hand, both propped up on a tubular cushion support. This is the least common pose and it is unusual to view the trio together this way. The other two, which are close by, along with several more from other centuries, are posed in the most familiar postures – standing and seated. The standing can be with arms to the side, the over-length Buddha-identifying arms and hands flat to the thighs or with hands held in one of the familiar *mudras*, or, as seen elsewhere at Polonnaruwa, with arms crossed over the chest.

By far, the most common Buddha pose, found in all sizes, all materials, located close to massive temple figures or, much smaller, tucked away in gardens, is the seated Shakyamuni. This is also true in secular art where seated Buddhas can be found as incense holders, wiener mascots (as with the Picton, Ontario product called Buddha Dog, see http://buddhafoodha.com) and the ubiquitous theme of countless cartoons of an ascetic under a tree or on a mountain top. An assortment of classic hand positions or *mudras* may be used, but the pose always shows Shakyamuni, sitting. Sitting in *padmasana*, sitting cross-legged, sitting straight-spined and sitting staring ahead.

Of course there are mythologic depictions of flying Buddhas, even flying seated Buddhas, or occasionally, Buddhas standing amidst a crowd of followers, engaged in one of his celebrated sermons. The least common pose, and the one whose absence presents as a large question mark for us here, is the walking pose. Over the centuries, less than a handful of depictions have chosen such a pose. An 11th century Japanese artist created the unusual standing Buddha, Amida Looking Back, from Zenrin-ji temple in Kyoto. It poses the standing Buddha, right hand in the wheel-turning mudra, and head glancing over the left shoulder, compassionately checking for suffering beings who may have been left behind. According to another story, this image startled a dozing priest, Eikan, who fell asleep while doing walking *nembutsu* practice. There is another beautifully slender Thai statue which presents Shakyamuni in full stride.

If a walking Buddha is rare, then the rarity is clearly compensated for by the image of Jizo Bosatsu, the walking Bodhisattva, which can be seen almost everywhere in East Asia. Even when he is not actually shown stepping along, he carries the *shakujo*, the pilgrim staff. This reminds us of his vow to walk through The Six Realms of Existence, bringing Dharma to beings, especially those unable to hear it due to the situation of their unhappy birth. Further, his figure is commonly located along roadsides, at crossroads or anywhere fellow walkers, travellers and pilgrims may need his assistance.

Even given the activity of Jizo, (whom we will meet more fully in Chapter 2), walking practices remain minor and usually adjunctive for most practitioners.

Herein lies the puzzle which occasioned this book: why are walking practices relegated to the back rows of Dharma practices? Consider the pre- and post-Enlightenment activities of Shakyamuni once he dismounted his beloved Kantaka and bade farewell to his loyal manservant, Channa:

> ...and so he passed
> free from the palace.
> When the morning star
> Stood half a spear's length from the eastern rim,
> And o'er the earth the breath of morning sighed,
> Rippling Anoma's wave, the border stream,
> Then drew the rein, and leaped to earth and kissed
> White Kantaka betwixt the ears and spake
> Full sweet Channa: "This which thou hast done,
> Shall bring thee good, and bring all creatures good."
>
> *The Light of Asia*, Arnold, 4th Book

There is no biography of Shakyamuni which disagrees on the facts. We have a description of his departure, his studies with the four renunciants, his near death and decision to seek awareness beneath the Vesak moon. We know of the temptation and victory. His choice to return to the world of *dukkha*, his various sermons. We know of his stops and addresses which spanned some forty or so years before his Parinirvana. Forty years or so of travels.

Imagine, if you will, an itinerary for the Buddha at almost any time of those forty years, with the exception of the 'rains' when they took shelter for that period of weeks. There would be time for seeking food and eating twice daily, time for sleep and, one assumes, the usual bodily necessities. There would be time for pauses on the way, perhaps to visit some royalty or other dignitary. There were periods of formal sitting meditation practice, in whatever grove or shade could be found. However, during most of the time spent over those forty-odd years they were engaged in walking. Lots of walking. Any scan of the maps of the Buddha's travels will confirm that there were major distances between sermons and stops, and so the majority of His and those of his followers' waking hours were spent wandering on foot hither and yon over the dusty roads of North India.

Again, as Arnold imagines:

> I choose
> To tread its [the Earth's] paths with patient, stainless feet,
> Making its dust my bed, its loneliest wastes
> My dwelling, and its meanest things my mates;
> Clad in no prouder garb than the outcastes wear,
> Fed with no meats save what the charitable
> Give of their will, sheltered with no more pomp
> Than the dim cave lends or the jungle-bush.
> *The Light of Asia*, Arnold, 4th Book

In some respects, the life of the Buddha is a model for the leader in chapter seven of The Lotus Sutra, mentioned above, who takes his followers on a perilous journey leading to the ultimate treasure. If we accept that Shakyamuni Buddha was the presentation of the Living Dharma, and that his every gesture was the expression of the Way, we must imagine the great amounts of teaching which occurred while the first Sangha walked and walked, year after year. Its inconceivable that during all that time there wasn't some structured practices of reflection, chanting or even question-and-answer that emerged. Could all that have been so trivial that it doesn't merit a place in the practice routine of the Buddha and his followers?

The question is worth noting, as we look into the performance of these practices. However, the deeper examination and possible answer to such questions belong to another, as-yet-undertaken study. For now, we raise the puzzle while we ourselves join the Buddha, feeling the Earth beneath us and "...tread its paths with patient...feet."

WALKING PRACTICE AS METAPHOR

Our journey here may not reveal to you the secrets of green mountains walking or an ultimate treasure, but we will most certainly follow Dogen's sage advice, and investigate clearly our own walking. Although walking might seem a minor practice, compared to the highly-praised seated postures, walking inspired the early Buddhist imagination in other ways. Way, path, vehicle, step. These are the prominent metaphors of Buddhadharma. Consider:

- The fourth of the initial and pivotal Buddhist teaching is, of course, the Eightfold Path, the *arya-arta ga-marga*. A *marga* is a well worn path, such as a wild animal would leave behind, and also suggests an expedient route, a passage or the proper course;
- Using another road metaphor, all the schools of Buddhism refer to themselves as *yanas*, vehicles. Hence, we have the Lesser Vehicle (*hina-yana*), the Great or All-Encompassing Vehicle (*maha-yana*), the Vehicle of the Thunderbolt (*vajra-yana*) and The Harmonizing Vehicle (*eka-yana*). The sense here is of practice as a conveyance, that is how one gets from here to one's destination; thus, these vehicles have the capacity to carry us to liberation or over the river of suffering;
- One of the most beloved books in the early Buddhist canon is the *Dhamma-pada*, literally, Dharma steps or footsteps;
- In the earliest Buddhist art, images of the Buddha were forbidden and symbols for the Teacher were used. One popular symbol was the *padanka*, the Buddha's footprint, which became an object of worship;

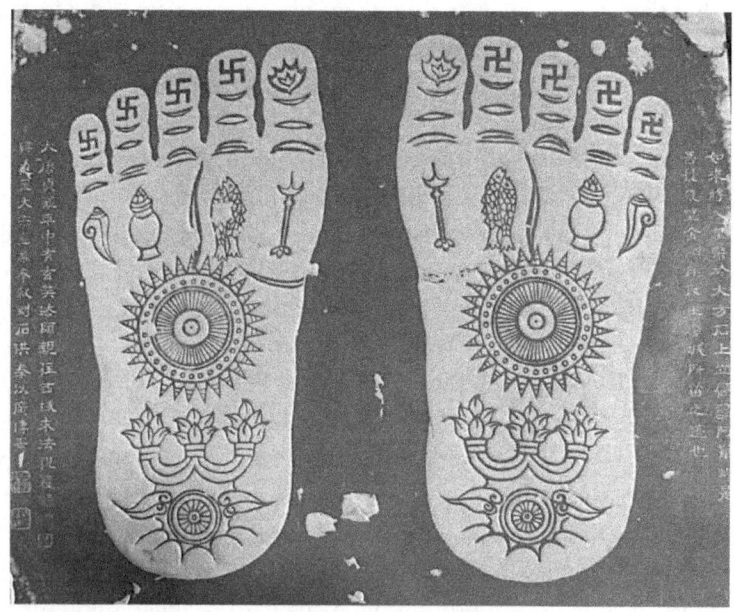

The padanka symbol

- The story of the infant Shakyamuni, following his miraculous birth, includes the detail that, unlike the awkward stumblings of most infants, he stood up and took three bold strides, symbolizing his conquest of the Three Worlds. As he stepped, brilliant lotus flowers sprang from the earth. Its worth noting here again that with all the possibilities of things he could have done to show his extraordinariness, it was walking which characterized this miraculous child.

Curiously, with all these road metaphors, the word for teaching remains Dharma, which is a symbol of something static, not moving. It suggests a pillar or foundation – a set of rules or a natural order. Perhaps the common contemporary (to the Buddha) usages of *Dharma* in Hinduism simply transferred over to Buddhist teaching. As Buddhism moved across into China and Japan, it became more associated with *Tao*, The Way, the foundational concept of Chinese religion which captures more of the sense of movement and flow.

WALKING AS A 'YOGA'

Walking practices, as we will see, are usually noted as adjunctive practices, such as a relief from sitting meditation, as with doing *kinhin*, as special practices, like the *kaihogyo*, which only the exceptional even dare to perform, or as instrumental, such as walking while doing *nembutsu* recitation. This book will take walking practices, not merely in these various ways, but as an integrated set of practices.

THIS HANDBOOK'S INTENTION: WALKING AS CONTEMPLATIVE PRACTICE

In a remarkable book, *Crossing and Dwelling: A Theory of Religions*, the socio-anthropologist, Thomas Tweed, proposes a metaphor to describe what religions are. He sets out:

> Religions are confluences of organic-cultural flows that intensify joy and confront suffering by drawing on human and suprahuman forces to make homes and cross boundaries. [These two] orienting metaphors are most useful for analyzing what religion is and what

it does: spatial metaphors (dwelling and crossing) signal that religion is about finding a place and moving across a space, and aquatic metaphors (confluences and flows) signal that religions are not reified substances but complex processes.

Crossing and Dwelling, Tweed, pp. 54/59

This intriguing and deeply satisfying conceptualization resonates strongly with a book about the place of walking in one of the world's great religious traditions, Buddhism. Space does not permit us to pursue Tweed's metaphors further, but he is successful in providing us with a suitable metaphor for this book itself.

We will adopt, in fact we already have adopted, this dwelling-and-crossing metaphor in two underlying ways: firstly, in conjunction with the 'three phases' metaphor introduced in our Preface, and the 'chapter-map' of our journey through Buddhist walking practices, the metaphor of crossing/dwelling enriches the journey metaphor, transforming it; and secondly, as a template for understanding the structure of any walking practice. We will see the dwelling/crossing frame can guide us in how to use the practices.

Let's look in a little more detailed way at how our journey will move us from dwelling to crossing and back again.

Part I: Preparations

Preface: Dwelling

We began in the known, the many rooms of and windows on our world, familiar and secure. In our meeting, The Preface, someone (myself) unexpectedly reports back with news from their travels. A question mark suddenly appears beside our calm world. A new way of being in that familiar world is proposed. The possibility of a new journey is raised, with something of how and why we might take it and what we might explore and learn. As in our usual world, this 'travel bug' must be scratched.

Chapter 1: Stirrings

We are now in the world of Shakyamuni Buddha, walking across North India, day after day, year after year. We step back from the sermons and the drama. We, who are his modern day entourage, observe his everyday life, treading dirt roads, resting in groves, finding a next meal. We step back and wonder what might this have to do with the Great Awakening. Could this to-ing and fro-ing really have nothing to do with being fully awake? Are the travels of Shakyamuni just filler, something to do around the real practices? In what ways has our 2500 year tradition formulated walking practices which we can employ on the Dharma Path? We will leave our comfortable dwelling and take to that road to join our Sangha-companions in their walk.

Chapter 2: Imaginings

A strange and compelling vision takes shape in our hearts and now our bodies. We begin to feel, in our bodies, the movement onto the highway. We recognize we are arranging our bodies for travel, and we need to remember the efficiencies of posture, step and breath. Although we may be walking alone, we remind ourselves that each step is *dogyo ninin*, two walking together. Who, we wonder, will be our silent companions? In whose steps are we following?

Chapter 3: Threshold – Foot and Step

With a deepened sense of how we ought arrange our bodies, before we set off, we check our most important equipment for the journey – our own body. Napoleon's army may have marched 'on their bellies', we will have to rely on ankle, foot, toes. Our strength will be our posture and breath. We will need to understand these intimately and we will use the lenses of both modern Western medicine and traditional Chinese medicine to inform our understanding. We will consider this journey as an exercise in bio-mechanics, and of ki-energy flow – one which takes place at the margin between earth and sky.

Chapter 4: Threshold – Preparations

Our determination set, having let go of habits and routines, we must gather around us the necessities of the road. We check equipment, pack knapsacks, re-fit boots with stout new laces. We consider our mentors –centuries of pilgrims, monks circling *stupas,* super-athletes coursing up and down a sacred mountain. They will recommend what we might need on our journey –can we really get by with only a begging bowl and a staff? We are struck by Jizo, the Eternal Pilgrim, trudging through the Six Realms of Conditioned Existence, his simplicity – the pilgrim's robes and his *shakujo,* the sturdy staff which supports his pace and whose jangling rings announce to all beings that the Dharma-messenger is approaching.

Some of us wonder whether we are fit for this journey. We wonder about old bones, injuries or even more permanent disabilities. Will these force us to stay behind. What can our predecessors advise?

Part II: Journeys

Chapter 5: Journey - First Steps

Our destination clear, all preparations made and a trusted map in hand, we take the first steps away from our daily lives and towards an adventure, a learning and, with luck, a transformation. As those who join the road do, we ponder the practice habits we know. Most of us turn to the archetype, the cross-legged monk, the seated Bodhisattvas and the Buddha, in repose on a lotus throne. Some may have tried the walks that divide rounds of sitting practice, some may understand how walking is the continuation of the practices of sitting. We frame our questions, we engage our curiosity, we have formed our intention for the road. Now on the road, we begin with our reliable and familiar practices.

Walking Practice 1: *Kinhin* **and Tai Chi**

Most styles of Buddhist practice include some form of formalized walking practice. The most common is *kinhin*, 'just walking'. It is characterized as the practice form used to vary periods of sustained sitting practice. It has its own posture and can be done in a variety of paces, from glacially slow to a near sprint. Since it is usually twinned with sitting, it is done indoors, contained within the actual sitting space. Others, most famously Thich Nhat Hahn, have promoted a moderately paced walk out of doors. His form breaks the traditional pattern of a line of practitioners. Video of him leading a walking practice resembles a swarm or wave moving across the landscape, with the Master Thay clutching one or two children's hands.

Normally, the *kinhin* line circles the outer edge of the practice room or, for smaller groups or individuals, a 15-20 pace extended loop, down and back the space.

When the Dharma entered China, it entered the territory of Taoist masters. Over the centuries, the two flowed in and through each other, leaving invisible links and overlaps. Like roads built over roads built over roads, no one can say what the substance of the final road may be. We pause to meet walking Tai Chi, a unique and companionable form of walking whose meticulousness and rhythm can teach us a new side to our walking.

Chapter 6: Journey 2 – Crossing

Evening the pace, feeling the freedom from former ways, we slip into the walking of our ancestors, all those monks who wove back and forth across the sandy trails between a deer park, a king's palace and a wealthy man's garden. Readily we come to appreciate the delights and demands of a meal on the trail. We are now immersed in a new life.

Walking Practice 2: Walking as Daily Life

Anyone who has passed a day at a Dharma centre will have engaged in *samu* practice. This term from Japanese Buddhism will have parallels in other countries. It refers to all the day-to-day duties a monk or retreatant undertakes to contribute to the Sangha. It is almost a stereotype of *samu* to be sweeping floors or cutting wood. The variations are as many as tasks in place. Virtually all of these require some walking. We will examine what we can bring to these work-practices. Only a few of us will pass much time inside a temple or monastery walls compared to the hours we spend at work elsewhere. We explore how we can make these periods of work opportunities for practice.

Walking Practice 3: Alms Rounds

No doubt, the oldest formal Buddhist foot practice is that of alms rounds. As Shakyamuni assembled his steady group of followers, they adopted the already accepted practice for wandering ascetics, that of daily visits to homes and estates to exchange the presentation of teaching, for some material contribution, most often food and drink. This is not begging, in the sense of someone down on their luck asking for support from someone more materially successful. Alms rounds are a recognition of the intersection of two distinct competencies. Those with material goods exchange them for the receipt of salvational teaching by those who specialize in that knowledge. The religious are not seen as 'needy', but rather in possession of specially acquired knowledge. Since laypeople were viewed as incapable (at least in earlier times) of their own religious education, the gift of teaching was the primary way they could benefit from the efforts of clergy. (It was, in fact, part of Buddhist vows to make efforts to present the Dharma to other people.) Providing for wandering ascetics was, of course, a means of acquiring merit, good *karma*. How the spirit of this walking practice can be transformed for our modern situations is an as-yet answered question we will ask.

Chapter 7: Threshold 2 – Turning Back

At some point, every walker must decide to transform the walk from a letting go to a coming back. We will take time to reflect on the symbolic and ritual meaning of this moment, what we previously called our journey's liminal or threshold moment. With our time behind us increasing, we come to appreciate the path-builders, the trail setters who preceded us. We understand their sincerity and effort, and will feel some gratitude. We turn to practices that represent that appreciation and thankfulness.

Walking Practice 4: Circumambulation

Circumambulation, for Buddhists, derives from the practice of walking around some sacred or honoured site. As part of the practice of venerating the remains of a great teacher, practitioners performed a walking and recitation practice which slowly encircled the *stupa*, in a clockwise manner. The recited material would be a familiar chant or a sutra. Such a practice not only deepens the practitioners mind-practice, but generates merit for themselves and others. Doing circumambulation is an essential part of any Buddhist pilgrimage.

Over time circumambulation around *stupas* or *pagodas* became possible around other sites, relics or statuary. In modern times, in its most extravagant form, it begins to merge with pilgrimage walking as circumambulation around sacred mountains becomes a practice.

Walking Practice 5: Walking Nembutsu

Nembutsu is a practice which emerged later in Buddhist history and is characterized by a reliance on a direct personal relation between the practitioner and a Buddha figure, most often Amida, the Buddha of Infinite Life and Light. It understood that human history had moved through an era where it had been possible for individuals to achieve Buddhahood by their own effort (*jiriki*), and entered a more decadent era (*mappo*) where it was necessary to rely on the intervention and effort of the Buddhas, that is, Other effort (*tariki*).

Because practitioners had to rely on super-human intervention, it became necessary to not only honour those figures, but also to request their generosity to aid struggling humanity. The new form of practice was this prayerful and personal plea for the Buddhas to employ their power to accomplish the work of Liberation. The address to Buddhas became the practice of *nembutsu*. The Jodo sects became the earliest formalization of this practice, although it found a home in other schools, especially Tendai, and even Zen.

Such entreaties could, and ought to, be made in and through every action. Nembutsu practice most frequently looked like extended chanting and silent prayer services. One version combined devotional chanting with walking practices. In some instances this would overlap or even replace sutra chanting during circumambulation. In others, it was a new practice form, that of walking *nembutsu*.

Prayer Walking

As modern walkers, we can draw on modern walking practice. One of the most popular is Mundy's 'prayer walking'. We will meet this Christian preacher and experience how his methods add a new devotional dimension for us.

Chapter 8: Journey 3 – The Long Road Back

Once our footsteps have turned to home, that stage of the journey may, in different moments feel the longest and the shortest part of the walk. We feel a growing eagerness to regain the familiar, yet resist abandoning this road and its freshness and richness. We can admire and imagine joining the millions who made the longest walks their practice.

Walking Practice 6: Pilgrimage

Pilgrimage, within Buddhism, likely existed from the time following the physical demise of Shakyamuni. With the appearance and promotion of *stupa* practice, it must have become desirable for early Dharma followers to re-trace the travels of Shakyamuni as part of the adoration of his physical life. Itinerant ascetics were nothing new in Northern India during that period, Shakyamuni himself was but one of countless, nameless men who left the relative comfort of towns and courts to explore the meditative life.

As Buddhadharma began its steady march, along the legendary Silk Road, across Asia into China, Korea, Japan and Southeast Asia, it set up a 'supply-chain' back to the great monasteries of India. There are many tales of monks returning to India to retrieve versions of *sutras*, *rupas* and other learning materials. Once these East Asian *Sanghas* became established, it became similarly important for Japanese monks to travel back to the home monasteries to retrieve teachings, *sutras* and religious objects for their own national centres. The giants of Japanese Dharma, Kobo Daishi (Kukai), Dengyo Daishi (Saicho), Dogen and many more, made the dangerous return trip to the Chinese home-base of Dharma.

With the establishment of Dharma centres at a national level it became more common and desirable for practitioners to undertake pilgrimage to places of importance. Pilgrimage in the Buddhist context is not different in form or in intention from those of many other faiths. It is a substantial endeavour for any practitioner, one that separates them from their normal routines, placing them on a super-temporal plane, a kind of symbolic level where their daily activities interpenetrate the cosmic realm of great human or super-human figures. In past times, pilgrimage was a dangerous and life-altering experience. In our world of rapid transit, high-speed rails and roads and helicopter charters, the risk has been dramatically reduced. Yet the symbolic importance of leaving one's life to become a pilgrim offers unique opportunities for practitioners.

Walking and Bowing

No doubt, greeting bows, the simple physical honouring of the Dharma in the presence of another, would be part of a monk's daily routine. The practice of formal prostrations, a structured sequence of bowing, is a well-established one in Dharma history, although one which needs coaxing for Westerners. Not only is there little tradition of bowing or prostration, there is overt resistance and hostility to the idea of even bowing to anyone or thing, let alone a full-out prostration. There are various styles from the more elegantly restrained Chinese-Japanese style to the all-out stretching prostration of Tibet. We won't take too much time to discriminate these differences here. We will describe the different styles and consider how to blend them in with a walking practice, be that indoor or outdoor.

Walking Practice 7: Kaihogyo and Kokorodo

Kaihogyo has been called the greatest physical challenge for human bodies, far more demanding than Western marathons. It belongs within the Tendai sect, and consists of rapid-paced daily walks, extending approximately eighty kilometres, up and down a steep and risky mountain route. Very few people ever receive authorization to undertake the training or perform the practice. It is an undeniable inspiration for all walking practices. It is, however, not something the majority of Dharma practitioners would even request.

We will not detail here, nor encourage this practices for most practitioners. *Kaihogyo* requires a substantial support-team, that is the involvement of many other monks, and, at certain stages of the practice, a whole lay community, to enable the completion of a super-human and life-threatening effort. It is not our purpose to facilitate such practices.

Kokorodo can be seen as a conflation and scaling back of both pilgrimage and *kaihogyo*. Not everyone can dedicate years or resources to daily marathon walking, or weeks to following a pilgrimage route. The *kokorodo* is an abbreviated version of these practices, where individual or groups of practitioners can share the endless road. It can be a taste of *kaihogyo*/pilgrimage experience that fulfills some of the same purposes. It removes the practitioner from the daily routine, even if that is a routine of a stationary retreat, and moves them into that symbolic/cosmic realm of the Buddhas and Bodhisattvas. The ordinary events of a 20 mile walk become transformed into an expedition into Dharma realms and heavens where century-old trees become encounters with sage-kings and Bodhisattvas; passages through cemeteries become confrontations with the intersection of life and death.

Unlike *kaihogyo*, the route may be familiar and less associated with great Dharma legends. It does not demand the rigour and repetition of *kaihogyo*, nor does it demand the extended commitment of pilgrimage. But like a pilgrimage, the practice may be a similar separation from daily routines and relationships.

Part III: In-Between Spaces

The metaphors of walking as journey, as crossing have been steadily with us to this point. Here we display a second powerful metaphor, that of walking in in-between spaces. Borrowing from another modern writer, novelist China Miéville, and his novel, *The City and The City*, we learn how walking can expose for us new dimensions in-between our day-to-day lives and spiritual realms which they parallel or intersect.

Chapter 9: Journey 4 – New Walking

As we see the landmarks that promise home, we begin to reflect on all the walks we've taken, their forms and benefits. Walking now enters a new realm – the symbolic. We envision and map out future walks into that realm. We expand our perspective and make connections previously unmade with other walkers. With the early Christian seekers we enter one of many labyrinth courses. Recalling the author whose words and walking passion opened our journey, we 'saunter' with Henry Thoreau along his beloved Marlborough Road, to where it intersects with the roads of our world. Finally, we find new meaning and enthusiasm for the walks which have been chosen by our present Dharma family to transform our world.

Walking Practice 8: Walking a Symbolic Landscape

The preceding practices all demand some amount of physical exertion and take place over a real, natural landscapes. The practices of this chapter take us into the realm of largely symbolic and less physical travels. Mandala and Pure Land visioning have deep roots within Dharma practice. Labyrinth practice is largely foreign to Buddhist experience. It is included here because, as a foot practice, it offers a great deal to Dharma practice, and because it is becoming increasingly familiar to Western practitioners.

Walking the Stations

Another version of a symbolic walk, in fact, a kind of symbolic/mini-pilgrimage is the structure of the Stations of the Cross. We'll pass up and down the church aisles to experience the possibilities of this important Christian walk.

Mandala and Pure Land

Mandala are symbolic patterns, sacred landscapes which describe realms, personages and relationships which invite us into another level of experience where we can participate in processes and adventures beyond the confines of usual time and space. Such experiences can supercede our ordinary body-bound experience and lead us to new understandings of the activities of Buddhas and Bodhisattvas. We will examine several noteworthy *mandalas* and their associated practices.

Pure Land recitation and visualization refers to meditative expeditions wherein the practitioner enters into a trans-physical landscape, one created through the meditative experience, and explores the otherwise inaccessible landscape of the Pure or Western Land of Amida Buddha. In these travels, we follow the practitioner who creates/enjoys a visit to an idealized world of sublime perfection, one intended to inspire and structure one's human realm practice. We consider how we can walk to such a land 'in this very life'.

Walking Practice 9: Labyrinth Walking

Labyrinths appeared in Mediaeval Europe, and possibly earlier, introducing Christian and pre-Christian symbolism into a highly structured walking practice. As Lauren Artress, the woman who single-handedly restored knowledge of and interest in the labyrinth, notes:

> The labyrinth is like teaching a fish to swim. It is easy and natural
> for most people to enter into a different realm of consciousness.
> *The Sacred Path Companion,* Artress, p. 25

Labyrinths are fixed-pattern walks, typically circular, which lead the walker through a complex series of back and forth circles which are designed to interrupt usual-mind thinking. One cannot predict the movement through a labyrinth, but one always has the confidence of completion. Labyrinths are not mazes. They require no solving, only walking. While they have little historical relation to Dharma practice, they have become familiar enough to Western practitioners that there may be value in learning to use them for Dharma practice. We follow our own footsteps through different shapes with different intentions, perhaps to find a way to blend this practice with our own.

Walking Practice 10: Sauntering with Henry

Thoreau has inspired countless writers, naturalists, meditators and environmentalists. During the middle of the 19th century, he re-located from a bustling commercial town in the North East of the US, into a small cabin not far, but far enough, from the town so that he felt part of a natural landscape. His reflections on his life, on nature, on civilization and on walking helped shape 20th century values and thought. In his book/essay, *Walking*, which first appeared in 1862, he begins:

> I have met but one or two persons in the course of my life who understand the art of Walking, that is taking walks, who had a genius for 'sauntering'… I think I can not preserve my health and spirits, unless I spend four hours a day at least, and it is commonly more than that, sauntering through the woods and over the hills and fields, absolutely free from all worldly engagements.
> *Walking*, Thoreau, p. 1-4

There is a distinctly 'spiritual' tone to Thoreau's work and so, as contemplative sojourners ourselves, it will be instructive for us to walk some way with him.

Walking Practice 11: Walking for Change

Many of the various waves of Buddhadharma arising in the West have tended to replicate Eastern practices. Contemporary Western Buddhists have carried on most of the traditional walking practices in some form. With the maturing of Buddhist thought and practice, teachers of all traditions found it critical to re-form walking to meet the needs, issues and familiar context of modern Western society.

From the worker's marches of the early 20th century, through the protests of the 60's-80's and into the 21st century, walking has found a place in the repertoire of social change advocates. Buddhists, East and West, have lead and joined marches for many causes, most often with peace and environmental issue focus. One radical and imaginative new form for walking is interpreted in Elias Amidon's *Mall Mindfulness*. He explains:

> [I had decided to invite my students...] to try something new – to contrast the grounded wisdom achieved through walking mindfully in non-human made nature with the lessons revealed through walking mindfully in that temple of human-made nature, the shopping mall.
>
> *Mall Mindfulness*, in *Dharma Rain*, p. 232

No less participants in this disjointed modern world, we can bring the historic adaptability and creativity of Dharma practitioners the world over to our engagement in the process of bettering our planet and society. Walking can be a vital element of that activity.

Chapter 10: Returning Home

Home, and the journey is over. And yet, are we at the end or only locating ourselves at another threshold? Can we ever truly dwell without some awareness of another boundary which we must cross, and the journey which will take us there? What have we learned on our travels? How might we begin or transform a personal practice with our new walking experience? Will the prospect of some new adventure thrust us into the company of that 17th century Zen poet-traveller, Basho, who could scarcely shake the dust from his feet before he abandoned his cottage once again for *The Narrow Road to the Deep North*.

Let us make preparations for our journey.

CHAPTER TWO
IMAGININGS

> There is a difference between a pilgrim and a wanderer. Buddhist teachings use 'wanderer' to refer to someone who is lost in the rounds of suffering existence, transmigrating through the six worlds... The difference between a pilgrim and a wanderer is to know the path and to set out on it.
>
> Jizo Bodhisattva, Bays, p. 118

This place of dwelling, this home of the hearth and security, is also the place from which we view the open road. It is out the window, over the back fence, below the balcony. It rolls out before us literally and metaphorically, not simply as a road, somewhere to visit, but as a path and the Path, which can relieve us of the irritation of The Question. One teacher of mine used to call it "the only question worth asking, who is this?" It irritates like a stone in one's hiking boot, suggests like an open door and calls like the roar of waves heard from the other side of a sand dune. We have to seek it out.

WALKING AS PRACTICE:
SITTING, WALKING; WALKING, SITTING

It is often said that what distinguishes Buddhadharma from the Abrahamic faiths (Judaism, Christianity, Islam, Bahai) is that they are founded on a set of beliefs; Buddhism is founded on a set of practices. I am not so confident that this is a valid distinction; however, it does point to the Buddhist emphasis put on structured and guided contemplative methods – what we incessantly call practices.

For Buddhists, we perform 'practices' and we have a 'practice'. We bring a certain disciplined attention to following a prescribed method of training, one which has been handed down to us by generations of previous practitioners as leading to deeper levels of insight.

It is important to recognize that practice methods are not a curriculum. Unlike many Western learning processes, where we move through beginner to junior to senior to master, Dharma practice is not a simple matter of working through a set of books or exercises. One individual can practice for decades and never penetrate much of anything. This is sometimes called 'dead sitting'. Another can progress (if that is a proper description) rapidly. Buddhist practice is no mere technique either. There are those who suggest that mindfulness, meditation and other contemplative practices are simply neutral and neural techniques. The proposition is we just need to do certain things, regardless of what we believe or understand, and the effects will follow. One might call it 'sleep-sitting' or 'sleep-walking' practice, rather than sitting or walking practice. They deny the fundamental triad of wisdom-practice-morality taught by the Buddha in his Eight-fold Path. All practices engage the whole person and, to be effective, require our full psycho-physical engagement in the context of the moral challenges of our day-to-day life.

The famous story of Hui Neng, the Zen patriarch, is an example. He was a monastery worker who picked up wisdom by watching and listening. His own determination and sincerity brought him great insight. When it came time for the abbot of the monastery to name a successor, he asked a typical Zen question-puzzle, and invited anyone in the vicinity to answer. The best answer would inherit the abbotship and the leadership of the lineage. The reigning star monk publicly presented his answer, apparently a worthy and studied one. He was thought to be the new abbot. This lay worker, Hui Neng, came to the abbot in secret and offered his answer, one which demonstrated superior insight. Even though Hui Neng had none of the star monk's learning or erudition, his greater insight was recognized by the abbot, who named Hui Neng as his successor. The authenticity of one's insight is confirmed by the master, not merely granted by the completion of a course of learning, by reading the latest best-sellers or ego-driven claims of accomplishment.

Another way of seeing this is to compare two contrasting concepts. In Western learning there is a distinction drawn between theory and practice. They are seen to be contrasted areas of expertise. Someone can be called a great theoretician, an ideas man or, pejoratively, an egg-head or ivory tower dweller. They are contrasted with someone who excels in applications, getting things done. These people are mythologized, especially in the North American environment, as those who fly by the seat of their pants, who are solutions-guys, or rely on instinct or wits, the only thing they know is how to get things done. The contrast is abstract/idealistic versus practical/realistic. Rarely does one progress from one to the other, or excel in both. No doubt this duality has some roots in Western ideas of knowledge and American values; we'll leave that to others to explain.

As one Sangha-leader likes to put it, Buddhists 'hold to no views whatsoever'. There is more of an inclusiveness of wisdom and practice. Wisdom, in the western sense of abstract knowledge, is pointless without some expression in practice; practice methods likewise are hollow actions unless grounded in insight or wisdom. Practice and wisdom are more like two sides of a coin than two poles of a magnet – complement rather than opposition. Therefore, when we engage in any Buddhist practice, we do so from the perspective of wisdom-in-action, and with the intention of elaborating wisdom through practice.

This is not to say that practice is abandoned once insight is attained. Its not that you've got your PhD and don't need to ever crack a book again. The connection between wisdom and practice continues without end. Wisdom would be false or incomplete if it weren't expressed in one's daily practice. One's practice may change and evolve, but remains the manifestation of wisdom.

Sitting and Walking

Buddhist practices take many forms. The saying is "there are 84,000 kinds of practice" – the Buddhist way of saying there are many, many forms. Different schools emphasize some over others, some schools see the different forms as identical leaves on a tree or different roads to the same destination. Modern Chinese Dharma teacher Chen Hua follows this direction:

> ...the Buddhadharma is one in essence, though it has many manifestations. In the first stage, you should gain broad understanding by reading everything you can. Later you can enter deeply into the door of knowledge which you choose according to your individual predisposition and preference...it is imperative that your studies embrace many facets, lest you someday be drawn into a sectarian mentality. Each Buddhist school has its good points, and each can contribute to the perfection of the others... The boundaries between them are never very strict... There is only one Buddhist religion, but it was divided into schools in order to suit the innate capabilities of different people. In studying Buddhism, the first thing is to 'vow to learn the gateways to the Dharma, though they be innumerable'.
> *In Search of the Dharma*, Chen-hua, p. 250

Thus, walking practices are one of many such gateways to the Dharma. We have already touched on the question of whether walking practice is a coherent whole, in the way that sitting or chanting have been seen. For now, we will assume walking practices do form such a coherent whole. If so, how are we to relate them to other kinds of practices, especially the much-vaunted sitting?

Posture

The question of proper posture first struck me only years after I had been sitting *zazen* in a Zen Sangha. We eager 'zennies' were taught, as generations of practitioners were and are taught, that the king of postures, the one Bodhidharma held for years in his cave, which Shakyamuni struck under his Bo Tree, is the full lotus, *padma-asana*. Hour after hour, I squirmed under the silent sneers of seniors who could hold it with ease, while my disobedient knees and ankles refused to conform. One *sensei* looked at me and barked, "if you're going to sit like that, you may as well go home!"

A few years later, when I visited the Land of Serendip, as Sri Lanka was once known, my first non-Western Buddhist environment, I was severally invited to join in with group meditation lead by a senior lay person or a monk. To my astonishment, no one even tried to effect a lotus posture, full, half or otherwise. People sat in what ever seated posture they could manage. Heads might be down, spines might be arched. No one cruised through the crowd with a *kyosaku* (stick of compassion) to adjust posture. The important thing was that you brought the mind to a state of attention. I smugly assumed my very sharpest half-lotus.

At my present level of practice maturity, I would recommend a standard somewhere between these extremes. I know that bullying my body into impossible (for me) poses, offers little strength for insight. I also have confirmed repeatedly that a certain formality and structure of posture proves much more potent for my sitting practice. What I have learned about sitting has also come with a maturing in walking practices, so I tend to see the two practice postures as inter-related. We only have one body, after all. This echoes the advice of one teacher who would describe simple indoor walking practice as identical to sitting in purpose and posture, with the exception of the movement of the legs. Holding that description gently for now, let's explore postures, walking and sitting. Apart from the arrangement of the legs, what are the key elements of the sitting posture?

- The spine is relaxed and uses its natural curvature for support;

- The balance tends to be slightly back-leaning;
- The chest is open, the shoulders back, to facilitate fullest breathing;
- The chin is tucked in, with the tip of the tongue resting on the upper palette;
- The spine is lightly stretched to relieve any compression in its bones;
- The gaze is straight ahead, eyes closed or in 'soft focus';
- There is no rigidity, the body will float gently with the flow of breath, adjusting its centre and balance with the changes in the upper chest;
- There is little other movement, no swaying other than this floating with the breath;
- Breath flows naturally, the belly swelling and collapsing;
- Hands and arms are stabilized in a supportive posture.

For most walking practice, the posture is the same. A good way to experience or establish the posture is to remove shoes and back up to a wall, with heels close to the baseboard. Stand with arms to the side, chin tucked in and follow all the other forms of sitting posture. Fall backward (as it were), into the wall, imagining yourself to be lying horizontally on the floor. Without changing anything above the hips, take a step forward. This is your walking posture.

At first it will seem awkward, but probably no more than what you felt the first few times you sat properly in meditation. The best way to introduce this posture is to use it for formal indoor walking or *kinhin*. As you come to understand the posture and the way the body balances and adjusts in walking, you will be able to employ the same principles for either indoor or outdoor walking.

These are the general principles of walking posture. When we examine other practice forms, we will need to make adjustments or allowances in this posture. For example, extended distance walking outdoors will abandon structured hand positions entirely, in favour of the use of some kind of walking support, such as a pole. Any practice which entails carrying some object, such as a *mokugyo* or *maktok* (the hollow wooden fish-instrument held with one hand and struck with a wooden striker in the other, and used for walking recitation), will require some variation. As with sitting practice, we are guided by the essential dignity of our posture. However and wherever we walk, we are each the companions of countless Bodhisattvas, and our practice, as with theirs, is the practice of liberating all beings. Our practice is the noblest of endeavours and calls for us to represent that nobility and dignity in how we stand and move.

The Hand Position

Hand position is just another element of posture. As with all the elements of posture, the hands influence or at least contribute to the overall posture. For example, the infamous urban text-walking posture illustrates a posture ill-suited to mindful walking (not to mention the inherent risks in traffic!). In this posture, the hands are extended at about chest height, cupped and cradling the mini-screen. The balance is forward, immersed in the changing display of the device. Awareness of the environment of the walk, of the feel of the step, of the flow of the breath is minimal or non-existent. As a 21st century Shakespeare might have said, "The screen's the thing!" Nothing could be further at odds with proper walking practice.

As we will see begin to see in Chapter 5 and following, there are several variations for each of the types of walking practice. The primary considerations of all hand positions are that they complement the overall balance of the walking posture and movement; they do not contribute distractions to the centering of awareness and the attention to the dynamic flow of body-awareness; and as much as possible, they sustain the strongest and most complete cycling of bodily energies, so the practice is invigorating, not tiring.

Different practices necessitate carrying appropriate objects, be that a *shakujo*-staff, a percussion instrument like a *mokugyo*, or a *mala* (beads for recitation). Circumstance may suggest an umbrella, a map, water bottle or identification guide at the ready. As much as possible these need to be portable without involving the hands, so as not to interfere with engaging the hands and arms in the broader posture of the practice. Various hooks, straps and packs are recommended in these cases. Master Thay is renowned for recommending walkers hold the hands of a child. The child will:

> ...receive your concentration and stability and you will receive her freshness and innocence...a child is a bell of mindfulness, reminding us how wonderful life is.
> *The Long Road to Joy*, THN, p. 36

There may be times when this hand-in-hand walking is of value, as Thay recommends. I would suggest that these instances are the exception, best reserved for more casual, short walks. In general, hands need to be free and arranged to support body posture, balance and stride.

Breathing and Walking

The action of breathing is not separate from the taking of a step. The lifting, swinging and placing of the foot necessarily involves the flow of in-breath and out-breath. A synchronicity between breath and step will support a smooth stride, which, in turn, will permit deep levels of concentration while engaging in walking. Conversely, a hurried, erratic or stop-and-start pace will interfere with relaxed breathing and the attention we bring to it and the activity of mind. Later on, we will examine more closely the performance of a synchronized breath-step and using counting or recitation to harmonize walking. For now, it is important to acknowledge the relationship and need to attend to breath with the first step, and to prepare body and breath for walking.

In his *Warrior Walking*, Josh Halzer suggest establishing the proper breath even before we begin. He describes 'embracing the tree', a simple *chi-kung* practice. *Chi-kung* is a set of affiliated, mostly standing, body-breath practices which are often used to build up concentration and body strength which one can use in preparation for a satisfying walk. He recommends we first assume the standing posture known to martial arts enthusiasts as the 'horse stance' (because you look like a rider whose horse has disappeared). The feet are set shoulder-width apart, arms are curved in and palms are facing and slightly curled inward. We squat slightly, with spine upright, we gaze straight ahead. This can be done sitting as well. From this stance we perform a dozen relaxed and deep breaths, attending to the in and out of each breath.

Some may recognize this as somewhat similar to the first few movements in Thich Nhat Hahn's Ten Mindful Movements. This set of very-easy-to-perform standing or sitting movements accomplishes the same pre-walk relaxation and breath awareness.

Depending on when and where and how far one plans to walk, one can turn to any sitting meditative practice, be that *zazen*, *vipassana* or mantra recitation. This is not the place to provide instructions in those disciplines, only to encourage walkers to use a brief period of sitting as preparation. Once again, we are reminded that walking and sitting practice have commonalities as practices. It is mostly the introduction of motion in the lower body and the stimulation of the energies in those regions that make the difference.

WALKING WITH JIZO

There is no greater model or exemplar for our walking practice than the Bodhisattva Jizo. Known elsewhere as *Kshiti-garbha* (Earth-Storehouse) or *Ti-Tsang*, this Bodhisattva is the eternal pilgrim, the walker *par excellence*. He is often portrayed carrying the *shakujo* or pilgrim staff and dressed either as a wandering monk or in the traditional white attire of a Japanese pilgrim. His path takes him through all of the Six Realms of Existence. His purpose is to bring the Dharma to those who cannot otherwise receive it or to share the merit of his efforts to lighten the *karma* burden of beings in dire circumstances. As told in the text known as *The Original Vows and the Attainment of Merits of Kshitigarbha Bodhisattva*, Jizo describes how he is dedicated to visiting all suffering beings, even in the worst of the lowest Hell-realms, and relieving their suffering. The sutra describes the many transformations, a king, a grieving girl and so on, that he assumes to fulfill his vow. He properly attributes this to the even greater vow and compassion of the Buddhas:

> Only through your transcendental powers am I then able to have transformations throughout millions and millions of universes to enlighten suffering beings to real liberation... I solemnly promise to fulfill your instruction to continue to relieve beings.
> *Kishitgarbha Sutra,* ch. 4

Though not clearly part of the sutra's imagery, the form of Jizo developed, over time, into that of the eternal pilgrim. Statues large and small, intricate and crude, appear at roadway intersections, in numbers at the front of temples and, in miniature, as medallions or portraits accompanying travellers. Chozen Bays identifies several ways that Jizo acts as the pilgrim-teacher:

- As a *living presence*, inspiring and guiding our footsteps on the literal and metaphoric Path;
- As a *companion*, walking each step along with us, encouraging and reminding us that we too are walking as and towards Buddhahood, we are never alone on our way;
- As a *protector*, transforming himself into whatever form is required to be of benefit to us on our journey;
- As the *path-clearer*, the one whose preceding efforts allow smoother passage for us.

In the journey we walk in these pages, we have borrowed Tweed's metaphor of religions as 'dwelling and crossing'. Our religious journey, the pilgrimage we walk, in search of a spiritual home or as the means of discovery itself, will take us through all of the Six Realms. At times we will make our way through self-indulgence, jealousy, instinct, desperate craving, utter agony and our very own humanity. Jizo demonstrates that this walking is our practice. Through it we can unfold the Way. On it we can express the Way. Sharing it we can fulfill and realize the Way. He reminds that we too are empowered through the energies and dedication of all the Buddhas.

DHARMA MASTERS GO ON FOOT

As we imagine ourselves pulling on our pack and crossing that threshold, we can hear the voices of our Dharma grandparents recounting the importance of their own journeys and urging us out onto the sunlit path.

> Do not ask me where I am going.
> As I travel this limitless world,
> Every step I take is my home
>
> Dogen Zenji, quoted in Bays, p. 141

It is obvious that they walked. Bodhidharma came from the West and spent years walking and preaching in China. Milarepa walked the treacherous mountain roads of Tibet. Saicho, Honen and the larger-than-life Kobo Daishi travelled up and down the mountain paths of Japan and into China. In fact, the mythology attached to the imposing pilgrimage around the island of Shikoku comforts all pilgrims with the assurance that, even though his pilgrimage took place centuries ago, Kobo Daishi continues to accompany each and every pilgrim who dares to set their feet on its rocky, wind-blown pathways.

Bankei was a Japanese Zen teacher in the 1600's. In *Bankei – Seventeenth Century Japanese Social Worker?*, English practitioner and mental health professional David Brandon writes a short biography of this unusual man. In a manner more resonant with the *myokonin* ideal (kindhearted, unsophisticated teacher) of Shin Buddhism, Bankei would rather help out in his community than study *sutras* in a temple. Brandon describes him:

Bankei had little time for the formal trappings of religious practice – the temples, the incense, the long hours of austere meditation. Bankei not only expressed compassion, he was compassion.

Bankei, Brandon, p. 240

We get the image of a busy community-worker, less a priest or monk. In one story, Brandon describes a walking practice not otherwise described nor endorsed by this writer! It concerns Bankei's reaction to being tricked out of a ferry transport by his jealous and spiteful brother:

When Bankei was refused entry to the boat, he said 'The ground must continue under the water', strode right into the river and struggled to the other side.

Bankei, Brandon, p. 237

Also in the 17th century, the poet-monk-teacher, Basho, like no one else, characterizes the wandering way. His many writings, especially *The Narrow Road to the Deep North,* carry us along with him on his many walks across the Japanese landscape. He acknowledges the power of his wanderings to free him of the turbulence of his mind. It connects him with fellow walkers, like the priest, Gyoki, who so integrated his walking practice into his life that his walking staff did double duty as the main support for his home. Crossing and dwelling seamlessly blend into 'this one moment'. Basho writes:

After many days of solitary wandering, I came at last to the barrier-gate of Shirikawa, which marks the entrance to the northern regions. Here, for the first time, my mind was able to gain a certain balance and composure, no longer a victim to pestering anxiety, so it was with a mild sense of detachment that I thought about the ancient traveller who had passed through this gate…(which) was counted among the three largest checking stations, and many poets had passed through, each leaving a poem of his own making. I myself walked between trees laden with thick foliage, with the distant sound of autumn wind in my ears and the vision of autumn tints before my eyes… Gyoki

is said to have used a [chestnut branch] for his walking stick and the chief support of his house.
Narrow Road, Penguin ed., pp. 105-107

Today, Vietnamese-French Dharma master, Thich Nhat Hahn (THN) is one of the few Dharma teachers to give anything more than a cursory mention of walking practice. He has produced another of his little gems in a multi-media product called *Walking Meditation*. In it he outlines his approach to walking, which is built on three fundamentals – the step, breathing and counting the breath.

The most important element of walking practice for him is coordinating the breath with the step. He recommends a counting method of three steps for in-breath, three steps for out-breath. One can count the numbers or use a phrase, like 'lotus flower blooms' or 'the green planet'. One can increase the number of steps for a longer breath. He comments:

> Walk leisurely, peacefully,
> Your feet touch the earth deeply.
> Don't let your thoughts carry you away,
> Come back to the path every moment.
> The path is your dear friend.
> She will transmit to you
> her solidity and her peace.
> *Walking Meditation*, THN, p. 5

THN does not distinguish indoor from outdoor, nor does he mention any other types of walking practice. We'll return to his advice in later chapters.

John Cianciosi, a disciple of the late Ajahn Chah, reminds us that some traditions, particularly the Thai Theravadin, have strongly stressed walking practice. He writes:

> ...in the area around each [monk's] hut you always find a well-worn meditation path. At various times of the day or night, monks can be seen pacing up and down these paths, mindfully striving to realize the same liberation of heart attained by the Buddha. Many monks walk for long hours and actually prefer it to sitting meditation. The late Ajahn Singtong, a much admired

meditation master, sometimes practiced walking meditation for 10 to 15 hours a day.

From *Mindful Nature Walking (One Step at a Time)*,
John Cianciosi

NON-BUDDHIST ADVICE

We are well instructed by several non-Buddhist practitioners who promote walking practices based in other faith-traditions. The first of these is labyrinthist, Lauren Artress. Artress is an American writer, walker and Christian who has re-kindled the ancient Christian and Pagan practices associated with the labyrinth. She writes:

> My lack of success with sitting meditation motivated me to find a more effective way to handle my chaotic mind. Walking – moving my body – drains of a great deal of excess energy. I can begin to slow down my thought process, become conscious of my breath and allow my awareness to rest in my body.
> *The Sacred Path Companion*, Artress, p. 5

She found walking in the highly structured environment of ancient labyrinth patterns was the key for her. For her it is 'a physical portal' into a symbolic realm and a psychological space. It is 'a watering hole for the spirit'. She lists the benefits of labyrinth walking as:

> ...quieting the mind...nurturing the capacity to reflect... engendering inner spaciousness...enlivening the body... integrating mind/body/spirit...and the realization that we all share the planet.
> *Companion*, Artress, p. 25

Her recommendations for preparing and practicing have noticeable deviations from advice here; however, her explanation of this unique practice, suggestions for meditative exercises and generous welcoming of all, make her worth reading. We will return to her and labyrinth walking in Chapter 9 – New Walking Forms. Another walker/writer worth reading is, of course, Henry David Thoreau.

Thoreau, (1817-1862), lived in the disappearing wilderness of North Eastern America as it began its transformation into an industrial giant. He had little use for the civilized and materially-obsessed world he inhabited. While some may find his writing pompous, judgmental or romantic, he has become a potent voice in caring for and about the environment, and as Thich Nhat Han might describe, 'interbeing' with his natural surroundings. We will set aside space for Thoreau later on, also in Chapter 9.

It would be unfair to neglect the handful of North American outdoor enthusiasts and non-Buddhists who have promoted the contemplative aspects of walking. Most are listed in the Bibliography at the end of this book. We should single out the above-quoted Halzer. His *Warrior Walking* steps out of the tai-chi discipline, and so his practices are more referenced to the tai-chi and martial arts practitioner. Nonetheless, he has great advice for walkers, with detailed body and posture descriptions. His familiarity with Buddhism is understandably cursory, since his interests lie in tai-chi and martial arts. He writes:

> [Strong sitting practice]...does not mean that meditation can only be performed while one is physically still and in a static position... It isn't all that difficult to attain some level of skill in rooting, chi projection and mental focus if you practice seated meditation and then only try to apply your skills in a similar environment of quiet, static posture and artificial tranquility... Being one in the hustle and bustle of everyday life takes real skill. This is why we must come to understand stillness in movement.
> *Warrior Walking,* Halzer, p. 114

In the *Spirited Walker*, race-walker, journalist and fitness advisor Carolyn Scott Kortge creates a blend of fitness advice, non-affiliated spirituality and a familiar kind of self-help, 'you can do anything you want' tone. She describes her entry onto the walking meditation path:

> ...walking crept under my defenses. Walking seemed so simple. I had no idea that these external steps would launch an internal expedition. Step by step, walking drew me into an adventure that travelled unmapped corners of myself. The tight lines that had

bound me inside the image of an athletic 'klutz' began to loosen... I had been looking at my body from the outside, as something to control with discipline and diet. When I stepped inside, I connected with a new self-image and a deeper knowledge of myself.

The Spirited Walker, Kortge, introduction

Elsewhere, beyond the 200 word fluff-as-lifestyle piece about how walking can restore some obscure biological fragment of your body or de-stress, walking advice is showing up in more and more print publications. The fine folks that brought us *Humour in Uniform* and *30 Years of No. 1 Country Hits*, the venerable *Readers Digest*, introduced *Walking* magazine in 1997 (sadly discontinued in 2001). Again, more in the 'lifestyle' than spirituality category, *Walking* offered a broad selection of perspectives on walking, some of which can be useful reference for our purposes. In 2000, they released *The Walker Within – Forty-five Stories of Motivation and Inspiration for Walkers*. In it, Greg McNamee, reminds us:

We were made to wander afoot...to keep moving. When we settle down, it seems, we tend as a species to become nastier rather than more civilized... Idle feet, it turns out are the devil's real workshop.

Walking, in *The Walker Within*, p. 10

Other publications related to walking are/have been *Walk!* magazine (now in blog version, more focused on competitive and race-walking) and *Walk – The Magazine for Ramblers*. This latter is the newsletter of The Ramblers, Britain's oldest charity supporting walking activities for more than 70 years. In print since 2004, it is also online. It focuses on environmental advocacy, and emphasizes adventure and fitness walking, gear, trails and expert advice.

There are numerous websites, Facebook pages and blogs directed at recreational, racing and adventure walking. An exceptional new resource is *Walkopedia* (www.walkopedia.net). This site lists hundreds of walking trails and paths around the world, providing reviews and ratings. If you are interested in a particular location, most regions have some kind of trail association which usually has some kind of newsletter and maps available. A final note: avoid *The Walk*. This is a fashion magazine, another kind of walk-way!

At the Crossroads

The famous apocryphal story of blues-music divinity, Robert Johnson, tells of him standing 'at the crossroads'. He had to choose between an ordinary and mediocre mortal existence or to sell his mortal soul to the Devil in return for an unearthly alacrity on the fretboard of his guitar. Legend has it that he chose the latter and, though he remains a legendary guitarist, he died while in his twenties, victim of a knife fight. Lucifer, it seems, demanded only the best for his band.

Thankfully, our crossroads choices are less consequential. Certain kinds of walking are very specific about location. Indoor walking is generally around the same space as the sitting practice takes place. Circumambulation requires a shrine, *stupa* mountain or some specific site to walk around. Pilgrimage is directed at a specific location. The *kaihogyo* walk is primarily done on the slopes of Mt. Hiei. Labyrinth walking does, of course, assume a labyrinth pattern. Yet the question stands. This way or that?

The choices can be as varied as our own quests and our reasons equally so. Most teachers prefer walking in a natural environment, where one can be in contact with the Earth, rivers and lakes, animals and plants. Thich Nhat Hahn suggests,

> When we practice walking meditation beautifully, we massage the Earth with our feet and plant seeds of joy and happiness with each step. Our Mother will heal us and we will heal her.
> *The Long Road Turns to Joy*, THN, p. 13

However, he acknowledges:

> You can practice walking meditation between meetings, on the way to your car, up and down stairs... This world has many paths [...and...] Every path can be a walking meditation path, from tree-lined roadsides to rice paddies in the back alleys of Mostar or the mine-filled roads of Cambodia.
> Long Road, p. 52

One extraordinary example, which we touched on early, is described in an article called *Mall Mindfulness* by Elias Amidon in the anthology *Dharma Rain, Sources of Buddhist Environmentalism*. He recounts an experiment with a group of his eco-psychology grad students. To contrast a prior nature walk, he takes them to a suburban mall to perform formal indoor walking practice. Perhaps the answer to the where question is similar to the Buddha's advice about practice – which practice you perform is less important than your dedication and sincerity in doing so.

Another choice for the contemplative walker might be expressed as – walking alone or with others? Buddhist literature frequently praises the lonely path of the solitary monk or uses the image of the Buddha as the 'lone elephant'. This may seem a simple issue; however, several Buddho-logical observations will qualify or refine the question. This is not the time or place for protracted theological discourse; however, we are exploring the contemplative dimension of the activity of walking, so some considerations of theological concepts can be helpful.

Firstly, our teaching directs us to interconnectedness and our inseparability from all beings. Other than in outer space, could one ever be alone? If we accept the notion of 'the activity of Buddhas and Bodhisattvas', we have to consider what alone might mean. Here I am speaking of more than the fantasy-realist vision of the sutra tradition, where magnificent and colossal Bodhisattvas emerge suspended in space, or vow to be endlessly active in the lives of sentient beings. While I don't discount that vision, we may also acknowledge Bodhisattvas as being fully active in our lives as something other than fantasy versions of humans-in-the-clouds. As Buddhists, or, in fact, as any kind of contemplative walker, we will have no difficulty allowing for the presence of compassion, loving kindness, healing and care-giving, for example, as vivid forces in our lives. May we not then, allow that Kwan Yin, Jizo and countless other Bodhisattvas are, in fact not just in metaphor, present and active in our lives, as not different from those familiar ethical abstracts. If we can allow for that, aren't these forces already with us, exerting themselves for our benefit as they vow they will. The question then presents itself whether our walking could ever possibly exclude the companionship of Bodhisattvas. Their vows are not dependent on our approval. We need not look for a colossal and magnificent humanoid figure ahead on the trail to experience the certainty of our being surrounded by compassionate care and embraced in loving kindness. Isn't the Buddha-presence displayed in the birds along our trail, the flowers that show our path and countless other guides we experience as we walk?

Secondly, Buddhist teaching excels at shattering our small vision of time. It does so in at least two ways. For one, it envisions time and space as non-linear. Beings can exist simultaneously in multiple times and dimensions. Thus, we might feel alone but only within a narrow time and space. On the other hand, the path under our feet may also be trod upon by others in parallel times or spaces. This may sound a bit too Star Trek-ish for some. Another way to understand this is to expand our usual frame of time. Its commonplace for my wife and I to walk a quarter of a mile apart because of our different paces and the interests of our three dogs. Although we aren't holding hands, we consider this walking together. If she were to walk the path this hour and I walk it an hour later, are we still walking together? At what point are we together or alone? Do we have to be in sight of each other, within arms' reach? Could we be together an hour, a day, a year, a century apart, and be walking together in some respect? Consider the impact of walking the same American trail as Thoreau or Daniel Boone or any of the English poets who traversed the Lakes District or the countless unnamed pilgrims who undertook pilgrimage after pilgrimage across the Spanish Compostello. In what way are we together with them? I suggest no matter what we call it, we are always walking with some other person or being. Since our practice is about opening ourselves to the environment, spatial and temporal, of our practice, we might need to reflect on the mind-state which encourages us to 'get away by myself'.

Walking Where?

Our journey seeks to explain the what, why and how of walking practices. A reasonable additional question is the 'where?' of walking. We won't spend too much time on this question, since it is mostly answered as where you practice. In a sense, we should be doing our walking practice wherever we can walk. Like all mindfulness practices, there are easier and more demanding spaces, but the practice is meant to be engaged wherever you are. Elsewhere, we discuss the range from Cuban beaches to Appalachian Trail, Sri Lankan desert to Japanese coast, Tibetan mountain, Tuscan foothills and Southwest valley. We discuss sites like *zendo* walking, garden walks, mall walking, labyrinth walks, 'walking for the cure' and 'random' walks. All are legitimate, powerful and worth doing.

Our most insistent source to express a strong preference for location is Thoreau who gives priority to walking in 'the wild', away from industrial civilization. Mundy, who explains prayer-walking a little further on, would hold the opposite view, I expect. For him, anywhere is appropriate to connect with the Divine. He would likely support anywhere which is available, affordable and, from an abilities perspective, walkable. As for many willing walkers, who walk as disabled adults, safety, rest stops and necessity of canes, crutches and walkers will limit locations.

Somewhat loosely in the Thoreau lineage, several modern writers offer similar advice and perspective, although for different reasons, for us when we ask a 'where?' question. Three in particular have shaped this work:

- Michael Pollan, *Second Nature: A Gardener's Education*
- Mark Coleman, *Awake in the Wild: Mindfulness in Nature as a Path of Self-Discovery*
- Richard Louv, *Last Child in the Woods: Saving Our Children From Nature-Deficit Disorder,* and *The Nature Principle: Human Restoration and the End of Nature-Deficit Disorder.*
- (NOTE: I would include Bill McKibben and John Seed in this company, although their work did not directly influence this book.)

What they share from a walker's perspective is an uncompromising insistence on the value of our walking in a natural environment and the importance of *acting*, not merely *being* in the natural world. For us as walkers, we understand we are interconnected with our walking environment. It is not a museum piece nor some unapproachable other where we as humans don't belong. As Pollan, who comes from a gardener's experience, notes about the late 19th century nature writers (Thoreau, Whitman, Hawthorne, etc.):

> Everybody wrote about how to be in nature, what sorts of perceptions to have there, but nobody about how to act there. Yet the gardener, unlike the naturalist, has to, indeed, wants to act.
> *Second Nature*, Pollan, p. 3

No doubt there are those who would quibble over what is a 'natural' environment, what is 'wilderness' or where the dividing line is between that and what Thoreau disparaged as 'civilization' or what some call 'human culture'. Pollan again offers:

> Americans have a deeply ingrained habit of seeing nature and culture as irreconcilably opposed; we automatically assume that whatever one gains, the other loses... This choice, which I believe to be a false one, is what led Thoreau and his descendants out of the garden... My experience in the garden leads me to believe that there are many important things about our relationship to

nature that cannot be learned in the wild. For one thing, we need, now more than ever, to learn how to use nature without damaging it.

Second Nature, Pollan, p. 4

For our purposes, the way we use nature is as the site, companion, inspiration and structure for our walking practice. We must distinguish that we are not consumers of nature. Unlike the disturbing modern trend to transform natural spaces into controlled/captured, marketable and capitalized commodities for 'experience consumers' to rent, lease or own, we walkers are obliged to treat the walking environment as a partner in our practice.

Coleman urges us to be aware of this interconnection in our practice. For him we are not simply observers of some wild other, where distance, disengagement and reverence are expected. He describes the natural world more as part of the plenum of loving kindness that we inhabit, that we draw on, and, by necessity, must contribute to as well. Walking in nature is a doorway into our own nature, if Buddhists can use that term, as much as being about nature. He reminds that the natural world is not exclusively majestic, innocent and pure, as the 19th century nature-writers might have presumed. The natural world offers us a view of 'this Great Matter of Life and Death'. He reminds:

> When opening our hearts [to nature], we expose ourselves not only to the joy that nature and life have to offer, but also to the pain... Walking in nature, we can reciprocate the love that we feel coming from the cottonwood trees...when birds fly past us, we can hold them gently in our hearts and wish that they be safe, healthy and well. This practice can connect us with the pulsing heart at the source of everything... Remember you are part of nature.
>
> *Awake in the Wild*, Coleman, p. 12

The third responder to the 'where?' question is Richard Louv. He coined the term 'nature-deficit disorder' to describe a gradual and unmistakable tendency in Western society to be disconnected from experience in the natural world. From closed or trivial playgrounds, to disappearing parklands, to the tragic ignorance of natural processes, our world is descending into one where the natural world is simply unavailable, a non-essential option or a consumer choice. He explains:

> Nature deficit disorder describes the human costs of alienation from nature, among them: diminished use of the senses, attention difficulties and higher rates of physical and emotional illnesses. The disorder can be detected in individuals, families and communities and can even change human behaviour in cities, which could ultimately affect their design, since long-standing studies show a relationship between the absence or inaccessibility of parks and open space with high crime rates, depression and other urban maladies.
> *Last Child in the Woods: Saving Our Children From Nature-Deficit Disorder*, Richard Louv, part 3

Louv moves beyond the 19th century romantics who idealized and separated us from nature and the wilderness. As with Coleman, he affirms that walking in nature is how we can connect with ourselves, as individuals and also ourselves as part of the larger natural world. The strong encouragement of this book, my answer to the 'where?' question, points firmly and enthusiastically at the natural world, whatever this means for each walker. For those lucky enough to reside in a rural setting, this is a less complicated choice. For urban dwellers, certain parks and protected spaces may be preferable. As Buddhists, there is no place which is not appropriate for our practice. No matter where we set our feet is the road for us. I suggest that one is more likely to connect with the call of the road when it traverses the natural world. Nonetheless, wherever it arises, that call of the road, that irritation in the hiking boot, is none other than 'the Voice That Calls' as Amitabha has been called. He, in his own form or that of his manifestation, Jizo, beckons us out onto the pilgrim's way. He invites us out onto the Way where:

> In ten directions everywhere, throughout the sea of lands,
> Every hair-tip encompasses oceans of past, present, and future.
> So too, there is a sea of Awakening, a sea of Buddha lands;
> Pervading them all, I cultivate for oceans of endless time.
> *The Vow of Samantabhadra,* Master T'am, p. 229

CHAPTER THREE
THRESHOLD – FOOT AND STEPS

As the mind works to focus on each section of the movement during a walking session, concentration becomes continuous. Every step builds the foundation for the sitting that follows, helping the mind stay with the object from moment to moment – eventually to reveal the true nature of reality at the deepest level. This is why I use the simile of a car battery. If a car is never driven, its battery runs down. A yogi who never does walking meditation will have a difficult time getting anywhere when he or she sits down on the cushion. But one who is diligent in walking will automatically carry strong mindfulness and firm concentration into sitting meditation.

The Five Benefits of Walking Meditation,
Sayadaw U Pandita in *This Very Life*

There is no path without a step. Our journey is only wishful thinking, a bold and lovely vision, until we set that first footstep over the threshold. Then that step magically, it seems, transforms our lives from dwelling to crossing, from home to the trail. Each successive step leads us deeper into the path.

WALKING WITH THE WHOLE BODY

Introduction

Even though only two feet are employed, it is as though there are an infinite number of feet each always ready for support as the body advances...walking is analogous to moving a load with a succession of logs beneath...the mechanical equivalent to a single wheel...

Tai Chi Walking, Chuckrow, p. 37

Chuckrow's metaphor of the wheel is a reminder of the dynamic flow of our stepping. Its not quite true in that, when we walk, we alternate between two feet and one foot in contact, but the image of a fluid support for the motion of the upper body is a fair one. Just as with a wheel, the evenness and balance of flow is responsible for the comfort of the ride.

When we begin walking, we engage the whole body, the whole mind. In a way different from sitting practice, which inhabits and demonstrates the space of attention, walking enters and exercises the space. If sitting is a sculpture of space, walking is a dance, a ballet.

There are four main body considerations involved in walking practice and we'll examine each below. Posture is no less important in walking than in sitting practice. It might seem obvious that foot and step need careful attention. In Chinese medicine, the foot is recognized as the contact point between heaven and earth. The foot, especially the sole itself, becomes another threshold for us to work with in our practice. More than just the structure of the foot, the step also is of importance for walking. The foot is the structure and the stride is how we make use of that collection of muscles, bones, tendons and ligaments. As we walk, we have to arrange and use our hands somehow, or they can interfere with the rhythm and balance of the stride. Hand positions are not simply a matter of personal preference, and we will see how each has its benefits and value. Finally, as with all practices, breath is of great importance to our walking. A poor alignment between step and breath creates a disharmony and an imbalance which disrupts and diminishes the value of the practice. As Thich Nhat Hahn says "Everything depends on the step."

Body Structure

Body Posture

> This illusion of movement and solidity is like a movie. To ordinary perception it seems full of characters and objects, all the semblances of a world. But if we slow the movie down we will see that it is actually composed of separate, static frames of film.
> From *Walking Meditation,* Sayadaw U Pandita

For most indoor walking styles, attention to a correct posture is as important as it is in sitting practice. As with sitting, the stamina, strength and benefits of the practice are directly related to the clarity, openness and balance of the posture. A good way to establish the walking posture is to back up to a wall, with heels close to the baseboard. Stand with arms to the side, chin tucked in and allow the spine to stretch upwards. Step away from the wall without altering the posture.

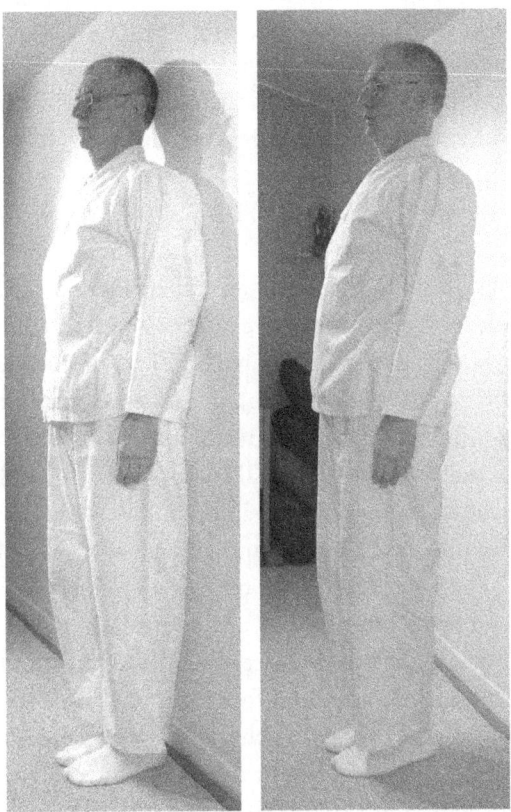

Proper posture for contemplative walking

In his instructions on Qigong posture, Zen teacher, Teja Bell advises:

> By paying attention to the integrity of structural alignment, the practitioner improves posture, increases relaxation and ease and develops what I call 'field awareness' of the body – the ability to be holistically aware of the presence of aliveness to what we

call 'our body'.... [you should] become present to the sensations of the weight of your body connecting with the surface you are standing on. Sense the three primary energy points of your feet...develop the feeling of connecting with the earth and with the quality of natural grounded stability... Sense the energetic 'centreline' that flows through the core of your body...a vertical axis that connects the three dynamic centres of the body – the head, the heart and the *hara* [lower abdomen]...[which] connects heaven and earth with the individual human in the middle...the physical and energetic being begins to come into harmony with itself and the environment.

Qigong for Meditators, Bell, in *Tricycle*, Summer, 2011

Our standing and walking posture and the balance of our stride rest on awareness of the feet as they shift our weight, through a steady stride and pace. Maintaining this dynamic awareness and balance in standing-rest is the beginning of that same awareness while in motion. In some respects walking meditation ignores or at least minimizes upper body motion. We stabilize the arms and hands through the fixed hand positions, as we'll discuss below. We do not engage any arm swinging as in the normal gait. Of primary importance is what happens from the hips down. More precisely, the hips and legs act as means of setting the stride in motion, but it is the feet, that is, the complex foot structure and mechanism which plays the most significant role in understanding a smooth, balanced and rhythmic stride. The feet, therefore, deserve careful attention. Both Western and Chinese medicine systems describe the foot structure, each in its own way. Our purpose here is not to promote one over the other, but to incorporate what we can from each to deepen our appreciation for the importance of the feet and the ways to make best use of them in our practice.

Structure of the Foot in Western Medicine

The human foot acts in concert with the rest of the body during standing and movement. It provides man with his most effective physical contact with the environment and is especially responsible for successful regulation of initial and final contact of the body with the ground. The foot must also provide adjustable support during the characteristic human occupations of manipulating the environment or of simply standing in line... Walking is more characteristic of human movement than running, since man has substituted cunning in the management of external devices for fast movement of body parts when speed is desired. The foot must constantly adjust to the varying loads imposed upon it. Particularly important are the stresses it must withstand at the initiation of contact with the ground and again at its termination.

Dynamic Structure of the Foot, Herbert Elftman, 1960

Western medicine describes the foot structure in terms of springs, keystones and other mechanical terms. These machine metaphors can help us to understand the complex flow and transfers that take place in every step. The foot consists of 28 bones controlled by 42 muscles and is held together by an almost unbelievable number of ligaments. In fact, the foot is:

> ...one of the most dynamic structures in the human body. The lively interplay of forces which makes its function possible is easily forgotten and it is too often treated like the graven image of a static structure.
>
> same reference

A brief summary of the structure tells us that we have:
- a complex arrangement of odd-shaped bones that compose the ankle (*talus*); these act to translate and transfer the forces from the hips, knees and legs along the rest of the foot;
- the heel (*calcaneus*) which connects the ankle, the toes and the large Achilles tendon which stretches up the back of the leg; it balances and pivots the step for maximal push;
- a span of long bones (the *meta-tarsals*) spreading out from the ankle which further transfer the forces into the ground through
- the ball of the foot, a structure of tissue and skin, located in the joints between the long and short bones and implicated with the tendons of the arch; the ball is the point of maximal force transfer from body to walking surface;

- a span of shorter bones (*phalanges*) which fan from the ball providing a stabilizing base for the step.

The simple process of stepping forward (or any direction), when looked at with more detail is actually a sequence of rotations (the ankle), rolling and balancing (the heel), a zig-zag transfer (the arch), an explosive thrust (the ball) and a spreading, springing preparation for the next step (the ball and toes). It would seem that, as Thich Nhat Hahn muses, the real miracle in life is that we can actually take a step.

Of course, we don't need to pass Foot Anatomy 100 to be able to perform contemplative walking. What this micro-description tells us is that there is a magnificent means for taking the forces and energies of the body and transferring them safely, efficiently and rhythmically. Such an awareness of the structure allows us to better feel the movement along the foot, from back to front as we step. It allows us to think and feel our way along our path. We will walk more completely when we can feel deep into the foot's movement and structure.

Additionally, some understanding of these details can help us to trouble-shoot problems and injuries that can occur with more active walking.

Structure of the Foot in Chinese Medicine

Western medicine excels at the former mechanical description, whereas Eastern or Chinese medicine more consciously attempts to place the human body and physical health in the context or setting of the natural world and Cosmos. Firstly, several large body systems or channels are responsible for balancing all the functions of the body. They run from the head to foot, side to side. The primary energy point in the foot is the centre of the ball of the foot, the so-called 'bubbling well', the point known as Kidney 1 (K1) or *yong-quan*. It is the lowest energy point in the body and one extreme of the Kidney energy channel which ascends through the body through the liver, lungs, throat and head.

In Chinese, the first character, *yong*, means surge, well up, gush. One part of the character points to water, showing water drops; the other shows a bud opening, suggesting strength. The idea of bursting forth with strength combined with water gives the meaning of surging water. The second character, *quan* means spring, fountainhead. The upper part is a rising sun, which implies, white, bright, clear. The lower part is water. Together, the bright white water is a fountainhead or spring.

It is the gateway to earth energy, sometimes called the 'earth surge' or 'earth thoroughfare' (what a great name for the foundation of our walking!), the balance of the frontal and rear lines, the upper and lower regions and the primary means by which we root our posture and make our connection with the earth.

As the lower or 'child' region of the Kidney channel, it plays a part in the flow of chi energy upwards towards the head, therefore implicated in mental clarity. Acupuncture specialists, Deaman, et al, tell this story:

> When the Kidneys are deficient below, pathologically ascending chi may rush upwards to harass the head. The powerful effect of Yongquan KID-1 on descending and clearing such excess is recorded in a story about the famous 2nd century physician Hua Tuo who treated General Wei Tai-cu for 'head wind, confused mind and visual dizziness'. Following the principle of selecting points below to treat disorders above, Hua Tuo needled Yongquan KID-1 and "the general was immediately cured."
> *A Manual of Acupuncture,* Deaman, Al-Khafaji, & Baker, 2007

Deaman continues by adding:

> According to a saying of Chinese medicine "The Lung is the canopy and the Kidneys are the root"...the Lung receives, via respiration, the clear chi of heaven in the same way that the canopy of a forest receives the light and air essential for life. Through the grasping and holding function of the Kidneys, the chi is drawn down via inhalation to the root below... Yongquan KID-1 is an important point in (meditative movement) practice. Directing the mind to Yongquan KID-1, or inhaling and exhaling through this point, roots and descends the chi in the lower *tanden* (also known as the *hara* or central abdominal energy so influential in meditative breathing) and helps the body absorb the yin energy of the earth.
> same reference

I approached New York acupuncturist, Karl Bowers, L.Ac., about *yong-quan* and he explained:

What can be said about the deliberate ways in which we walk in *kinhin* and the concentration that we hold in each step, there is a greater stimulation of the [*yong-quan*] point than during sitting practice [when chi comes up through the perineum]. We are actually dropping our awareness into the feet. This awareness, from my opinion, increases the flow that occurs naturally, which is the Yin coming up from the earth...walking also moves the chi and blood, they flow together, so the act of walking helps to move that energy into the *tanden*. (This being the centre of gravity, with all movements to and from this centre, we remain balanced and not wobbly, and the spine sits naturally on it.) This is aided in the steps we take, not a huge gait to the walk, rhythmically and consistently pressing heel, outside of foot, to the inside, assures that all aspects of the foot are pressed evenly and easily into the floor (like meditation, not tilted left or right, front or back) and as we walk, the pressure is dynamic, never staying on one area of the foot for longer than needed, keeping the movement forward. It says a lot for the act 'putting pressure' on KID-1, stimulating it and promoting its 'grounding' effects.

(Private communication, 2011)

What this tells us is that the *yong-quan* is more than just a focal point in the ball of the foot. It is one critical node in a major channel which transfers our life energy (*chi*) from the earth into the head, providing clarity of thought. It is an essential component of the larger system of the body and affects our relationship to the movement and flow of cosmic energy fields within which our bodies live, and through which we walk.

In his study of religious themes, French religionist, Rene Guenon, describes the Chinese doctrine of 'the great triad' (*The Great Triad*, 1994). This is the division of the cosmos as heaven-man-earth. I will not offer any extended explanation of either Chinese metaphysics nor Guenon's work here. The central insight for us is related to the inter-mediary function of the step in our relationship with heaven (however we want to define that) and earth (however we may define that). Since humans began walking upright, abandoning the trees and the quadruped life forever, we have experienced our bodily place in between heaven and earth primarily through our feet. For the most part, our mobility is a constant negotiation on behalf of the part of us that waves in space like a blade of grass and the surface which literally 'grounds' us. A step is rarely a single phenomenon, rather part of a rolling, stroking action whereby we seek a new point of stability and harmony between heaven and earth. The 'bubbling spring' represents the key connection of this relationship.

Hand Positions

Walking is seated posture in motion, so to speak, and how we hold our hands must reinforce our posture every bit as much as when seated. In zazen postures, experience teaches us the power of the *zazen mudra*, that hand position represented in Buddha images and taught widely. The strongest hand position in walking is derived from that same sitting hand position.

You know that the sitting hand position is with the hands held in the lap, palms up, flat and parallel to the ground. The left hand rests on the right. The fingers are extended and the thumbs form an oval above the palms, with their tips gently touching. One teacher used to say we should pretend we were balancing a grapefruit on our fingers, with the thumbs stretched over the top. This structure is strong, never rigid, allowing the hands to rest in the lap. Properly done in combination with a suitable sitting posture, there is no strain on the shoulders, and one can sustain the posture for long periods of practice. Those who study the flow of psychic energies of chi-flow explain that the *zazen mudra* creates and reinforces a cycle of energy in the frontal line of the body, and that this builds deep strength within the *hara (or tanden)*, the spiritual centre of the body, located behind the hands in sitting posture. The mudra also acts as an alert for the practitioner. The quickest indication that one's concentration is failing is when the hand position begins to collapse, with the thumbs dropping.

Our primary walking hand position begins with the *zazen mudra*. Curl the left hand fingers inward, enclosing the left thumb with the fingers. Wrap the right hand fingers around the left, continuing to cradle the left with the right. Place the right thumb on top of the left thumb. You now have the correct arrangement. Raise this hand arrangement upward to rest lightly over the heart. This, then becomes *shashu*, the walking hand posture. Another variation called *isshu*, has the left hand held parallel to the floor and the right resting on top of it. I haven't used this and can't see its advantages.

Each of us is blessed/cursed with our unique body shape with curves, contractions, bulges and cavities. Should you be living with the consequences of

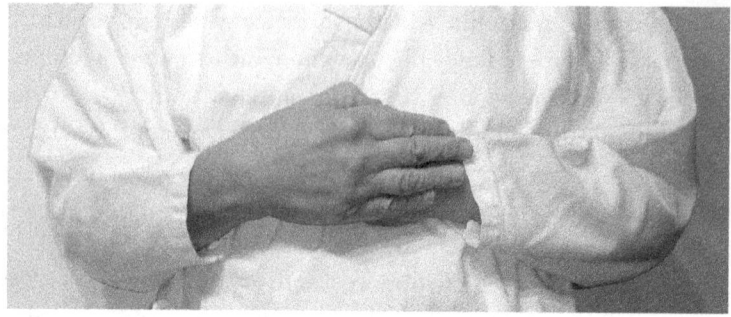

Shashu, the walking hand posture

an upper body injury or disability, you will have your own architecture to work with. Exactly where you place the hands will then be a matter of experimentation. Usually one will feel the hands 'click' into the right place. This is equally true for the walking posture itself.

There is a second hand posture which can be used. It is simpler and many people prefer it to the *shashu* position. This style comes from Pure Land, and is used for walking chanting, including circumambulation. It is not hard to recognize that this position is a slight variation on the *zazen mudra*, one which releases the mudra and turns the hands flat onto the body. Place the palm of left hand over the lower belly, with fingers extended. Place the right hand over the left, slipping the right thumb in between the thumb and forefinger of the left. Both hands lie flat against the body. The arms are held loosely. Again, the precise up or down location of the posture

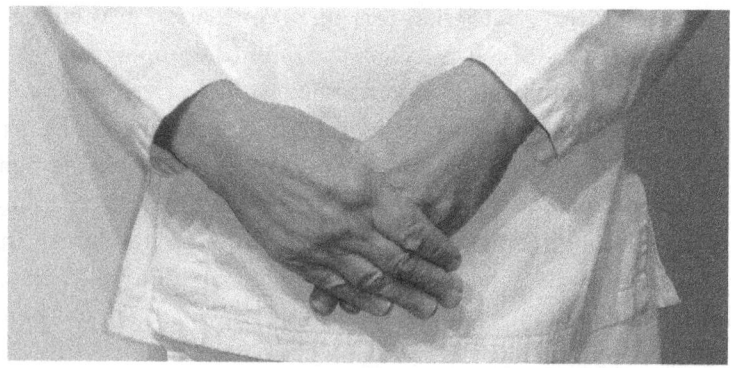

Alternative walking hand posture, based on the zazen mudra

will be determined through experimentation. A variation of this is repeating the position, but placing the hands behind the back, so they rest in the small of the back.

There are those who will quibble about the relative left-right priority of the hands, regardless of the position used. In some Buddhist schools, right over left or the reverse expresses a particular symbolic power relationship, expresses a principle of the flow of cosmic energies. In some elements of Chinese medicine, the left represents the public self, the right the inner. I have also heard people insist that men should place left over right to stabilize the preponderance in men of strong right hands or the need to balance the *yang* (male, right side) energy with *yin* (left, female). Doing so, it is claimed, balances the energies of the body. Conversely, women will be encouraged to put the right on top for the opposite reason. There may be a time when this detail matters; however, for beginners, experimenting with either positioning will not be disastrous.

If you watch Thich Nhat Hahn in his *Walking Meditation* video, you will observe yet another hand position. Its not clear if this is idiosyncratic for Thay, if he recommends this as a standard or simply uses it during this lecture. In any case, he interlocks his fingers, with the right index finger as the first finger on the top. His left thumb is lowered to rest on the right index finger, his right thumb touches the place where the left thumb joins the left hand. He holds this position at about waist height. It is a comfortable position and worth experimenting with. The closest thing I can guess is a variation on what is called the Sign of Unshakable Inner Strength (*vajrapradama mudra*) which apparently has special preference in Laos and Thailand. Comparing it with the

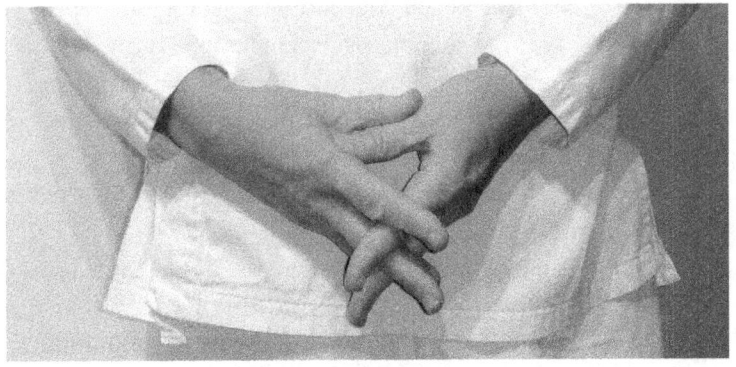

Second alternative walking hand posture, as used by Thich Nhat Hanh

zazen mudra, one could speculate that it is a more stable version of the sitting mudra, where the interlock holds the mudra in place, and the thumbs contact the same energy points on the hand that the fingers do in the *zazen mudra*.

One may dismiss all the specifics of hand positions as fussiness, as Asian folklore or unnecessary for the modern practitioner. On the other 'hand', we may too quickly dismiss the relation of the hands and the parts of the hands to the larger balancing systems of the body as described in the classics of Chinese medicine. I encourage all walkers to take some time to allow themselves to learn and use these various positions and, based on sufficient practice experience, determine what is most supportive.

Hand Position and Chi-Flow

We mentioned above the importance of the 'bubbling spring' (*yong-quan*) point in the ball of the foot and its centrality in our dynamic relationship with the realms of heaven and earth (however we define those). The placement of the hands, and their contact with the body and each other plays a small but noteworthy part in this moving drama of walking. Here, we'll consider the static positioning of the hands during the slower walking practices, primarily *kinhin* (see next chapter).

We earlier mentioned that several large body systems or channels are responsible for balancing all the functions of the body. They run from the head to foot, side to side. We emphasized the *yong-quan* in the foot as the primary chi-energy location in the feet. The hand-arm areas of the body are the location for two meridians or channels which concentrate several points in the hands. As we'll see, these points have a role in pain management, breathing and the moisture associated with breathing.

The hand contains the first five of a series of acupuncture points, the Lower Intestine channel (LI1-20) located at:

- LI-1 (*shang yang*), found at the tip of the index finger; involved in pain and inflammations;
- LI-2 (*er jian*), found at the knuckle where the index finger joins the hand;
- LI-3 (*san jian*), found just below LI-2; involved in cooling the face and throat and in stabilizing the lower intestines;
- LI-4 (*hoku*), found in the webbing where the thumb and index

finger meet; with LI-3 involved in improving chi-flow, especially involved with face and head;
- LI-5 (*yang xi*), found at the base of the thumb; involved in management of wrist pain;
- LI-6 through 20 are located up the arms into the centre of the face.

The hand, then, contains the *hoku* point (LI-4) which relieves mental confusion, obsessiveness and various digestive upsets. It is highly recommended by acupuncturists to relieve headaches, as well as joint and muscle pain anywhere in the body. This, and the others, are the points which receive a light but steady pressure in the recommended walking hand positions. Thus, when we adopt the proper hand position, we are promoting improved joint performance, energy flow and alertness in the face and head.

Another set of points close to the LI set runs from the top edge of the thumbs up to the shoulder. The series, the Lung Meridian or LU is eleven points. The three positions in the hand are LU-9, (*tai-yuan*), located at the base of the wrist, LU-10, (*yu-ji*), located quite close to LI-4 and LU-11, (*shao-shang*), located at the outside of the tip of the thumbs. The LU-10 point, called 'fish border' is important in managing throat dryness, improving breathing, and chi-flow.

To create a strong energy environment while walking, we need also to be aware of a third system which runs down the sternum or breastbone, called the Conception Vessel meridian (CV). From the bottom of the rib cage to the throat, there are ten CV points. These points are important in managing breathing and energy flow. This channel is important to our walking posture because we are placing the hand cluster directly over this channel as we walk. Not only are we building strength by putting the hands in contact with each other, but building an energetic circle of chi across the chest. As you explore and experiment with these hand positions, you will begin to discover the precise points of energy in your own body and experience the harmony and balance of the hand positions we suggest.

This detail is not intended to empower you to perform any kind of acupuncture/pressure treatments on yourself, but only to indicate the presence of important energy points in the hands. When we hold our hands in front of the body using the described positions, it is clear that we have the opportunity to work with the core energies of the body. These energies transit through our bodies, between the earth and sky, and keeping the energy flow unimpeded and strong allows our walking to be stronger, and the resulting mind states stronger as well.

In the previous chapter we recommended the use of some type of hiking pole. As we have seen in considering hand positions, the involvement of the hand reinforces rather than weakens the energetic dimension of walking, especially the *yong-quan* point in the ball of the foot. With the use of poles, the proper grip, regardless of handle type, will be the placement of the pole between the thumb and the first finger. This lever point in poling will further engage hand positions of the LI and LU channels that parallels the *yong-quan*. The position between the thumb and the place where the first and second fingers joins the hand, in effect, forms a complimentary chi-point. We need not be too obsessive of whether we are holding the pole in the correct point. This relationship is suggested here to remind us that when we walk, the whole body, all of its energy points and movements are involved. Whether we are describing hand positions in slow walking or poling grips for more active walking, the hands are not simply going along for the ride. They are important and active participants in the whole body experience we call walking practice. We ought not dull or ignore the major role played by the hands as we walk the Dharma path. If using poles, we must be clear not to grip the handles with the whole hand, as we might on a brake handle or axe. We need a light hand, a dynamic hold which frees and directs the energies of body-mind.

Walking and Breath

Those who have experimented with sitting practices already know there are numerous ways to work with the breath. There are counting the breath, 'bamboo-breath', 'wheel-of-winds', 'stopping the breath', 'throwing strength into the *tanden*' and many more. Such techniques are less of interest in walking practice, because the primary demand is maintaining an even pace and stride. Balance, flow and rhythm exceed stability and groundedness. This is not to suggest that breath-control and attention to the breath are unimportant, for they are not. Only to say that of greater importance is the relationship between that practiced breath and the step.

The breath acts as the primary support for the step, it connects the step to the broader movements of the body. We know that breath is not something added to or even parallel to the awareness of body. Not only are body and breath two of the Four Foundations of Mindfulness (along with speech and mind), the separation or duality of body and breath is a convenience of thought, not a reality. We cannot be aware of the breath except through the awareness of body. Awareness of body is always mediated through awareness of breath.

When walking, we work with breath in two ways, first, layering breath and step, and secondly, pacing breath and step.

Layering means the relationship between the phases of breathing and the phases of each step. The relationship between breath and step can be illustrated as in the following chart:

Phase	Breath	Step
1ST	Lifting the foot	Drawing the breath in (inhalation)
2ND	Swinging the foot forward	The filled-lung inter-breath pause
3RD	Shifting the weight into the planted heel	Pushing or releasing the inhaled breath
4TH	Rocking the weight along the foot in the transfer of weight.	The emptied lung inter-breath pause.

Those with some familiarity with movement activities, be they martial arts or dance or sports, know that the inhaled breath accompanies preparation, the exhaled breath accompanies exertion. The in-between breath phases are those mid-action pauses, important for contemplation and decision. One teacher of mine used to say that the in-between phase was the most valuable, not the in or out breath. He believed that in the silence, stillness and pregnancy of that middle phase represented *akasha*, (infinite spaciousness), that place where anything/everything was possible. He encouraged us to look deeply into that space. (Later in the book we consider another dimension of such in-between spaces as a metaphor for one sub-set of walking practice). Thus, in its simplest terms, we coordinate the lifting of the foot with inhalation, we coordinate the shifting of weight with exhalation. The forward thrust is driven by the pushing out of breath. Likewise, the mid-step pauses represent not only the necessity of alertness to change of direction or attention, as is familiar to martial arts practitioners, but also a crucial point to attend to the whole space of walking, to contemplate direction and purpose, and to re-commit to or alter one's course. As we attend to and explore the mid-step phase, the more it expands and opens as an ever-expanding space in our consciousness and the more it provides opportunities for insight.

The phases are not that discreet, however, and should not be bluntly separated. Rather they flow one into each other, in sequence. This means that the final filling of the lungs is also the beginning of the forward movement of the foot. The inter-breath pause is quite brief and hangs in the air like an arrow pulled back on a bow.

The fullest point of the exhalation is the planting of the heel and the commitment to the weight shift. The emptied lung pause is similarly brief and not as sustained as it usually is during sitting practice. Finally, the full shift of weight onto the forward foot and the lifting of the rear foot for the next step are not separate. It is more of a rocking movement, where the body is balanced in a fluid way on both the forward and rear feet. Only in the slowest versions of indoor walking would there actually be a point of poise, where the forward foot is held up

It is obvious that this layered step is a slow pace, one best suited to indoor or structured pattern or track walking. The very slow and balanced movement compliments the mental attention, breath and movement become one. Once we shift to open outdoor walking, such as you might do in an informal contemplative walk, we would likewise shift to a different step-breath pace. Thich Nhat Hahn recommends this through a counted step. He instructs that we should multiply steps-to-breath, so that we take between 3-5 steps with the in-breath and then again with the out-breath. He acknowledges that most people have a slightly longer out-breath so there is more of a steps-plus-one on the out-breath, in fact:

> If your lungs want four steps instead of three, please give them four. If they only want two, give them two. The length of your in-breath and out-breath do not have to be the same... If you feel happy, peaceful and joyful while you are walking, you are practicing correctly.
>
> *Peace in Every Step*, THN, p. 28

This step-to-breath pacing relationship remains flexible so that we can adjust it according to how fast we need to move. What this gives is a reinforcement to both step and breath, so they can act as foundations for the contemplative activity, whatever that might be. Later, we'll look at how Thich Nhat Hahn suggests using phrases, silent or spoken, to even further stabilize the breath-step relationship.

CHAPTER FOUR
THRESHOLD: PREPARATIONS

These handcrafted waterproof hikers perform on or off the trail. An upper of waterproof leather, and breathable Air 8000 mesh is matched with a waterproof breathable Goretex® liner, helping your feet stay dry. The improved Ortholite® sock liner has a special anti-microbial treatment and wicks moisture so your feet stay dry. Vibram® rubber outsole grabs and breaks on hardscrapple terrain. Made in Italy. Available in Tuscan Olive, Dark Mulberry or Blue Quartz.

Ad copy from an L.L.Bean outdoor wear catalogue, 2011

Eighty pairs of straw sandals are allotted for the 100-day term... For the longer Imuro Valley course, *gyoja* (trainees) are allowed the use of one pair per day. During the Great Marathon, the monk can use as many straw sandals as necessary, usually going through five pairs a day...most *gyoja* have their sandals made by a pious old grandmother who lives in Sakamoto – her sandals are treasured as being both comfortable and good luck. In sunny dry weather, one pair can last three or even four days, but in heavy rains, the sandals disintegrate in a few hours. Thus, the *gyoja* carries one or two spares.

From *The Marathon Monks of Mount Hiei*, John Stevens, pp. 63-64

Those with experience of regular participation in any contemplative practice will understand that the practice begins well before you even enter the room. This might be limiting the timing or menu of the meal before practice. It might be a change of clothes, even a shower or bath. If the practice requires materials, such as a *zafu*, mat or book, one has to collect those. This will also mean maintaining those materials in a condition which is clean and ready for use.

Then there are subtler mental and emotional preparations. For example, one might keep the car music turned off en route to allow the mind to clear. There can often be an agreement of silence in the assembly space, just outside the door. Some may have a silent prayer, a bow or final deep breath before the hand touches the handle into the practice space.

Inasmuch as we are taking walking as a contemplative practice, we can likewise recognize the importance and appropriateness of several special preparatory activities.

The only exception would be indoor *kinhin* style walking. Since this takes place within a sitting environment and routine, it really flows out of the sitting itself. In that sense, the sitting meditation can be said to be the preparation for the walking, and vice versa. All other walking forms will benefit from some preparation.

Someone once quipped that anytime two walkers meet on a trail and, after they exchange comments and advice on the trail, they will launch into a detailed discussion of their equipment. No doubt we would not have trouble finding exhaustive examinations of footwear, packs, rain-gear, eye-wear, poles, GPS, head coverings, underwear, shirts, shorts, pants and on and on. This is not our purpose here, so we'll limit our equipment considerations to poles or staves, winter walking and documentation.

This chapter looks at some of the preparations one might make for walking. There is no intention here to describe or recommend items like boots, packs, clothing or the like. There are numerous resources which address that more fully. Our concern is with items and activities specific to walking as a contemplative practice. Every step on creaky old knees and hips, and memories of past back and knee injuries remind me of the differences between my walking in my twenties and now, in my sixties. So, at the end of this preparations stage, we acknowledge the differences that present themselves with different bodies, strengths, ages and abilities.

EQUIPMENT, STICKS AND POLES

What to Carry? Old and New

The traditional travel kit for a Buddhist monk was a pretty basic checklist:
- a bowl for meals, drinking and wash water;
- an extra set of robes;
- *juzu* or *mala* – set of beads for recitations;

- a razor, for keeping scheduled hair cuttings;
- tweezers for picking creatures out of food;
- *sutras* or texts;
- all carried in a simple over-the-shoulder cloth bag.

Since monks were forbidden to handle money, there was no purse or wallet. Appropriate to climate, there might be additional clothing. One can imagine there might be a small supply of medicinal herbs.

Observing modern monks, there are only a few changes. Wallets are more accepted. Cellphones may be carried. Even the Dalai Lama has raised the fashion bar with his trademark visor.

For those of us walking in such footsteps, we will choose what we carry based on the form of practice. A short half-day walk needs very little; a day-long will require more. An over-night not much more, beyond typical hiking gear. A longer pilgrimage needs considerable preparation. For example, *henro*-pilgrims on the Shikoku will participate in a formal orientation at Temple 1, where they are told how to behave and what they need as equipment. They can also acquire those items. These details are beyond the scope of this book, but can be found in numerous resources appropriate to each pilgrimage.

Essentials

Modern equivalents to traditional Items

It is unlikely for most of us that we will choose monastic robes, unless we are in fact clergy. Assuming we are not, we'll want something appropriate. As we will see later the Japanese *kaihogyo* marathon practice and pilgrimage requires a special, all-white costume. This might prove impractical for all but the most rigorous. Nevertheless, the principle of white is that of simplicity and purity, both of person and purpose. We can easily apply that and opt for similarly simple, clean and dedicated clothing – that is, dedicated to the walking practice alone, and not used for other activities. For example, lay *henro*-pilgrims are allowed to get by on a simple white vest, combined with their staff and hat. As well as putting the pilgrim into the proper attitude for the experience, such minimal details make it possible for pilgrimage neighbours to identify them as pilgrims and as appropriate recipients of charitable donations or *settai*.

We can take another tip from East Asian monks with the use of the *kesa* and *juzu*. There are numerous styles of *kesa*, but the idea is the same – a simple coloured band or collar worn around the neck. This custom emerged, we are told, during times of persecution of Buddhists. Since robes were an obvious target for attacks, monks reduced the robe to such a collar, easily worn under acceptable clothes. When needed, the monk could slip the collar on top and assume his clerical role.

These days a *kesa* (also called a *wagesa*) is worn by monks over sect-specific robes, a reminder that one is engaging in religious acts. *Kesa* are now also worn by lay people who have taken formal refuge, that is undergone the ceremony wherein they announce their dedication to the Three Jewels. It reminds them that they have come to a crossroads in their lives and set their feet on a unique roadway, the Buddha's own Path. They make these pledges:

> I vow to abstain from harming others, committing violence, and I will work to promote peace.
> I vow to avoid misappropriation and exploitation, and to be generous with my time and money.
> I vow to abstain from sexual misconduct.
> I vow to avoid false speech and speech harmful to others.
> I vow to be moderate in all substances and not to lose awareness.

If you have taken refuge, it would be quite appropriate to wear your *kesa*, especially on a longer walk. If you have not yet done this, you might designate a special shirt or scarf as one to remind you of the sacredness of your walk, and keep it set aside exclusively for that purpose. The refuge recitation might also be set aside, as discussed below in dedications.

The companion to wearing a *kesa* is wearing a *juzu*. A *juzu*, (also called a *nenju* or *mala*), is a wrist bracelet worn for maintaining count in recitation practices. They typically have 108 or 27 beads, with some different, larger bead, the 'Buddha bead', which marks the completion of a recitation sequence. Longer ones can have extra strands used to mark sets of recitations, that is the completion of 10 or 100, for example. *Juzu* etiquette varies and is beyond our scope here. It is sufficient to note that a *juzu* is not just another nice bracelet worn to match clothing or as a fashion accessory. The *juzu* is a reminder of commitment and, like the *kesa*, is reserved for practice times. It is an appropriate addition to our small collection of walking items.

Should you choose to carry these items, they must always be treated with respect, kept in a bag (a clean plastic sandwich bag might make sense for the trail) when not being worn.

Nordic Poles

It is surprising that the regulations which apply to the 1000-Day/Seven Year *kaihogyo*, the apex of all secular or sacred walking practices, define walking supports, like poles, as excluded for beginners. They are only allowed when "the monk earns the title 'White-belted Ascetic'," which follows his 500th day of walking (*Marathon Monks*, Stevens, p. 71). This is even more daunting when one views the challenging mountain-side landscape of the *kaihogyo* course.

Kaihogyo-ja aside, poles make eminent sense for most walkers. More particularly, I am recommending the use of Nordic walking poles for anyone walking more than a couple of kilometres over relatively level ground. Colin Fletcher, author of *The Complete Walker*, remarks that these poles "reek with cunning" (3rd ed., p. 80). Nordic poles (referred to as poles from hereon) are a modern invention that are constructed with four distinctive features, from bottom to top:

1. A hardened steel tip used for piercing soft surfaces or gripping/levering on ascent and descent; they allow the over-attachment of an optional rubber tip. These tips are useful for preventing slipping on hard surfaces, like pavement or large rock-faces. Tips can be a nipple-style, or a rocker-style.
2. An in-shaft spring-shock device that provides 'bounce', thus reducing hand-wrist fatigue.
3. A three-part light-weight shaft with two-screw-and-lock mechanism which allow an adjustment of the overall length from between approximately 28" to 54". This adjustability distinguishes these poles from something like a Nordic ski-pole or a solid material pole, say bamboo or wood.
4. The most common handle, a straight molded rubber handle that fits the hand, as contrasted with a cane-style with its characteristic hook handle. It is usually constructed from a moisture-absorbing and cold-insulating material. Built into the head of this handle is an adjustable strap, one of the pole's most useful features. Proper use of the strap eliminates fatigue and strain on fingers, hand and wrist, very important for a longer walk.

There are variations on the handle that include an optional screw, hidden under the cap, which allows mounting of a camera or other add-ons.

For those not familiar with Nordic poles, the advantages may not be clear. Firstly, consider the advantages your dog has over you in covering difficult, elevated and uneven surfaces. As the pigs in Orwell's *Animal Farm* chant triumphantly, "Four legs are better than two!" These revolutionary pig are correct, although for different reasons than the ones they cite. Apart from being in better shape than you, the most obvious reason your dog does well is the use of four rather than two legs. This distributes the weight and maximizes the strength, balance and flexibility. Poles effectively convert you into a 4-wheel drive walker. Secondly, this re-distribution both increases efficiency and reduces fatigue. Others can explain the science of this; let's take it as true.

Pole novices invariably use them improperly. They tend to grip the handles tightly with the hands, holding the pole vertically, with arms extended out in front of them. They end up walking like an uptight giraffe or a heron in tall grass. I recommend a short course at the local recreation centre, outdoor store or walking club. There are also excellent free video instructions online. We won't try to train you here, but will stress several key points:

- get a matched set of two, you'll feel the difference on the trail;
- for a short flat distance (less than three kilometres) one pole is enough; otherwise, use both;
- correct pole length is the distance to the ground from your outstretched palm, held parallel to the ground, with elbow on hip;
- pole length increases on a steep descent, decreases on a steep ascent;
- adjust the strap so it provides the grip, not the handle;
- balance the pole handle between the thumb and first finger, the rest of the hand is usually uninvolved;
- plant the pole tip before you stride, so you benefit from your arm push-off;
- plant the pole tip so it hits just behind the line of the opposite heel;
- except on steep climbs, never reach out with the pole;
- the pole or poles should swing gently as you walk along, never rising above the level of the hips;

A final note on poles is the recent arrival of the Chuk-Grip, developed by Chuck Lewis, a dedicated American poling enthusiast. This radical new pole handle is described as:

> ...a multi-positional, ergonomically correct pole handle. Works wonderfully for hiking, walking, cross-country skiing, mountain climbing and snowshoeing. It [ensures] proper positioning of hand and wrist in relation to the poling stoke...its comfortably shaped main grip is angled to enable the user to keep the pole in close to the body, increasing the power and efficiency of each pole plant.
>
> From the ChukGrip website

I have tested these out in short and longer walks. My impressions are highly favourable, especially for those with thumb-wrist based pain or arthritic conditions as I experience. I have found they live up to the claims and are at least as good, and probably for many walkers a superior choice, for poling purposes. They are available in a retro-fit handle, or in-place on a pole. There is a choice between a walking or cross-country ski-pole size. Chuck Lewis is currently working on improvements to make the grip even more comfortable.

The Walking Staff or *Shakujo*

There are many symbols for Dharma activity – the *vajra* (thunderbolt or sword), *kalasa*, (vase of plenty), *pasha*, (rope) and so on. Various Buddhas and Bodhisattvas are associated with different ones, such as Manjushri and the sword, Kannon and the vase. Only a few Buddhist figures are associated with a stylized walking staff called the *shakujo*. Of the hundreds of possible figures – Buddhas, Bodhisattvas, Jinas, Vidyarajas, Deities and Taras, Dharma-guardians, Hell-Kings, World-protectors and great human teachers – less than ten are associated with staves. As we saw in Chapter 3, most immediately identified with a staff is Jizo Bodhisattva, the Eternal Pilgrim or his 'aspects', such as Muhenshin, Hoko-o and Keiki.

Others who carry the *shakujo* are:
- Mahakashyapa, the Buddha's great student and founder of the Zen lineages;
- Sindura, one of the twelve warriors of Yakushi Nyorai, the Lord of Healing;
- Kuja-shonin, a monk-figure associated with Amitabha;
- Hachiman, the warrior-hero-protector of temples and emperors;

- Senju-Sengen Kannon, the 1000 armed Bodhisattva, who carries a *shakujo* in one right hand; and
- both Fukurokujo and Joroju, two of the seven Chinese gods of good luck, who carry crooked staves, not quite *shakujo*.

In its non-martial arts form, the long-handled *shakujo* can stand a foot or two above the head in length, and is surmounted by an elaborate head-piece. This head-piece is usually a metal loop with a cross bar. Atop the loop may be a Buddha figure. The bar in the loop supports a set of six or more cast metal rings, symbolizing the realms of being (*bhava-chakra*), the precepts or some other reminder. The martial arts version would incorporate a spear-tip or sword blade into the head-piece.

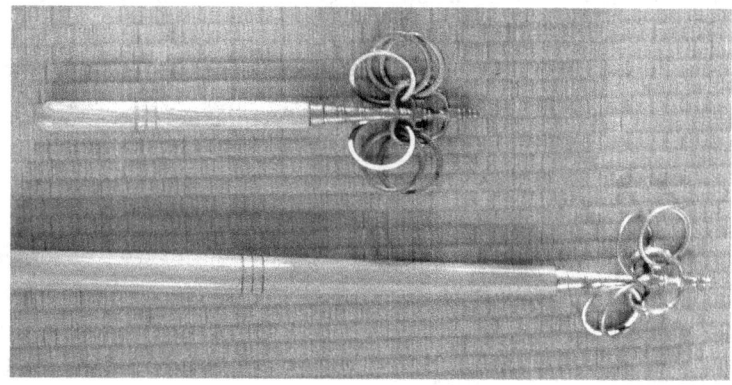

Short- and long-handled shakujo staffs

The *henro*, pilgrim or walking monk would plant the base of the staff onto the ground with a loud clinking sound with three purposes. In general, the sound will warn animals of the walker's arrival, avoiding any opportunity for harm either way. When used during a *takuhatsu* or alms gathering round, the clinking calls householders to the door where they may offer food stuffs in return for the gift of Dharma provided by the monks. When used in conjunction with walking and chanting, the clinking can mark the rhythm of the chant.

In this last form, there is also a smaller, shorter *shakujo* used inside a temple as an instrument in a chanting practice. One chant declares:

Now I wish that in the Ten directions, all sentient beings hear the shakujo; that the lazy become diligent; precepts-breakers keep them; doubters obtain belief; the stingy donate; the angry express compassion; the ignorant obtain wisdom; the arrogant find respect; the idle establish concentration.

Kujo shakujo, in *Tendai Buddhist Services*, p. 37

Acquiring an authentic *shakujo* can be both difficult and expensive. Often the dealers advertise in Japanese only. Even the smaller one can be costly. I do not really recommend it unless you are regularly leading a Dharma walk. Those wanting to incorporate the *shakujo* into walking practice or give a Nordic pole more religious quality can use less expensive options:

- use small metal rings from a hardware or saddlery store to fabricate the bar of rings and attach this to the handle of a pole;
- attach a small Buddha or Bodhisattva 'charm' to the pole;
- paint a *bija* or root syllable (shown in many books or online) on the pole; perhaps the most appropriate might be the 'ha' syllable for Jizo;
- print a small Buddhist symbol onto a piece of adhesive, transparent plastic and wrap that around the pole;
- hang a Buddhist flag from the pole;
- paint on or wrap thread or wire around the pole, using traditional Dharma colours (red-green, blue-yellow and white-black);
- use an adhesive window sticker.

Chanting Materials

As we will see later, in Chapter 7, walking and chanting are natural companions. The rhythm of the stride and the flow of a chant can support each other and deepen the contemplative quality of any walk, indoor or outdoor. Every tradition has developed its own specific chants which, if you are already affiliated with such group, will be handy and easy for you to incorporate. (Interestingly, 'incorporating' chanting, literally *in-corporare*, from the Latin for taking into or blending with the body, applies here to blending voice with body while we walk.) Non-Buddhists will not have difficulty in drawing from the liturgy or scriptures of their own faith for appropriate material. We'll look at Christian prayer-walking in Chapter 7. A small journal or binder (see below) can have chants printed out and inserted within. If you have decided to bring a portable MP3 player, many excellent recorded chants are available online or you can record what you prefer. No matter what collection you bring along, there are three Buddhist chants which have been adopted by virtually all Mahayana traditions. These are, of course:

- the *Heart of Perfect Wisdom*, (aka The *Mahaprajnaparamita Sutra*). There are dozens of English translations available online, and even some recordings. My recommendation would be using a Japanese version. This is easily memorized and has a wonderful rhythm. Like Zen teacher Norman Fischer, many practitioners learned this in Japanese for that reason before ever learning the English meaning;
- the *nembutsu*, or Amida Mantra, which is essential to all devotional practices. There are other Bodhisattva mantras as well. We'll touch on them later. Your own practice will determine your final choices;
- the Jizo mantra *(om namu jizo bu sa, om namu jizo bu sa, om ha ha ha vi sma ye svaha)* has a wonderful flow and rhythm and fits perfectly with our walker's relationship with this Bodhisattva.

PURIFICATION AND DEDICATION

Walking practice is no different from any other practice. It is strengthened by framing the experience with traditional rituals, particularly purification and dedication.

Purification is not a cleansing of sin, nor applying some magical protection. Purification has to do with the actor, not the act or the equipment. All we are doing is separating the practice activity from the secular or mundane, designating ourselves as engaged in practice. The purification can involve a purifying substance and a purifying declaration. Clergy may also know appropriate *mudras* (hand symbols) or recitations as part of the act. Purifying substances might be a dot or smear of water or incense powder taken from a temple altar, or one's home altar. The smoke from a stick of incense would work as well.

The dedication is a spoken or silent recitation at the outset of the walk which acknowledges one's spiritual purpose, and transfers whatever merit which might result from the practice to the benefit of all beings. If one is accustomed to some type of devotional or Bodhisattva practice, the dedication could be an invocation of that figure and an invitation that your and their efforts function harmoniously for the benefit of beings. It might act as the start of a longer sub-practice. For example, the dedication could be part of the Ten Recitation Practice described by Master Lin Kuang, a Pure Land master. Notice the method has a purification, washing up, built in. As is often done in Pure Land, a repetition can be done for a day-long walk at setting off, mid-morning, before and after meals, mid-afternoon and at the conclusion.

> If the cultivator is very busy...he should set aside a specific period... After washing up, he should bow three times to the Buddha (if he has one, if not, face west). Then standing erect, he should join his palms and single-mindedly recite the words 'Namo Amitabha Buddha' as many times as he can in a stretch [breath?], each stretch counting as one recitation. He should recite thus for ten stretches, and then utter the following stanza:
> "I vow that, along with other Pure Land cultivators,
> I will be reborn in the Land of Ultimate Bliss,
> See Amitabha Buddha, escape birth and death,
> And rescue all, as the Buddha does."
> After reciting, he should bow three times.
> *Pure Land Zen*, Master Yin Kuang, p. 62

WINTER WALKING

Snow-shoes, Skates and Skis

Winter walking, particularly where winter means lots of snow and cold, can be both a rare and beautiful experience and an impossible challenge. There can be many days and even weeks when walking means wading through deep snow or risking frostbite. For this reason, shifting walking practice from boots alone to specialty winter sports equipment can turn the impossible and impassable into one of those rare and beautiful experiences. If the trail or roadway is clear and safe, then good winter boots will be adequate. Strap-on ice-grips can be used for the determined walker. People use skis, of all kinds, snowboards, skates and snow-shoes to navigate their sub-zero climates. Lets evaluate these latter options for our purpose.

Right away, I would eliminate down-hill skiing, snowboarding and those activities which provide an exhilarating high-speed winter experience and are great for that. As for a contemplative experience, the kind of pace and urgency involved would nullify any contemplative value.

I would give a reserved nod to Nordic or cross-country skiing. If the style is racing, skate-skiing or precision styles like telemarking, the skier may be similarly distracted as in snow-boarding or alpine styles. Arguably, one can do a leisurely skate or telemark, and only the skier can judge if they have the same degree of concentration to engage in contemplation. Certainly, one can have a very leisurely ski with the old-fashioned diagonal sliding technique. Provided the terrain does not raise any danger, one could engage in contemplation.

The same argument holds for ice-skating. Competitive figure skating, while demanding concentration, is far too much performance-oriented to allow reflection. I wouldn't suggest the hockey rink, or a crowded indoor or outdoor rink as promoting contemplation. There are some environments, such as the popular and local Rideau Canal skate in Ottawa, Ontario, providing the surface is in good shape and there is no danger of colliding with anyone. Not having ever used the newer long distance skates, I can't speak from experience; however, I would expect they would facilitate a graceful contemplative experience, provided ice and crowds allow. The measure of appropriateness is whether one's emphasis is contemplative practice or athletic.

"Jogging is My Meditation"

Whenever I've taught walking practices to newcomers, especially those with little experience in Dharma practice, there are invariably those who say something like this, substituting biking, tennis or whatever their favourite sport might be. They explain how these activities bring them focus, deep experience of body or respite from whatever stresses fill their lives. With all due respect to all the proponents of the Zen of running/biking/tennis/etc., these activities have clear value but they are not truly contemplative, nor are they substitutes for plain old walking, and they are most definitely not in the company of foot-based Dharma practices.

Consider the most preliminary forms of meditation, such as those that belong to secular mindfulness programming, yoga and martial arts environments. We see these in the early North American transformations of meditation, the Relaxation Response or Transcendental Meditation, for examples. These practices emphasize cultivating states of lowered heart rate, modulated breathing and mental attentiveness, especially to body and breath. Their purpose is stress-reduction or cognitive awareness or bodily relaxation or focus of energy, not penetrating the question of human existence or fundamental suffering.

What most amateur athletes and weekend warriors experience can be a deep state of mental relaxation, a releasing of the endless mental distractions which occupy us most of the time. It can be an exceptional state of focus or one-pointedness, where one is fully engaged in one's activity. Some call it 'being in the Zone'. The relation between meditation and elite professional athletics could be something different; however, relatively few of us, myself for sure, belong in that elite and well-paid company. In short, such activities may produce a deep sense of calm or focus or both. These states belong to the very simplest and preliminary stages of meditation. Those of us following the Buddha-way cultivate these states early on and use them as a foundation for deeper and richer investigations of the Great Matter.

Further, those who engage in Dharma practice know the importance of reducing distractions. Stable practice, especially as we are in the early stages, requires minimizing interruptions from ringing phones, text message alerts or sensory-physical distractions such as strong smells or cold drafts. There are very few outdoor sports activities which eliminate distractions. Traffic, other participants, concurrent activities, environmental noise, signage, etc., all impinge on the simplicity of a meditative space. Perhaps some people can arrange to jog in complete isolation on a surface that does not require a vigilant eye, however, most do not.

Finally, it is rudimentary to Dharma practice that one follows a pre-established and well-worn path. We all begin counting the breath, measuring chants and working with centuries-old mental exercises, such as *koan*. It is a given that the path is itself the Way, and so there is no short-cut or compression or weekend seminar that substitutes for working one's way along the path. Personalization follows experience. We are only in a position to modify our practices after we have engaged with them, struggled through them and been confirmed by a senior as having sufficient mastery to move on. There is a marketing-promoted assumption in the West that everyone can play in the NHL or the Olympics or whatever elite level we want by means of a cash investment – expensive equipment, pro-guided lessons, stylish clothing or other irrelevancies. It is absurd to think we can play a little weekend softball and this prepares us for Major League baseball. Hollywood repeatedly tells the story of someone 'making it' because they 'want it more than anyone' or they 'have more heart'. This is just wishful thinking. Some insist we can learn the Dharma by reading a few books written by those who know about Buddhism from reading others who know about Buddhism. The result is a lot of minimally-informed people sharing their cursory knowledge with others, as if it were true teaching. It results in posers, wannabes and charlatans. As the saying goes, 'you gotta pay some dues, if you wanna play da blues'. Its completely backwards (although part of Western mythology) to think that if we call what we enjoy doing meditation, that makes it so. We can't define whatever we like as meditation and definitely not as Dharma practice, without some reference to, and deep experience in, traditional practices combined with some validated context in traditional practice methodology. This is true for body practices likewise foot-based practices. Sorry joggers, jogging is just jogging.

With all due respect, I'm afraid I must disagree in part with my distinguished elder brother, Thich Nhat Hahn. In his *Walking Meditation* mini-guide, he comments on jogging. I guess you could apply this to some other 'fitness' activities. He does allow:

> The way you can apply mindfulness into your jogging experience is to jog at a comfortable pace while still being able to count the numbers of steps you take with each breath... In this way you can continue to jog and hear some acorns falling, see the squirrels chasing each other and feel the warmth of the sun... you will feel calmer and your mind will become clear.
>
> *Walking Meditation,* THN, p. 45

I am less generous in my estimation of what joggers can and do while jogging. I maintain that jogging, as for most other energetic fitness activities, especially when elements of conditioning, interval training, competitive aspirations and electronica are involved, is not compatible with walking practice. Brother Thay gives with one hand, and later pulls back somewhat with the other:

> Although jogging can be quite pleasant, it does not replace slow walking meditation...jogging...can never slow down your mind to the same degree as slow walking meditation.
>
> same reference

COMPANION DOGS

The same holds true for walking the family dog. Dog walking may be relaxing, it may promote the bond between humans and animals and it may clear some mental space from one's daily stress, but it does not, in and of itself, equate to meditation. That said, actual walking practice can be enhanced by sharing it with a companionable dog. Not so differently from the human walker, the limits will always reside with the disposition and preparation of the dog.

I am blessed with a perfect example of a companion for walking practice. My boy, Joshu, is a five-year-old male Havanese. This breed is intelligent, intensely loyal, fun-loving and vigourous beyond their 10-15 pound size. They were bred as herding and alerting dogs, and so running hard and endurance come naturally. He will never turn down a walk. On the trail, he will stay within twenty feet of me, always checks to see if we are together, and obeys his basic obedience commands. If I respect how he does his practice, it is very rare for him to interrupt my practice with having to search or call for him. He won't run off or chase down wildlife. I cannot count the ways he has inspired me and taught me lessons of the trail. Like most dogs, he demonstrates being both single-pointed and in this moment with every step.

I've had different breeds as companions at different stages of my practice, none as companionable (or perhaps its me that's become companionable). As the saying about the teacher appearing when the student is ready, this particular dog arrived in my life and practice at the moment of ripeness. He usually accompanies my Sangha when we have our 45 minute walking practice from the *zendo* space to the nearby lake. He will heel-walk when he needs to, scramble when he can, urge all of us forward. He is rarely a distraction, more often he embodies the mantra we use on our walks:

> your presence, small friend, is like a mindfulness bell,
> returning me to my breath,
> reminding me to be careful in my travels.

In contrast, I have witnessed other owner-dog teams who are totally unsuited for walking practice. In particular I would cite owners who have spoiled their dogs, overfed them so they are (usually both) unfit for even a light walk and, most grievously, failed to teach even the most basic politeness and control. Such combinations are hopeless on a contemplative walk. If you are lucky and considerate enough to have a well-prepared dog, they can illuminate walking practice.

DOCUMENTATION: CAMERAS AND JOURNALS

At the conclusion of the gorgeous and touching Korean Buddhist film, *Spring, Summer, Autumn, Winter...Spring*, the grown-up monk-hero decides to carry a giant Kwan Yin *rupa* (figure) to the summit of a mountain, in penance for childhood misdeeds. The film ends with him, sitting beside the *rupa*, looking out over a scene that captures eternity, purity and innocence. Environmentalists in the audience might tut-tut for his obvious violation of the oft-heard nature travelers' code 'Leave nothing behind, take nothing but pictures'. Without a doubt his dragging this massive figure carved a path in the side of the mountain, and he transformed the mountain top, some might say desecrated it, with the Bodhisattva of Compassion as his accomplice. (I can't speculate on the karmic consequences.) Does the spirituality of his intention excuse his actions? If we take our contemplative practices into the natural world, are we constrained by ethics of non-interference and stewardship? Few of us are disposed to dragging giant *rupas* up mountain sides. Ought we be ruled to take nothing and leave nothing?

Cameras

That above-quoted code allows us picture taking, and there are no direct harmful consequences for the environment from such documentation, unless the scale approaches that of The Nature Channel. Should we then squeeze some kind of camera into our tiny travel-sack? If we are to take pictures, how might this impact on the purpose of a walking practice?

The least inconvenience would come from the least of cameras, a point-and-shoot model or the one on a cell-phone or tablet. The technology is such that these can take excellent snap-shots, ideal for recording an outdoor adventure. The larger and more complicated the camera and equipment, the larger the intrusion into one's walk. Video is no different from the perspective of bag-space.

How might a camera support one's walking practice? Alan Mirabelli is a semi-professional photographer in Eastern Ontario who specializes in what is called 'large-format photography'. This is what the legendary nature photographer,

Ansell Adams, used to capture the majesty of the American Southwest in the 1940's. The equipment is larger and more cumbersome than a point-and-shoot, even with today's improvements. Alan once spoke about his day of shooting by explaining that he began walking and sitting in the woods alone. He would mostly walk and sit, trying to harmonize with the rhythm and mood of his environment. He brought no distractions of music, books or anything and did little more than observe and absorb. He had no preconceived notion of subject or technique. Only after 4-6 hours in the field would he feel in tune with the area and begin to capture the dozen or so images he wanted. This seems to capture the benefits of a camera on a walk. We are not using the walk to transport us to our subjects. The engagement with the subject precedes the photo and, I think Alan would agree, might be of equal or greater value to him than the photo.

Conversely, adding a camera to one's sack has the potential to interfere or even side-track the walk. For example, my own picture-taking habits are completely incompatible with walking practice. I tend to follow a trail, possibly doing some *nembutsu* as I walk. This is incidental and of short-duration because, unlike Alan, I am constantly scanning the landscape for possible images. Once I find an area, I will take 50-60 images from various angles and detail. In my case I am seeking images that are evocative of a place, time and emotion, and so the walk is mostly the means. My walking practice always leaves the camera at home. One must assess what is the purpose of bringing the camera. If it is more like my approach, it would be wise to leave the camera at home or break up the walk into walking and picture-taking phases. Most undermining would be if the picture-taking broke the flow of the body-mind practice of walking.

A final note on camera-phones or tablets. These small electronic devices are multi-function and include still and video capacity. This raises the larger question of cell-phones and portables on a walk. A cell phone could have a place in one's sack if one is committed to some emergency role, say a physician with high-risk patients. If one is planning a multi-day or very long one-day walk into territory where one is at potential risk – say, winter storm conditions, wild animals and the like – safety might recommend a phone, provided there is some agreement of respecting privacy and solitude.

The central question is whether the possession of the device raises the possibility of an interruption to your concentrative and interior process. There are newspaper stories of people experiencing a reaction like drug withdrawal when separated from their portable devices. If this resonates with you, this seems the strongest possible argument for leaving the device at home. Our purpose in any contemplative practice is to experience our life in the rawest, most direct manner, to facilitate insight into important spiritual questions. Mediated experience, literally experience with media, has no place in such a journey.

Another leave-at-home for walking practice is any kind of audio device. Modern walkers have become very attached to their personal audio players, much to the detriment of the walking experience. Is this mis-guided multi-tasking? Is this a means of blocking all the sound pollution that fills our ears? Some have called it the ultimate triumph of Muzak. It really doesn't matter what the cause of this may be. As Shakyamuni responded when asked how walking practice differs from everyday walking: "When we walk, we know we are walking."

If our purpose is to work with body, breath and mind, there is no room for distractions of music, radio or talking books. Imagine the reaction if you strode into any practice hall anywhere in the world with a set of ear-buds tucked into your ears. Walking practice is no different. As Dr. Peter Chuckrow advises in *Tai Chi Walking*:

> The addition of music is superfluous when the mind is thoroughly in the moment…listening to uplifting, inspiring music and communing with nature should be separate experiences, each requiring total attentiveness.
>
> *Tai Chi Walking*, Chuckrow, p. 114

Journalling

On the contrary, bringing a journal or notebook seems quite apropos, possibly even worthy of encouragement. The caution would, of course, be the same as for media devices. The journal has a place if it supports or deepens the walking practice. This it can do in a number of ways. In her standard on labyrinth walking, *The Sacred Path Companion,* Lauren Artress suggests some worthwhile journal exercises. She provides blank exercise forms and structured self-studies. She delineates four categories of walking journal activities: healing, shadow work, soul assignment and initiatory rituals. These middle two are not really Buddhist activities, however, perhaps they all have something to offer. She comments:

On **healing**:
> [Walking]...offers a blueprint for connecting the mind, body, and Spirit to support the forces of healing.

On **shadow work**:
> *(Note:* Jung defined the 'shadow' as the unclaimed parts of ourselves that we cannot allow into our conscious awareness.)
> [Through a walking journal exercise]...you can get glimpses of your shadow, of what hinders you and sabotages your relationships with others and often with the Divine.

On **soul assignment**:
> We need to align our lives with the life-giving forces that bring Light, healing and peace to the world... What are you to dedicate yourself to?

On **initiatory rituals**:
> These are structured experiences designed to give us entry into a new stage of life. They are the other end of healing rituals, whose purpose is to conclude. In her book Artress gives several examples which illustrate this point. Here, I will substitute my own example, which I believe was a profound experience for me. I understand it as the completion of my own healing, but primarily the initiation of the next, and what has become the most fruitful and rewarding stage of my journey. In the case of the labyrinth and many other initiations, the form of the journey is clear and well-defined. Mixed as it was with healing, uncertainty, insight and resolve, this initiation journey was less well-defined.

In the late summer of 2002, a few years after leaving a Zen group which had been my focus and refuge for nearly a decade, I was unclear of my practice direction and distracted by emotions of disappointment, anger and disillusionment. I was living again in a rural environment at least an hour from any organized Dharma group and frustrated that Sangha meant a long drive. I had failed to find any practice companionship close to my home community. Determined to take a proactive approach to this frustration, I arranged a visit to a couple of Dharma centres in the Vermont area. New England, while still distant, had promised many Dharma flavours, surely one for my palate. New England also resonated with me from many boyhood adventures. Our family camping trips often led us into New York, Vermont, Maine and its bordering landscape in southern New Brunswick. Even if my search for Dharma-family were to prove fruitless, I could at least avail myself of an excellent day-hike in the Appalachians.

The centre visits, while pleasant, proved unsatisfying in addressing my search, and so I headed for the White Mountains whose delights I knew from past walks. I set off up the cool late-summer trail with my conundrum as my only companion. The walk took about five hours, with a turning point at a silent lake on a mountain-top. As we'll see later in the book, turning or pivot points in any walking practice can be decisive, rich with understanding and resolve. I think they can be instrumental in the soul assignment that Artress proposes.

I still recall that moment. I was sitting in the doorway of a hikers' overnight cabin, gazing out over a beautiful and peaceful lake. Sunny stillness, out of time, as old forests can be. It was one of those moments when you think you could rest there forever. As it inevitably does, the trail called, and with it the lack of resolution in my practice need. I re-hefted my day-pack, slipped on my poles and began the descent. I hadn't noticed how the wet and cool summer had affected the trail on the ascent. Walking with, rather than against gravity soon reminded me how treacherous a trail can get. Mossy rocks were without grip, leaf-deep ground turned to patches of skating-rink. The whole path became a kind of diabolical sliding run. The trail demanded full concentration. Each step had to be planned, felt and risked. Every ten minutes or so, the trail caught me again, sending me sliding and stumbling, slamming my backside into the mud or smashing my knees into roots, rocks or dirt. Sore, tired and bruised, but thankfully uninjured, I got up each time and set off once more. Paradoxically, this focus simultaneously brought me back again and again to my religious path and my lack of traction on the Way. I cannot say exactly how or when it happened but, in the midst of what seemed endless falling and rising, it was very clear to me that no one was going to do this work for me, I would have to answer the need myself.

It bears noting here that mediaeval East Asian Dharma produced a radical theological notion, *jiriki-tariki*, the contrast between one's own efforts or Self-power (*jiriki*) and the ceaseless flowing of the liberative energy of the Buddhas, Other-power (*tariki*). The most eloquent spokesperson for Other-power, the 12th century Pure Land patriarch Shinran Shonin, teaches that humans, as karmic beings, are powerless to effect their own Awakening. The Dharma Path is one of total surrender to the Vow of Amitabha Buddha which ensures Awakening to all.

This is not the place to address such a theological controversy. Perhaps what I can say here is to interpret Self-Other from the perspective of my slippery descent. In simple walker's terms, I was reminded of the place of humility on the trail; one can never force one's will onto the trail. By the same token, I was reminded that the trail presents itself to transport the walker. Patience and trust are rewarded with certain arrival at the trail's end. I learned that my own path, while it promises Awakening, offers no guarantee of a smooth, clear or trouble-free journey. As with my own understanding of the Self-power/Other-power question, the walking path and the contemplative path both present themselves as the Way. They do not, however, perform the walk or promise a flawless transit. It still comes to us to walk, in our sometimes clumsy, sometimes graceful way along whatever the trail places beneath our steps.

As I finished the descent, the conundrum had been shattered. The search for Sangha evaporated as did the peril of that descent. I was firmly dedicated to the establishment of a Sangha where I lived. I didn't know what it would look like or how it would practice, but I knew it was the answer to my search. As is the case with most of our walking experiences, the arrival at the end of one trail suggests the starting point of the next. This, for me, was my initiation into what has become much more than I ever expected when I set off up the mountain. High five, Moses.

Other

Other appropriate activities that involve journals on a walking practice might be sketching and painting, collecting (eg. flowers, leaves) and bird watching. All of these can be wonderful exercises in mindfulness. Each requires us to be alert and investigative of our walking environment. No less an inspiration or exemplar is Thoreau, who remarks on this as being an important part of his walking practice.

One of my early teachers used to assign a five-sense walking exercise to learn mindfulness. We were instructed to take a walk and begin it by selecting one sense to filter our experience. We were to carry our journal and simply jot down each experience as it occurred. Not only did this refine our senses as the means of attention, it also left each of us with an instant poem that captured the unique sensory dimension of that walk.

DISABILITY CONSIDERATIONS

Many of us in parts or all of our lives are dealing with some kind of physical disability. This need not necessarily restrict or prevent contemplative walking. My Sangha-partner, Jisei Dick, was born with cerebral palsy and learned contemplative walking late in life. Here are her reflections on the subject.

> Most people, when doing a walking meditation have an awareness of placing their feet up and down as they move forward their arms are placed together, the spine is straight, their eyes focused ahead. There is a deliberate grace to these movements whether one walks alone or one is walking with a group of people. There is a symmetry to these motions that is beautiful for people to experience and to be a part of. One's mind has focus; breathing is automatic as this walking meditation continues.
>
> I was encouraged by Innen Parchelo to contribute here, because I have a perspective which is informed and guided by the fact that I live with a physical disability. There will be a brief explanation of what brought me to mindfulness and meditation practices in the first place and then I will provide a detailed account of my walking practice. This 'difference' will be acknowledged and explained by the way I have adapted the walking practice to account for the limitations I have. The following information is given, in the hope that anyone may benefit from these practices. There are adaptive things that one can utilize despite the circumstance of being disabled. Accommodating for and adjusting for mobility challenges during a walking practice are possible.
>
> My journey into the world of meditation practices began in the Spring of 2010. At that time I was experiencing dissatisfaction in my life and was seeking relief so that I could enter my sixth decade with more grace and dignity. I had overcome previous obstacles in my life. Significantly, learning to live with a

Jisei Dick, with Innen's walking companion, Joshu

permanent disability, this was the result of injury at birth; and despite the fact that I had adapted well to these circumstances, I felt frustrated that my world was shrinking and that I had no purpose or direction. I was miserable and saw no end to these negative emotions. I am intelligent, have enjoyed a long-marriage and have good friends. Why then, this disconnection? I have realized two years later, that my ego and sense of entitlement were the driving forces behind my discontentment. I am content today and have found activities and practices that enrich my life and the lives of others who share their time with me.

How, does the 'walking meditation' practice inform my daily

life and specifically to my situation? Generally it is difficult for me; however, I adapted this practice to make it meaningful to me. What surprises me the most is the fact that my awareness of my body and its movements are heightened. I had always thought that I was aware of my body and the gait that I use continually. How wrong I was! Prior to walking practices, I know now that I moved on automatic pilot without any thought to what or how I was moving. In fact, truth be told, I barely walked at all, unless I had to and could only walk for less than five minutes at a time and then needed to sit down. Two years later my walking has increased to 10 minutes of continuous motion.

Paying attention and walking with purpose is now very deliberate. This sounds like the description earlier, doesn't it? Yes and no, because I shuffle my feet, my hands are placed on my two canes, my spine has a curve in it and I see only from the right eye. When first learning this particular walking meditation I was very self–conscious, felt inadequate, and thought that because I could not pick up my feet, have my arms in front of me and have peripheral vision as other people did, I could not participate in this specific form of meditation. When I let go of my need to do this correctly, I embraced my walking practice and celebrated my overall improvements to walking longer than five minutes. I am not as tired and walk with a confidence I have never known. I still shuffle, have a curved spine, etc. However, these limitations are now in the background and do not hinder the experience of my walking meditations. When I am walking in this way, I am truly free to explore my body and how it responds on any given day. Finally, whether I am walking by myself or in the company of others, I feel self-acceptance and a sense of belonging that is profound and sustaining. I encourage anyone, with limitations or not, to learn about mindfulness, meditation practices and/or the Dharma as I have during the past two years.

CHAPTER FIVE
JOURNEY 1: FIRST STEPS

In Bodh Gaya, India, there is an old Bodhi tree that shades the very spot where the Buddha is believed to have sat in meditation on the night of his enlightenment. Close by is a raised walking path about 17 steps in length... When reading accounts about the lives of monks and nuns in the time of the Buddha, you find that many attained various stages of enlightenment while doing walking meditation.

From *Mindful Nature Walking (One Step at a Time)*,
John Cianciosi

FIRST WALKING PRACTICES

The bell rings to conclude another round of sitting meditation. You release the legs, perhaps massage the stiffness away and then rise to standing. Either you return to informal life or you take some kind of pause and prepare to go back to the mat. Indoor, outdoor, blank wall or mountain view. Theravada, Mahayana, Buddhist, Christian, no-name. Its always the same. In the early stages of practice we are thankful for the pause or break. Later, as practice deepens, we strive to sustain that meditative state, to extend it into whatever we do after a round of formal sitting.

This is the moment when we need and discover our first walking practices. For most practitioners, it takes the form of a slow, silent and mindful walking movement. In this chapter, we encounter *kinhin*-style walking, as it is called in the Zen and Japanese traditions. This structured form of walking is used in all traditions, each with variations that fit their practice intentions. We'll look at the basics of the walking form, considering the relative preferences for different paces as most notably associated with the two major Zen schools, Soto and Rinzai. Once we've circled the room a few times, we'll take it outside and apply that form to less structured environments. We'll weigh the differences between solo and group walking and offer some suggestions for those leading a walking round.

Since we are introducing ourselves to basic walking, this is an ideal time to look beyond formal Buddhist walking and try out two other contemplative walking practices – the Eight-step walk of Tai Chi and what Halzer calls 'kung walking'. These two offer valuable insights into both the mechanics of walking but also the importance of walking 'in your body'.

WALKING PRACTICE # 1
KINHIN

Kinhin or indoor walking meditation is the Honda Civic of walking practice, the baked potato, the 'little black sweater'. Anyone and everyone who has investigated walking meditation in any Buddhist environment will have practiced *kinhin*. In some groups, it is nothing different than ordinary walking, in others it can be highly structured and formal; in some traditions it is painfully slow, in others, it is a race around the practice hall; in some traditions, it is a 'break' inserted between rounds of sitting; in others, it holds an equal or greater value to sitting practice.

Formal kinhin

Kinhin can be performed in indoor or outdoor contexts. In its more formal versions, there is an outdoor 'track' set aside for that purpose. Typically, this is a flattened ellipse, approximately 12-15 paces in length and wide enough that two walkers will not interfere when they pass. There are temple halls and courtyards where *kinhin* has been done for centuries, and where countless footsteps have worn a smooth groove in stone. Less formally, it can be done in a rectangular, square, oval, or other pattern. Outdoors, it can also follow the shape or contours of whatever space is selected.

In previous chapters, we've already covered the basics of posture, hand position, the structure and movement of the foot, including the four-part step. All of this applies to *kinhin*. Perhaps it is good here to remind ourselves that *kinhin* walking is not a break but a practice. The word means something like 'walking the sutra', or as someone fancifully suggests 'walking the talk'. Some instructors mistakenly describe it as nothing more than a way to stretch the legs and hips, to relieve the rigors of sitting and to interrupt any dull mind states that can build in seated practice. This is greatly under-estimating the benefit of walking, however.

Just as we do when we alter our seated practice between breath-focused, visualization-focused or word/phrase-focused practices, we do not relax or treat any practice as filler or relief. We bring full body-mind to that practice. Likewise, walking practice expects our full attention and the involvement of whole body-mind. Less than that reduces it to the level of any other non-contemplative activity.

The Five-Part Step

This is a good point to introduce what I call the Five-part Step. This is a way of experiencing the step in a way which ensures the full execution of the step and which sustains full balance throughout the flow of the step. As with any contemplative movement activity, it is artificial to dissect the movement into component parts because we aspire to perform it as one fluid motion. Doing so does, however, remind us of the complete step, so we can attend fully as we walk. The five component parts of a normal step are:
1. The placement of the heel;
2. Rocking the weight forward along the outside edge of the foot, adjacent to the arch;
3. Transferring the weight across the foot to the ball;
4. Spreading the forward motion of the ball into the span of toes; and
5. Pushing off with the toes/raising the opposing heel to start the next step.

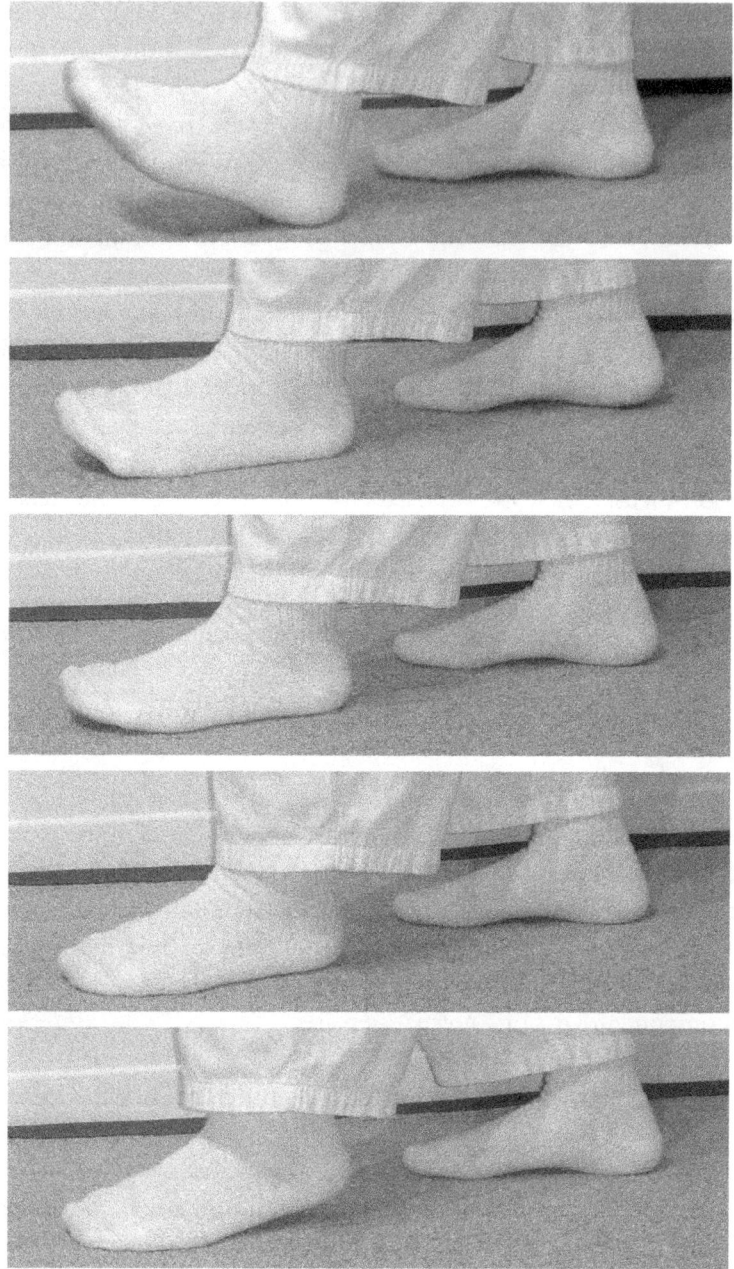

The five-part step

This full action is the correct movement which maximizes the mechanical design of the heel and foot, a design which translates the weight of the upper body, the rocking and propulsion of the hips and knees, into efficient forward motion. An incomplete or constricted action will create physical problems in the body and will constrict the attentional processes of the walk.

Most casual or non-athletic walkers don't pay the slightest attention to their gait or the fullness of their step. They assume that the way the learned to walk from childhood is without variance. The truth is awkward walking, incomplete stride and poor balance develop over one's life-span and can be corrected to refine the capacity for contemplative walking. I would suggest you return to previous notes about balance and posture, since these need to be correct before one even sets off.

I was walking with a companion recently and we sat at the conclusion of the route. She had recently begun more and faster walking for fitness reasons. She commented that she was experiencing some neck pain since increasing her routine. I asked if she had considered her balance and step as contributors to the pain. I had observed her from a few steps behind and at the side and noticed that she did not properly begin the step, but rather began with her weight into the middle of her foot. I noticed her head swung from side to side and her overall balance was thrust forward as she stepped. I explained this to her and suggested how she might correct things. Within a week, her pain had cleared up and she recognized her stride and rhythm as being more balanced and efficient.

The least exploited parts of the Five-part Step tends to be the final two. Most walkers roll their weight onto the ball without finishing the full transfer of weight through the toes. The toes provide the push out of the rocker of the ball and their spread provides the balance into the next step. As we complete the step, we need to squeeze the toes, in a sense gripping the ground, and pushing forward. Its not so different from the use of shoe straps on bicycle pedals. Strapping the shoe in allows for the upward motion of the pedaling stroke to be used, not just the downward push. This creates a fluidity in the pedaling, with more force and efficiency. This is also true of the walking step. The gripping and pushing of the toes coincides with the raising and swinging of the preceding heel and establishes a continuous flow. Back and front feet communicate push and balance, powering the full step and sustaining balance as we walk.

The Walker's Gaze

Before setting off with the first step, it is important to assume correct posture. In Chapter 3 we learned that our formal standing/walking posture mirrors sitting posture. The key elements of the sitting posture are:
- The spine is relaxed and uses its natural curvature for support;
- The balance tends to be slightly back-leaning;
- The chest is open, the shoulders back, to ensure clear breathing;
- The chin is slightly tucked in, with the tip of the tongue resting on the upper palette;
- The spine is lightly stretched to relieve any compression in its bones;
- The gaze is straight ahead, eyes closed or in 'soft focus';
- There is no rigidity, the body will float gently with the flow of breath, adjusting its centre and balance with the changes in the upper chest;
- There is little other movement, no swaying other than this floating with the breath;
- Breath flows naturally, the belly swelling and collapsing.

We also covered proper hand position, breathing and the five-part step in Chapter 3. Here let's return to correcting the gaze. Because the head is tilted due to the lowered/tucked chin, it is not possible to stare ahead. Matthew Flickstein in his *Journey to the Center: A Meditation Workbook* instructs "Look down at the ground at a point about three feet in front of you." This, I would suggest, is a bit too tight a perspective. It pushes attention inward, encouraging an imbalance between mental and physical-spatial awareness. I would recommend a gaze directed at a point between 8-10 feet ahead. This encourages a wider, more broadcast attentional field that takes in the immediate body-space, the longer distance and the peripheries. One is thus walking more in a field, than in a body-space.

Of course, there is a difference with gaze if one is walking alone or in a widely spaced line, as opposed to walking in a tighter group-line (that is, with less than three feet between walkers). In that case, directing the gaze out to 8-10 feet should be corrected to a focus on the back of the head/shoulder-blades of the person in front. Under no circumstances should we make eye-contact with others. You will often see beginners casting their eyes around a practice space when they do *kinhin*. They have not yet recognized that the unbroken gaze in walking is the same as in sitting, and relax into the distractions of the altar, pictures or a view out a window. It's a short step to shopping lists and memories of last night's sports event. As we develop a walking practice, we maintain that same strength of 'open gaze', attending to the walking space, not the objects in it or the mental distractions which can arise.

The walker's gaze

Regardless of the number or closeness of walkers, the gaze is an 'open gaze'. That is, in the same way as our view in sitting, we are not looking at anything. The eyes are merely open, we are receiving whatever arises in the visual field, without judgement or discrimination. As walking practice develops and refines into a whole body experience, you will find less need to watch where you're going. This is more true indoors or on a structured track, for example, in a labyrinth pattern. Needless to say, outdoor walking must adjust to the quality of the track. The role of the leader in a group walk is especially crucial, as we'll see below. This is not to suggest we walk with eyes closed, as we may do in seated practice, although blind walking offers its own benefits. In walking, open gaze and receptivity, not discrimination and judgement, are the major standards.

Regardless of the number or closeness of walkers, we use a wide perspective. It is different from the driver's perspective, where we are scanning the horizon for signs, traffic and patterns in anticipation of danger. It is the perspective we use when we meet a panoramic ocean or mountain view, openness without caution or decision. The eye-balls can even be deliberately turned slightly outward and upward. With the position of the head, slightly lowered as the chin tucks in, we naturally have to look slightly upward anyway, but this orientation has an added benefit. According to neuro-scientists, holding the eyes upward directs the brain to engage in more imagination and creativity. Holding the gaze outward, they would also suggest balances our brain's attention to past and future, a more present-moment attention. The combination, a slightly elevated, slightly outward gaze, keeps our practice alert, non-judgmental and less prone to distracting and wandering narratives.

A receptive gaze means, once again in the same way as in sitting, that we are not 'looking at' anything. The eyes are merely open, we are receiving whatever arises in the visual field, without judgement, searching or discrimination. As you attend to this aspect of practice, you will recognize how active the eyes are in the search for distraction and fabrication of self-narrative. This is not surprising, since we, as animals, give priority to visual information.

Cultivating a receptive gaze is challenging in the same way as cultivating a open breath while sitting. In a sense, we are over-riding the patterns of the brain to allow an un-managed behaviour, be that open breath or open vision. This is part of practice, in that it releases us from some of our habitual behaviours and fosters an alert openness to each moment of experience.

Indoor and outdoor track-walking (not free-form walking on a outdoor natural path, of course) can be richer in a dimly-lit or darkened space. One of my favourite *kinhin* experiences is indoor walking in our New York temple before dawn. One can barely make out the general form of the person in front. There are no visual distractions and body awareness is at a premium. In fact, an experienced walking meditator is able to close their eyes or walk in the dark for several steps, without stumbling, because the balance and pace are so complete, that visual cuing is less important.

A practitioner can deepen this low-vision sensitivity by practicing *kinhin* around the perimeter of a table. Take a position at one corner of a long, rectangular table (like a folding banquet table, for example). Assume your walking posture, but allow your inside hand (usually the right) to drop so that the outside of the hand, (usually the wrist-bone, back of hand or knuckles) gently brushes contact with the table's edge. Close your eyes (or use a darkened room) and practice the *kinhin* slow pace around the table. Pay attention to your own body's balance, not the table. Gentle and occasional contact will correct your stride and pace and address any insecurity that may distract. As you practice, you will discover improved balance and correction with the table will become less and less necessary. In time you can return the right hand to the hand posture, and use occasional contact of the hip or thigh to act as the correction.

Pacing - Thai or Soto Pacing and The Rinzai Pace

In the previous chapter we learned the pacing which is most commonly practiced and is associated with Thai *vipassana* teaching and Soto Zen. This is the breath-and-step pace where one counts the parts of the step in some relation to the in-and-out of the breath. Thus, the foot is raised on the first part of the in-breath; the foot is planted and weight shifted with the push of the out-breath.

Most commonly, *kinhin* is practiced using that somewhat slow pace, one that lays on top of the breathing pace. Thus, as described above, each step relates to the normal flow of in and out breathing. An exception to this is within the Rinzai style of Zen practice, where walking takes on its own unique format. The practitioners stand at the ready, then with a clap of the wooden blocks, they move off to the left at a rapid pace. They circle the room (or garden, if outdoors) at this steady, urgent, almost break-neck pace, until the double clap returns them to the start. The circuit is often U-shaped rather than circular. The space between walkers does not vary from the seated spacing, and there is little room for error. During the rounds it would not be unknown for someone to stumble or walk up the back of the ankle of the person in front.

Some commentators casually attribute the difference to a matter of chance. My experience in the Zen environment suggests chance and choice have little to do with it. Not to suggest that other Zen schools, like Soto or other Japanese Buddhist styles, are sloppy in the matter of walking, only to say that there is a more insistent rigourous precision in Rinzai practice. The Rinzai style is usually characterized as concerned with sudden dramatic breakthroughs of insight, wrought through intense and often mentally frustrating practices designed to shatter our reliance on careful linear thought. One might say in Soto (and others) we practice on the flat surface of the sword of insight; in Rinzai we balance on the finely-honed edge.

As such the Rinzai style tends to use a rapid pace to keep one's 'feet to the flame', as it were. A practitioner cannot dawdle nor afford distraction, mental or physical, lest they end up stumbling onto a mat or smashing into another walker. My experience with this emphasized full-body and larger-space awareness over any subtleties of foot or breath. I was much more keenly aware of motion through space, of the turbulence of arising-and-falling away. In the context of the parallel sitting practice, which similarly tends to precision and rigour, this walking style heightened one's sense of open space, and, as a result, the openness of experienced awareness.

In the final analysis, this is a style of walking available to us. Its value, I think lies in its relationship to the sitting style, rather than any intrinsic value. I have taught this to beginning practitioners primarily to have them experience the surprise and uncertainty of its rapid changing pace. There is great value in recognizing that walking (and sitting) practices are not little techniques which we can fuss over, as we might a tennis grip or a golf swing or a brand of running shoe. We don't 'master' them, they master us.

ALTERNATE CONTEMPLATIVE WALKING

Eight-step Tai-Chi Walking

Although not a traditional Buddhist walking form, a style of walking taught by Tai Chi teachers is worth learning and using. This form can be done indoors, however, in the spirit of Tai Chi, outdoor practice is always valued over indoor. The posture, movement and pace are different from *kinhin*. The great value is in deepening the resonance of breath and movement, and in intensifying the full-foot and full body awareness of the walking path. In some respects it may provide more of a similarity to sitting practices than traditional *kinhin*. I should stress that what I mean here by Tai Chi walking is not simply practicing Tai Chi principles while you walk (although this too has great value). In his book, *Tai Chi Walking: A Low Impact Path to Better Health*, Robert Chuckrow explains the mechanics, variations and uses of many walking exercises, using Tai Chi principles – such as naturalness, mindfulness, centredness, precision and continuity, to mention a few. These are all worthwhile walking experiments.

What we mean here by Tai Chi walking is a specific version of Tai Chi which employs a structured and compacted stride, careful weight transfer and a hand push that reinforces the step. It is sometimes called the Eight-Step Walk.

What distinguishes Tai Chi walking is its skater-like or s-curve stride and a raise-and-push arm movement. *Kinhin*, as we've seen, relies on a straight-ahead stride, where the feet remain parallel, and the forward step begins with a heel-plant just ahead of the overtaken foot. If it weren't for the slight spacing between feet, the stride would resemble a tight-rope walker, one foot following the other. Tai Chi walking, by contrast, relies on a careful weight transfer to swing the back foot into the body as it lifts off and moves towards the front foot. As the weight shifts forward, the rear foot passes the body's centre-line and the front foot, and advances ahead of the former front foot, it swings away from the body, describing a flattened s-curve. The familiar 45-degree step is the model. The feel is like the swing of a skater-stride, feeling the weight shift from left to right and back as the feet advance. While *kinhin* has a distinct linearity, eight-step walking has a lateral swing.

Both styles of walking (*kinhin* and Tai Chi eight-step) begin with a similar stance, the Mountain Stance (described above). As with many Tai Chi movements, the steps go out in slight angle or curve from each other. To start, from the standing position, the first foot (let's use the left for our example) turns out. The weight, again as in many Tai Chi movements, leans back onto the stable right foot, the knees are slightly bent to keep the weight low. The left foot slides out, away from the centre line, in a 45-degree angle from the centre-line and the heel barely touches. Chuckrow refers to this as 'stepping out like a cat':

> ...the foot should first touch the ground for a finite amount of time before any weight is committed (separating *yin* and *yang*)... If you become content to take smaller steps and lower your body somewhat, you will see that stepping like a cat can be done... [And] you are much less likely to fall and you can achieve a much deeper state of relaxation of your legs.
> *Tai Chi Walking*, Chuckrow, p. 42

There is a premium on balance in this form of walking. At any point, the weight can be shifted, the stride adjusted. In true Tai Chi/martial arts fashion, the walker is ready to respond and move in an appropriate way as the circumstances dictate. This is quite different from *kinhin* walking, where the premium is on continuity and rhythm. *Kinhin* walking emphasizes a steady mind-state, one that promotes meditative activity. Tai Chi walking fosters a spontaneity and deeper, more responsive body experience. In this way it may have more in common with the above-described Rinzai pace.

Accompanying the foot and leg movement is an upper body movement. From the stance, the arms are allowed to relax by the sides. With the heel plant, the arms bend gently upwards, towards a 90 degree angle, held out in front of the chest. As the weight shifts to the forward foot, the hands should be at shoulder height. The shift of weight in the hips and legs is accompanied by a downward thrust of the hands. Its as if you are doing a double-pushing off with Nordic poles, without the poles. As the weight is fully shifted, the arms return to a resting position at the sides. Remember, unlike any other walking, the arms do not swing alternately but in parallel, nor are they held immobile in front of the body as we do in *kinhin*. It seems that the arm movement is not always included. Further, I have seen some video where the step is quite exaggerated, the raised foot coming up along the shin to the alternate knee before being extended out as a step. I have seen one video of such walking which, to my untrained eye, resembles a stumbling drunkard! Tai Chi seems to allow for considerable stylistic interpretation and I would presume teachers vary in how they instruct.

Kung Walking

Josh Holzer has been a martial arts teacher for more than twenty years. In his book *Warrior Walking: A Guide to Walking as Exercise, Meditation and Self-defence*, he describes a practice called walking chi-kung, or simply walking kung. Chi-kung is a whole Asian body-mind discipline that emphasizes proper breathing and slow movements and is most often used as a preparatory practice, supporting martial arts styles. Many of the movements in Thich Nhat Hahn's Ten Mindful Movements are based on chi-kung.

He describes the importance of proper breathing and draws on the aikido school of martial training. This begins by imagining the breath as a long continuous thread, resisting any habit of fragmented or puffing breathing. Breath is drawn in through the nostrils and exhaled out the mouth. He suggests placing the tip of the tongue on the palate and drawing breath with the lower abdominal muscles, the *tanden*, a practice familiar to those who have spent much time doing sitting meditation. You may want to re-visit the section Walking and Breath in Chapter 3 for more on this.

Holzer elaborates considerable detail on the proper breathing technique, describing position of the shoulders and use of the belly. This is familiar to any martial arts enthusiast and worthwhile advice for enthusiastic contemplative walkers. The remainder of the book has some excellent suggestions and 'finer points' on walking technique. In particular he explains the practice of a 'pulling step'. He begins from a standing position, the mountain stance mentioned above, and directs us to 'grip the ground' with the toes. With this tension, we can, in a sense, pull the step forward with the toes. There is a simultaneous tensing in the inner thighs, with the two legs squeezing towards each other. This leads us towards what I have called the skater-like s-curve in the above description of the eight-step Tai Chi walk. A final 'fine point' he makes is the importance of the heel plant in one's stride. When we lower the foot in the forward movement, there is a temptation to drive the heel backwards, to use it to propel the step. More correctly, because the weight is not thrown forward in the step but lowered, we need to similarly lower the heel. This is a straight down motion. As we lower the heel, the weight is rolled over the heel – its proper function as a transferring ball – as the weight is transferred along the foot onto the *yong-quan*, it is the toes which will pull us along. We have described this in the idea of the five-part step, above.

Interestingly, Holzer does not acknowledge the contemplative value of walking, locating himself at the more casual end of the spectrum of contemplative walking:

> However, no one wants to think that every single time they go for a walk they are undertaking some form of meditative ritual.
> Holzer, p. 85

I would agree, as I have affirmed elsewhere here, that there is a value in distinguishing recreational walking from contemplative walking.

LEADING A FORMAL WALKING PRACTICE

> The practice of mindfulness meditation can be compared to boiling water. If one wants to boil water, one puts the water in

a kettle, puts the kettle on a stove, and then turns the heat on. But if the heat is turned off, even for an instant, the water will not boil, even though the heat is turned on again later. If one continues to turn the heat on and off again, the water will never boil. In the same way, if there are gaps between the moments of mindfulness, one cannot gain momentum, and so one cannot attain concentration.

The Benefits of Walking Meditation, Sayadaw U Silananda in *Bodhi Leaves No. B 137*

During one of my first 10-day Tendai *gyo* trainings, we set aside one day for our *kaihogyo* practice (to be discussed in Chaper 8). This is an extended vigorous walk, which can take the better part of a day (and much longer in some contexts). Our group of 15 novices set off, single file, with the walk-master at the lead. His step coincided with the thump-clank of the ceremonial walking stick or *shakujo*. Every 45 minutes or so, the leadership would pass to the next in line, and the leader would move to the back. As a comparative new-comer in that *gyo*, my turn came later in the day. By that time, my legs were aching, my energy fading and my concentration fluctuating. It was remarkable how, when I received the *shakujo*, and stepped off in the lead, I suddenly became energized in body and mind. I felt the deep responsibility to sustain an energetic pace, to inspire those behind and set an example of determination.

Whenever you stand at the head of a line of other walkers, your own walking takes on new consequence. The walking leader may also be the leader of a longer practice or retreat and, so, their duties transfer from that role too. At other times, the walking leader is a rotating, handed-off or special role, so they need to assume responsibility for practice at that time. They are the heat under the kettle of each walker's practice and their responsibility is to maintain an even and adequate energy for the practice.

For formal indoor practices (and their outdoor counterparts) a leader has three responsibilities – timing, pace and direction. In the instance of outdoor walking, away from a prescribed path or circuit, the leader might have an additional duty of defining the route.

Timing means two different things. It means setting the length of the walk, but also means announcing the start and finish. Typically, for indoor *kinhin* practice a leader uses the *han,* a pair of hardwood clappers which are slapped together, once or twice to start the walk, twice at its conclusion. During the walk, the clappers are held still in a modified walking mudra. The length of the walk is based on several considerations. If the walking is part of a multi-session period of practice, the walking is used primarily as a shift into body-intensive meditation and, secondarily, as a relief to stiff muscles. In this case 5-10 minutes usually suffices. In a longer training period, such as a retreat or *sesshin,* the time may be longer, more like 10-15 minutes. For some practice formats, often in *vipassana*-style retreats, indoor walking can take a position of equal importance to sitting practice, so alternating rounds from 20-40 minutes (or longer) may be used.

Other than the Rinzai pace discussed above, where a rapid pace is the rule, a walking leader has the option of different paces. Most often the pace will be set to mirror breathing. Here, the leader needs to attend to possible differences between their own and that of other walkers. An experienced walker may have a longer breath, and thus a slower pace than newer practitioners, who may find that pace distractingly slow.

At times, a leader may prefer to alter the pace to enliven a practice session. Directing the line to double the pace can have many benefits when a group has become dull or settled. It may also serve to sharpen the line's attention to instruct them to close their eyes for one or more breaths. This can restore a sluggish pace. Likewise, an overly energized pace may need some reining-in. Beginners usually err in the extreme of too slow or too fast.

Directions during a walking round may be necessary and should be given for specific purpose and done briefly so as not to distract the line's attention. If the group is inexperienced, the leader may need to demonstrate elements of posture, hand-position and step at the outset. The leader needs to explain whether walkers have permission to break out of the line for washroom stops or not. If this is permitted, it is best to remind walkers to step out of the line at a doorway and, on re-entering the practice space, to wait to re-join in the same place they left. With less experienced groups, a leader may need to remind walkers to keep an even distance between themselves and the walker in front and behind. The leader needs to stay alert to distractions in the group. This will show up as walkers staring at objects in the practice space, fussing with clothing or hands or inattentive decrease or sloppiness in the boundaries of the circuit. Directions might include changes of pace which the leader calls for their own purposes. The leader should bear in mind that the walkers look to them to model the practice. Each step, each turn, each bow is a critical teaching opportunity. If bowing is included in the circuit, the leader's bowing needs to be timely and crisp. If the circuit uses squared corners, the leader needs to model this at every turn. If the practice space has windows which allow for visual distractions, the leader models focus and non-distraction. If chanting is included at any point, it will normally be the leader who initiates, that as well.

Returning to my *kaihogyo* walks, and, so I don't leave the impression that walking as a contemplative practice unfailingly fills us with superhuman spiritual energy, let me complete the story. The next year, our *gyo* schedule came around to another *kaihogyo* day. Due to a combination of increased length, more varied terrain and the progress of arthritis, my second experience was less energizing and more demanding. In short, it was everything I could do to put one foot in front of the other and complete the walk. Unlike the experience above, this one tortured me with thoughts of personal failure, aging and disappointment. It further brought me guilt and shame that my declining strength was causing the whole pace of the practice to slow.

In this case the walk leader was a gentle and loving man who knew the trail well and himself lived in a mountainous community in Vermont. He never uttered a sharp word, never suggested I should give up or couldn't do it. This walk presented an entirely new lesson and illustration of leading a contemplative walk. As with our own journeys, the *kaihogyo* and all contemplative walking are not solitary accomplishments. There are no gold medals for the first place finisher and no one 'lets the team down'. We look to Jizo Bodhisattva for example. He walks without end, through all times and spaces, ensuring all beings receive the Dharma and his encouragement to persevere. As walk leaders, it falls to us to ensure each and every walker walks to their highest level and that we begin and complete the walk together.

CHAPTER SIX
JOURNEY 2: CROSSING

If one does no work for a day, one should not eat for that day.
                                            Zen patriarch, Pai-Chang

WALKING AND WORKING

We have learned the first of our walking practices by looking at those we do alternately or in combination with sitting practice. These practices balance off and, I would propose, complement extended periods of immobility and sitting with movement. As we saw, mental activity and awareness of breath are supposed to remain consistent in walking or sitting. In this chapter we consider walking within the less formal daily routines of a Buddhist practitioner. Familiarizing ourselves with a highly structured routine can suggest ways we spiritual seekers, less framed by religious structures, can insert contemplative walking into our day-to-day activities.

We begin by following the footsteps of monastic life, ancient and modern, tracing how Buddhist monks might incorporate walking practice into their daily routines. Next we follow those footsteps more closely, into the daily routine of acquiring food by walking through the community. Later, we will explore how this ancient daily act has been translated into modern life and how those of us practicing in non-Buddhist environments might bring this practice into our world.

Before we do so, some orientation is in order. The Buddhist Sangha (community) began with the followers of the historical Buddha in the 5th century BCE. They were initially wandering groups, following their teacher in a minimally organized manner. As did many other wandering religious men (*sadhus*) of the time, all over Asia, they moved from place to place, living on the generosity of others, be they common people or nobility. These early Buddhists owned nothing but the clothes on their backs, their eating bowls and a few other religious items. They owned no property and slept where they could. We often read of their passing time in a grove or in the garden of some noble family. They were not seen as vagrants or beggars. On the contrary, they were seen to be fulfilling an important stage in human cultural development. Leaving behind one's family and position in search of Truth was (and still is in India) seen as a praiseworthy action. Their lives were seen to offer blessings and merit for others, and so there was an implied social obligation to support their efforts. They might be seen as individuals residing in that space in-between the everyday and the heavenly.

As the Sangha grew and passed the seasons, the early Buddhists found it too difficult to travel about in the rather harsh and challenging times of monsoons. During 'the rains' any traveler could experience days of continuous downpour, with floods, washed out roads and no possibility of sleeping under the open sky. Over the years, with the permission of the Buddha, these wanderers took to hold a time of seclusion during this season. They would remain in one site, often a donated place, until travel was again easy.

With the further growth and expansion of the Sangha also came the challenge of continuing to locate itself as part of this tradition of *sadhus* or wandering pilgrims or as a more anchored monastic life. We can appreciate their dilemma. The first teacher emerged from and taught within a wandering ascetic tradition, where near-wild men learned, taught and practiced away from settled society for the most part. His first followers joined that way of life. At the same time, the preaching of the Dharma came to expand beyond this community of self-exiles and into contact with that settled society. The sutras describe the Buddha teaching in the gardens of wealthy patrons or near towns, as well as the isolation of some wild peak or forest. More and more, they must have found themselves moving from the fringes to be part of settled villages and towns. The growth of the monastic Sangha was their response to this predicament. This is a bigger question than we can address here. Suffice to say, a decision was made to direct a mobile Sangha into a true monastic lifestyle, that is, religious men, and later on women too, located in a permanent monastery. Over time, as more monasteries arose, monks became part of a large network of institutions. With this network, the rules that had first developed on the road likewise became firmly established. These rules or *Vinaya* code instructed monks about all the aspects of their lives. They were told when to eat, when to sleep, when to collect food and how to behave so as not to disturb their sacred work.

There is no evidence of specific rules about walking. What the rules of monastic life do tell us is that, from early on, the Sangha had many tasks to accomplish. Like Napoleon's army, the Sangha 'marched on its belly', so one task that stood out was the daily search for food. And like Bonaparte's soldiers, the early monks had specific instructions of what to do and what not to do to acquire it. With the growth and spread of Buddhadharma, monastic life became more elaborated and qualified by the country of its practice. Below we will consider how the daily search for food changed in East Asian environments.

WALKING PRACTICE # 2
WALKING AS DAILY LIFE

As with those in Western Christian countries, Buddhist monasteries operated as largely autonomous mini-villages. A Buddhist monk or nun living within the walls of a monastery or convent lived with the rhythms of the overall community. Each person had a role in the administration, workshops, gardens, schools, building maintenance and so on, not to mention their duties in the many religious services provided by the monastery or temple to the nearby lay community. These would most often be blessings of planting or harvest, children or marriage, holding funerals and memorials, providing medical treatment or simply providing religious instruction.

The overlap of religious and everyday life within the walls of a monastery or convent was meant to bring a sacredness to that daily routine. It provided a means by which a way of life separate from, although not always isolated from, lay life could be lived. Monastic life was created to blend the sacred and the everyday into one experience. Early monastic life was as low-tech as one would expect, and so walking continued to be the predominant mode of mobility, especially in activities that did require travel. Thus, ordinary monastic life was one of walking. No garden tractors, no fork lifts, no pick-up trucks. No vacuum cleaners, no conveyor belts, no elevators. Just about every task in a monastery or fulfilled by its monastics outside the walls meant some walking. In modern times this has changed little, since monasteries remain places of religious life, not productivity. As Koji Sato notes in *The Zen Life*: "In present day monasteries there is little effort to promote more efficient methods for realizing enlightenment" (p. 151). This applies equally to the daily routines. Meals are still taken in the same formal methods that have been practiced for years.

There is in this a recognition that everyday tasks are not in opposition to contemplative life, nor are they subordinate to it. In fact all of our day-to-day activities, many accomplished in motion, offer us moments of attention, awareness and insight. The Zen tradition is replete with examples of awakening experiences which occur in the course of daily routines – filling a bucket, carrying firewood, chopping vegetables and so on. The Zen saying goes: "Before enlightenment – chop wood, carry water. After enlightenment – chop wood, carry water." From our perspective, we could add: before enlightenment, walk; after enlightenment, walk.

Only a few of us will spend much time in a monastic environment. More will enjoy a quasi-monastic environment through a retreat or *sesshin* experience. However, the majority will not even seek out such an experience. What then have we to learn about spirituality and movement from these centuries of monastic lives?

The answer returns us to the same point as those living inside monastic walls. A very large proportion of our lives is spent in some form of movement. We walk to the bus or subway. We walk between the car to the office or shop. Our jobs may actually be walking. We walk the aisles of the grocery store. We walk the kids, the dog, or, with a view to our own improved health, we walk ourselves. (If you're not walking a lot in your life and have the physical means to do so, you would do well to compare that with your satisfaction with your physical health).

We need not layer such ordinary walking with matters of hand positions or directing the gaze. Nonetheless, many of our previous lessons hold true in the most mundane of walking experiences. Formal walking practice coordinates step, breath and overall body awareness. Why wouldn't these also apply to directing the lawnmower, walking behind a grocery cart or pushing little 'Shnookums' in her stroller?

Here's a small example for grocery day. Once you enter the store, whether you are using a cart, a basket or carry bag, and before you start collecting goods, stop and stand briefly, out of everyone's way. Close your eyes and, in Mountain stance, feel your own body balanced where you stand, Take one relaxed in and out breath. Exactly as you do in the *zendo*, feel the weight evenly balanced on both feet. As you take your next in breath, shift the weight onto the right foot and slide the left foot forward. Open your eyes and with the out breath begin to move the body forward into the step.

Depending on the time you have for shopping, the busy-ness of the store and your own comfort level, you can repeat this little walking practice as often as you care. If you are using a cart, you can use it to stabilize your stride and lean back a little in the stride, as we do in a formal environment. If the store or aisle is not too busy, you can even briefly close the eyes and allow the cart to pull you along for a few steps. This is an excellent opportunity to feel the movement of the body, attend to the colours, sounds and smells that surround you. Anytime you stop to take something from a shelf or display, you can insert a slight pause and breath, hefting the weight of whatever you take, noticing the texture and smell, especially with fresh produce. This transforms a common task into our version of chopping wood and carrying water.

WALKING PRACTICE # 3
ALMS ROUNDS

To give alms is nothing unless you give thought also.
John Ruskin

Traditional Alms Rounds

In most monastic settings, meals must be completed before noon. This usually means a dawn breakfast and a meal just before noon. Depending on the country, the meals can be prepared in the monastery using food donated from outside or purchased by the monastery. In some places, eating depends on the gathering of donated food each day. This is true alms-gathering.

Completing the alms round means that all or most of the monks form a line, with their bowls in hand and proceed to the nearby community. When I experienced this (as an observer) in Sri Lanka, this meant an hour long walk down and back up a rather steep hill. In the village, the monks pass through the village, going door-to-door. This is always done on foot and the monks will use the time for walking meditation or sutra chanting. As they pass, homeowners will wait for the line to pass and serve out whatever food stuffs they have to share. Monks are officially not permitted to discriminate over what they receive and so the onus is on the donor to ensure it complies with the demands of a non-meat diet. We can only hope the tale of the monk, Makakasho, who approaches a leper for alms is metaphoric and instructive, rather than historical. As the person offers food to him, his leprous finger drops off into the bowl. The monk could not refuse. It gives the expression 'finger food' a whole new meaning!

In the Japanese traditions, alms gathering is called *takuhatsu*, (the word-characters literally saying 'pilgrims' and 'holding bowls'). This is because there is a kind of deliberate transformation which takes place when monks go out for food. In Japan, on certain days of the month, monks will change from their monastic robes into the traditional pilgrim or *henro* outfit. The outfit is referred to as *unsui* (cloud and water). This means over their regular robes they layer a white jacket and pants, straw sandals and *tabi* (one-toed socks), white leggings and arm-bands and the over-sized wicker hat (*suge-kasa*). This is the costume of the *henro*-pilgrim, someone who has abandoned their life, lay or monastic, and chooses to live on the road and on the charity of others, at least for a period of time.

The henro-pilgrim

It is only the Japanese monks who have adopted a particular specialty headwear, an over-sized wicker hat, that resembles a large round basket. Of course other pilgrims in Japan or elsewhere can be seen wearing sun-shade hats or carrying umbrellas, but the Japanese custom is, I believe, unique. There are even some versions called *komuso* which resemble a complete helmet, covering onto the shoulders, with a fine mesh eye-hole. The result is that the mendicant monk can not make direct eye contact with donors. If one purpose of the alms round is to dissolve self-identification, then turning the monk presence into a neutral, even generic, 'monk' makes sense. Why then, is it only Japanese monks who do this? The answer may be more a reflection of the Japanese social convention of avoiding eye contact. Westerners, used to the opposite convention, are often surprised to learn it is considered rude, even aggressive to look someone in the eye. I recall in my clerical training there are several instances where we are instructed to keep the gaze low and averted, only rarely staring directly at the altar Buddha. One exception during my Soto Zen training, during the many periods of *dokusan* (face-to-face conversation with the teacher), we would often be silently doing zazen looking directly into each other's eyes. Here, within that training moment, full and complete exposure between teacher and student makes perfect sense.

Someone in the *takuhatsu* line will carry a bell to notify laypeople that they are approaching, the bell also being a symbol of generosity. The leader carries the *shakujo* staff which further symbolizes the pilgrim role. We will explore this further in Chapter 8 when we examine the *kaihogyo* or pilgrimage practice. One could speculate this transformation is how Japanese monks maintain and preserve the two traditions of monasticism and mendicancy, the dilemma we mentioned above.

The *takuhatsu* is very much the reconstruction of a daily necessity into a daily practice. While the monks walk, they will chant and continue their regular practices, be that awareness of the breath and step, *nembutsu* (devotional chanting) or *koan* (contemplative questioning). Sato describes one Zen monk, Byakuin, who maintained his *koan* practice while doing alms round. His was a 'mixed' experience, you might say, and typical of the drama of many enlightenment tales:

> ...he came to a house where an old woman lived. The old woman refused to give him any alms, but still Byakuin refused to move on. This angered the old woman and she took a bamboo broom and brought it down hard on top of the wicker hat...the moment he regained consciousness, he was able to solve the various koan he had been given, thus achieving full enlightenment.

In our walking practice we would be wise to emulate such behaviour with caution. The highway and the trail possess many unexpected encounters and enlightenment may not be the consequence for everyone!

The Meaning of the Alms Round

> ...[alms] practice does not teach us to be dependent upon society, asking for something that is not earned, or pressuring a community for an entitlement to food or goods. Rather, it teaches us the fundamental lessons of the Buddha: to be dependent on everyone, to live our original homelessness, to include the homeless in thought and deed, to share everything, to accept what comes to us, to be generous, to be humble in society, to recognize the timid, to resist fame, to be modest, to resist the acquisition of goods, to throw off ego, to have the courage to be fully visible in practice.
>
> *Takuhatsu in America*, Eido Carney, *tricycle*, 1998

It would be a gross misunderstanding to view alms rounds, as they are sometimes mis-represented, as begging rounds. The Western practice of alms-gathering comes from an old European tradition of providing money or goods given as charity to the poor. The Old English, Latin and Greek meanings embody 'pity' and 'mercy', even compassion. In the European context, religious life, monastic and clerical, is equated with Christ-like poverty, and alms represent more of an act of pity for their suffering. As Carney notes, alms-gathering in the Buddhist tradition carries different meanings. On the one hand, it relates to the practice of walking to deliver the Dharma, which dates back to the historical Buddha. On the other, it relates to the Asian tradition of providing foodstuffs in return for the meritorious activity of religious wanderers (*sadhus*).

Well before the Buddha and continuing into the present there remains an Asian tradition of the wandering saint or wiseman (*sadhu*) and the mendicant or pilgrim. This person has taken the difficult step, in more ways than one, of leaving their home, in fact, abandoning their identity in pursuit of Truth. Like saints or shamans and perhaps even witches, they choose to dwell outside the norm, psychically and physically. As with Frost's road less-travelled, they choose the unfamiliar.

Although they step outside the norm, and typically step outside regular village habitation, they do not step completely outside of society. In fact, they are part of the fabric of ancient Asian life. Thus, it is common for such individuals to interact with settled people and represent to them the possibility of extraordinary contemplative life. Further, their dedication to a contemplative life qualifies them as individuals of extraordinary religious knowledge, strength and merit. We will not take time here to elaborate the Asian theory of merit, its acquisition and transfer, which is part and parcel of the Buddhist worldview. Suffice to say, the wandering wiseman brought both wisdom and acquired merit in their travels. Thus, if one were to meet such an individual, one would want to reward their extraordinary effort and also to benefit from being close to such a meritorious individual. The offering of alms to the wanderer is, therefore, more of an acknowledging gift for their effort than any demonstration of pity, as Europeans might view it.

More specifically, in the Dharma context, we have to refer back to the Buddha story itself, and three details in particular. First we recall that as the layman-prince Siddartha reaches the end of his tortuous quest. He has denied himself almost all nourishment and finds he has only succeeded in risking his own death. A peasant girl, Sujata, takes pity on him (more like the European meaning) and provides him a refreshing meal. From here, he makes his decision to practice only meditation until he can make the final breakthrough. He seats himself beneath the Bo Tree, on the banks of the Filgu River, near Bodh Gaya. He swears he will not rise until he has reached his goal of full awakening.

Once he becomes the Buddha, he sets off on the road to teach the Four Noble Truths and Eightfold Path. The road then becomes something radically different than simply the place where one lives as or where one encounters a *sadhu*. With his setting out as the Great Teacher, the road now becomes his Dharma-hall, his class-room. Thus, in the activity of the alms round, we are not encountering some physically impoverished saint upon whom we should take pity. On the contrary we are entering the Dharma-hall and monks on alms rounds are continuing the salvational work of Shakyamuni. On their rounds they are not so much seeking something for their sustenance, but rather offering us the most nourishing food possible, the food of Liberation. In return, the alms provided by householders is more of an exchange of what they have to offer for what the monks (as Buddha-surrogates) have to offer. If there is pity or mercy, it is more clearly the monastics who take pity on suffering beings and go out on rounds to bring the Dharma for their relief. In this way, as Carney notes, *it teaches us the fundamental lessons of the Buddha: to be dependent on everyone*. The activity of the alms round underlines the notion of dependence and interdependence, and thus becomes a real-life teaching lesson which points both monk and householder to that truth.

Finally, its important to reflect on the communal aspect of alms rounds. Not all alms rounds are done in a group, there are countless stories of individual monks or teachers on the solitary road. Nevertheless, the majority of alms gathering takes place as a group experience. The cultural image is a 'line of walking monks', people walk together. One could speculate many reasons for this including security and safety, the greater impact of a group or plain organizational reasons. We could also add that it represent a re-enactment of one of the most fundamental Buddhist stories, one which connects practitioners to Shakyamuni himself. As a ritual, it is an activity by which we re-affirm our collectivity as Sangha.

Does Alms Gathering Make Sense to a Modern Lay Practice?

Our study in this book is of walking practice and so we need to ask ourselves this question: does alms gathering make sense to us as a modern lay walking practice? If we want to cultivate our walking practice as a contemplative way for ourselves in our (probably) non-Asian environment, is it possible to either transpose this Asian practice to our world, or is there some way to re-shape it to fit?

For those reading this who have a location which supports some form of Buddhist alms-giving, you will have the means to join in such a practice. For most of us in most Western settings, this is not the case. A few teachers have tried to transpose alms rounds, with, as I am aware, very little success. I believe both Sangharakshita (World Buddhist Order) and Dharmavidya David Brazier (Amida Trust) tried it early on in their experiments with bringing Asian practice to England. Both concluded it was not a comfortable fit. The evolution of the modern welfare state changed the connection between donors and receivers into one largely mediated by institutions (government, religious groups like churches or Salvation Army, and non-profit fund-raisers). Carney notes:

> Begging is legal (in our community) as long as one does not engage in aggressive panhandling. In the United States, religious begging has all but disappeared, begging has been institutionalized in the form of fund-raising, conducted by every church and nonprofit corporation in America. Giving is no longer a direct transaction from the donor to the begging bowl. Americans make appeals

through the mail...there is no contact, no communal prayer, no immediate direct eye-to-eye gesture.

The question of why begging/alms rounds have disappeared in general, and more specifically why *takuhatsu*-like practice is not supported, is a larger one. Carney again offers:

> Why is it that Americans have embraced zazen meditation and yet do not incorporate *takuhatsu* in their practice? Even many Japanese teachers say, "*Takuhatsu* is impossible for Americans." Perhaps the deepest, most debilitating notion – and one that hits the entire nation, not just those contemplating takuhatsu – is the terror of being perceived as, or associated with, the poor.

Whatever the reasons, it is probably not possible at this time for those of us looking for meaningful walking practice to look to *takuhatsu* in its conventional form. How, then, might we adapt the practice to our modern environments? An answer might be found within the purposes for alms rounds – to bring Dharma to those who will benefit from it:

- to provide an opportunity to acquire merit through generosity (*dana*);
- to provide an opportunity for combining chanting, *koan* or other mindfulness practices with movement;
- to extend the merits of our practices to others;
- to perform a community-building ritual for faith practitioners;
- to provide a meaningful experience for individual and groups of practitioners;
- to make face-to-face contact or at least, some personal contact with suffering beings;
- to sustain the cycle of interdependence, that is, where beings can contribute to and receive from each other.

Keeping those purposes in mind, along with the strong social and historical disincentives for public begging, it seems doubtful that replicating Asian-style alms rounds will have a place in our collection of modern walking practices. That said, we need not exclude it entirely, only that culturally-informed version. What then, could we adopt to benefit from a *takuhatsu*-like practice that would make sense from an Western individual and group perspective?

I would suggest we in the West ground ourselves in the above-listed purposes and in what has already appeared in our social context. And before looking at examples, we need to re-formulate the mode of exchange of modern alms rounds. Undoubtedly our society is no longer supportive of individuals or groups seeking public material support in a door-to-door encounter. In fact, the antipathy to front door or street contacts by Hare Kirshnas, Mormons and Jehovah's Witnesses has become commonplace. The more likely formulation of a modern alms round would redirect or reverse the donation of materials like food or money. Here are some possibilities:

Charitable Walking

Every year and in communities all over the Western world people take to highways, paths, trails and urban streets to raise money for some favourite charity. The Walk of Life (heart disease), the Walk of Hope (breast cancer), the Walk for the Cure (various conditions). As I write this, in about two hours, I will be joining others to walk for our local hospice. These and hundreds more encourage people to act on behalf of others – survivors, health care workers and facilities, shelters, families and more, to raise funds for the advantage of others. This is a re-direction of the alms spirit. Walkers act as a conduit, a mediation between giver and receiver.

The pre-walk activity in charity walks usually means approaching friends, co-workers and other to act as sponsors. Here, we can recall the alms round spirit and make a simple invitation for support, rather than the kind of flashy self-marketing that sometimes people embrace. We should remember to express thanks, in advance for any donations and to refrain from a judgment of what others offer, or indeed for those who decline the invitation.

Individually or as a community or Sangha activity, we can take part in these charitable walks as part of our contemplative practice. To do so, we can forego the head-phones and other electronics and whatever hoopla may accompany the event and focus on finding a place and a pace that is appropriate to a more contemplative approach. We can plan our route to allow for some breaks along the way to insert some sitting practice or some gentle movement practice, whatever allows us to sustain a careful and concentrated mind. For those who embrace devotional practices, we can reserve periods of walking for that (more on this in the next chapter). We can begin the walk with our own quiet meditation. I often recommend people walking outdoors set themselves a 'sense-filter' for their walk, and this could be used for a charity walk too. A 'sense-filter' means we reserve some time, say one hour for each of the senses. As we walk we filter our experience by focusing on one sense at a time, noticing all the sounds or colours, for example, in a block of walking.

If walking as a group or Sangha, we have even more strength to bring to a contemplative walk. As in the *kaihogyo*, we can alternate leadership, so the followers can dedicate greater attention to chanting, *koan* or whatever practice they use. When we choose to change from walking to a brief period of sitting or movement, we are less likely to be disturbed if we are part of a small group. If the group chooses, they can dress in robes or meditative costume or borrow the all-white scheme of the *takuhatsu,* even have the leader carry the *shakujo,* or something similarly symbolic.

Care-taking Walks

In alms rounds, the walkers are collecting sustenance for themselves, sufficient food to feed them for the day. Food then, especially fresh food, is the collectible. However, our world is beset with more than food as food. The aftermath of grocery shopping can be piles of plastic bags, cardboard and bubble-packs. Packaging seems to go along with our food. This new food-collection walking practice is a variation on practice described in the literature of Morita therapy. Morita practice is a Buddhist-inspired practice which engages people in purposeful work, especially work that contributes to the overall well-being of the community. For example, a typical Morita exercise would suggest that an individual help a neighbour by sweeping their walkway or shoveling the steps of a senior.

A food-collection walking practice variation would direct us to construct a walk with a purpose, for example, picking up all the packaging left by the roadside. In doing so, we need to prepare with bags and gloves and appropriate recycle bins at the end. As we walk we can remind ourselves of the long chain of interdependence that travels from the food 'in the ground' to our use, the materials and resources that lead to the packaging, the chain of transport and delivery, and the impending decomposition of materials.

In most debt-burdened cities these days, activities like street and sidewalk maintenance are low priorities. In another variation, our walking care-taking can take the form of weed removal, grass trimming or removal of stones and broken curbs. Institutions, such as hospitals, shelters, seniors homes or clinics might be approached with an offer of a care-taking walk. Finally, there is no reason why such care-taking walks need be limited to the human environment. Care-taking walks along public trails, river banks or other walkways, either city or country can be done. Most animal shelters and rescue facilities have many more animals than companions. A care-taking walk might be negotiated with the facility to add animal companionship to a walking activity.

A Sangha Food Campaign

Even if we don't recommend unannounced door-to-door alms rounds, there is no reason why a group or Sangha cannot organize a pre-structured alms round. Sadly, communities in every developed country rely on some form of food pantry or food bank to help low income people find sufficient food. A walking group could assume responsibility for canvassing a part of a city on behalf of the food bank. With proper attention to advertising and fore-warning to the community, a *takuhatsu*-type walk could follow a prescribed route where residents would be expecting their visits, just as they do in Asia. With a combination of proper identification and an alms discipline, the experience could benefit the food bank and provide a meaningful contemplative experience for walkers and donators.

CHAPTER SEVEN
THRESHOLD 2: TURNING BACK

THE TURNING POINT

In Chapter 5, I described my Appalachian walk along a trail up into White Mountain National Forest. This for me was a true pivotal experience, and I noted the spaciousness in the ascent/approach, an urgency in a not-yet-answered question and a possible resolution in a descent. Whether it is a mountain walk, a full pilgrimage or the course of a labyrinth, in the turning point we realize the journey's first ending; we have reached our goal, we might say. This ending reveals, however, that we are but taking the first step in our return journey, one of equal import to the first half. It is almost that the out-going part of the journey is the right-brain stage, where we are feeling freely, open to novelty, looking for inspiration, patterns and opportunities. Then with the turning point, comes the left-brain stage – analytic, engaged in solution finding, less emotional and more decisive. The turning point is the bridge, the threshold, the bracket between two stages and two mind-states. The turning point can be one of those 'one-thought-moments' that Shinran describes, where time and timelessness intersect.

In Chapter 1, when we first stood facing the path, we said:

> We are not driven onto the road, we deliberately step onto it with reasons and aspirations unique to ourselves. At some point we reach the limin, we become liminal. This liminality has an ambiguity..."liminality is not only transition but also potentiality, not only 'going to be', but also 'what may be'." The final phase is the re-entry, re-crossing the threshold back into the home we left. It is a re-connection, and yet, because of what we have become on the journey, we recollect how we are different.

The turning point in any journey is full of paradox. We may reach a point where there is no turning back, and yet at another point turning back is all there is. The middle of the journey is, in some ways, the end; the turning point at the middle is, in some ways, another threshold.

WALKING PRACTICE # 4
CIRCUMAMBULATION: GOING AROUND IN CIRCLES

Circling What?

Most of us spend enough of our lives metaphorically running around in circles. We might well wonder why we would deliberately do that, and in the colloquial everyday sense, the expression has negative connotations. Yet exactly that practice has a long and noble history in Buddhist and other traditions' walking practice. In the Lotus Sutra, for example, we read:

> Thereupon, five hundred myriads of kotis of great Brahmas went into the lower regions with their palaces to enquire about this phenomenon, carrying heavenly flowers in their robes. They saw the Tathagata Mahabhijna-jnanabhibha on the terrace of enlightenment sitting on the lion seat under the bodhi tree. He was respectfully surrounded by humans and such non-humans as devas, naga kings, gandharvas, kinaras, and mahoragas. They also saw the sixteen princes requesting the Buddha to turn the wheel of the Dharma. Then all the great Brahmas bowed until their foreheads touched the Buddha's feet and then circumambulated him one hundred thousand times. They scattered heavenly flowers on the Buddha, and the flowers they scattered were piled up as high as Mount Sumeru.
>
> Lotus Sutra, Chapter 7

This kind of honorific circling seems to have been part of East Asian culture and of Buddhist social interchange. Jacobsen notes:

> The circular procession has a different function from the linear. The circumambulation marks off the space around the object as

sacred. The area around the temple is marked as the territory of the god.

South Asian religions on display: religious processions in South Asia, Jacobsen, p. 201

Apparently, in secular contexts, part of an Asian leader's designation of a conquered property took place when a king, prince or general walked around the conquered space, rendering it as his own. So, going around something has multiple levels of meaning. In Buddhist practice, it appears as a ritual involving Buddhas and also sacred spaces. In different traditions we read of circling specific relics, such as the bones or ashes of a Buddha or some great follower of the Buddha.

Early in Buddhist history, such relics were covered by mounds that marked a location. These were the first *stupas*, or burial mounds. Over time the mounds became more elaborated, with dome-coverings, fences, raised walkways, art-work and so on. The great *stupa* at Sanchi, an exquisite Buddhist site in North India dates from the 3rd century BCE. It features stonework piled in a dome pattern, a ramp leading to a walkway around the dome, and a carved stone gateway opening onto the walkway. There is a stone fence or balustrade around the whole structure and it is capped with a parasol-like construction representing the Indian convention of identifying royalty by a parasol. We won't go into the historical development of these structures, but only note how they traveled to the Far East and became the structure we know as the *pagoda*. They added roofs and towers, rising to ten and more layers. They normally marked the location of important religious objects, such as relics and even sutra libraries.

Another form of sacred object, appropriate for circumabulation was a significant natural object. The various sacred trees that attract Buddhist pilgrims to India, Japan and elsewhere, represent the sacred Bo tree under which Shakyamuni reached his own Enlightenment. They are likewise encircled with carved stone fencing, and all kinds of colourful markings to designate them as sacred. Another natural feature that hosts circumambulation are mountains. These can take on mythologic importance as residences of specific Bodhisattvas and deities, or as sources of extraordinary spiritual power in themselves.

For example, Tibet's Mount Kailash is often called the 'centre of the universe', and is the sacred mountain for four different religions. Pilgrims will follow a pilgrimage to Kailash known as the *kora*. The *kora* consists of a 32-mile path that circles the mountain and typically takes five days. The Kailash pilgrimage has a

Mecca-like importance in a Buddhist's life. It has been said, "One circuit is believed to erase a lifetime of sin, while 108 circuits is believed to ensure enlightenment."

In Japan, many less imposing but equally cherished mountains, Mounts Koya, Hiei and, of course, Fuji-san hold sacred positions. In a typically Japanese manner, these mountains are referred to by the respectful suffix *-san* which suggest a kind of personal relationship between a person and some venerable old wise man. Some traditions treat the mountain as a sacred being in itself.

The Practice of Circumambulation

Since we designate a circumambulation object as a location of spiritual power, this practice is not simply walking around it, as we might stroll around a museum or shopping mall. The whole sequence of approach, acknowledgment, circling and separation constitute a full practice. We create a direct personal relationship with that space or object, and our practice is not a private one, but rather one of locating ourselves in relation to it and grounding ourselves within the larger space at which the object occupies the centre. It is not so different from how we behave when we enter a temple or *zendo*. We mark off that space as a separation from our secular lives and an entry into something sacred, at least for us. Some may also recognize the parallel between such circumabulation and our approach to our teacher.

This brings us back to our metaphor for walking and contemplation as a journey – the threshold, the setting off, the turning point, the return and the threshold again. When we circumabulate, we repeat this in miniature. We decide to engage with the site and may prepare in advance. We may change clothes, may let go of certain burdensome objects (cellphones, wristwatches, etc.), may cleanse ourselves especially. We may gather practice objects – flowers, incense, a *mala*-bracelet, a sutra-text – for use at the site. There may be some ceremony we perform, participate in or have performed for us which signifies the approach to the site.

Once more, we arrive at a threshold and all that signifies. As we mentioned, these can be marked by a gateway, as at Sanchi or the *torii*-gates at Mount Koya. We begin the walk and proceed around the object or place. For simple locations, like a *stupa*, this will be a matter of a few hundred feet. I recall walking around the many *stupas* at Anuradhapura in Sri Lanka in a single afternoon. Others, will be more complex and will actually transform the circumambulation into a pilgrimage. (We will discuss pilgrimage in our next chapter).

In most traditions, the direction of the walking practice is of importance, if one wants to overlay some formality or ritual value to it. Typically, we move in a clockwise manner, moving off to the left of the circumambulated object, keeping it on our right. This reflects a curious pattern of preference for right over left in multiple cultures. It has been speculated that this comes from the holding of a weapon with the right hand (in our right hand dominant species), and so keeping a trusted person on the right is a display of openness, vulnerability and trust. Much has been written about right-brain/left-brain explanations. Some have pointed to the common Asian association of right with purity, left with defilement. In Asian Buddhism there is a frequent distinction made between right as expressing common, public or ordinary spiritual power (exoteric – that is, common knowledge or practice) and left as expressive of special, secret or privileged spiritual power (esoteric – that is, knowledge held within a specialized cultic practice). Thus, in the practices of Japanese Buddhism called *mikkyo* (secret rituals) there is a tendency to assign potency to the left hand in certain hand positions (*mudras*) and acts. This activates certain forces within a ritual act. There is probably a great deal more to be said about handed-ness but this is not our purpose.

A wonderful pop culture example of this appears in the 1999 Japanese supernatural thriller, *Shikoku*. The Shikoku is perhaps Japan's most famous and arduous pilgrimage walk. It circles the island of Shikoku, following a 680 mile route past 88 temples. It was said to have been created by Buddhist saint-legend, Kobo Daishi (Kukai), in the 8th century CE, and who is said to continue to walk its treacherous coastal trails. The normal route is clockwise, for the ritual reasons mentioned above. In this film, the main character is a modern-day husband whose wife has died leaving him heart-broken. He decides to walk the pilgrimage route in reverse order, counter-clockwise, in the belief that if he does so the prescribed number of times, he will open the gates to the underworld and be re-united with his wife. He is successful, but not in a happy way. We walkers need to be careful where we set our feet!

All of this to say that we needn't trouble our practice by worrying too much about direction. The common practice is to move in a clockwise manner. Even on the Shikoku, thousands of *henro*-pilgrims choose a reverse order without apparent consequence. Should we decide, for whatever reasons, such as differences of surface grade or walking into the sun or a strong head-wind, that a counter-clockwise path is best, we needn't fear the sudden and calamitous opening of the gates to the underworld!

WALKING PRACTICE # 5
THE SOUND OF WALKING – WALKING NEMBUTSU

If you have done silent sitting practice, you already know that the body has its own sounds, even at our stillest moments. We can hear the beating of the heart, the gurgling of fluids and gases, the popping and cracking of joints. Its no surprise that we 'sound'. Pythagoras, the Greek philosopher of the 5th century BCE and father of mathematics, proposed a broader theory about universal sound, which was still common belief in Shakespeare's times. He asserted that there were crystalline spheres within spheres that composed the universe. Each of these vibrated in a unique way and all together they sustained a musical harmony, the 'music of the spheres' that found its expression in numerous Elizabethan dramas and philosophies.

Next door to the Greek philosopher, Pythagoras, in Northern India, even centuries earlier, philosophers understood that vibration and sound were not just ways to understand the universe, but physical ways to experience its form and rhythms. The syllable *OM* is now part of our culture, at least as a cliché for the meditative way. It is the combination of three sounds – actually four. "A" (spoken "ah") is the primal breath, the first letter of so many alphabets, the so-called 'mother of sounds'. "O" is the middle sound, as a circle, as a symbol of infinity, as a symbol of fullness makes up the mid-sound of the *OM* syllable. As the mouth closes, as the breath subsides, as the universe wanes, there is "M". The fourth part of *OM* is, as any good Indian philosopher would know, the background silence, the emptiness from which *OM* arises. In Sanskrit, the sacred language of Asia, *OM* stands for all sounds; it is the entire alphabet of human and cosmic sound. That alphabet begins as does ours, with 'A' and ends with 'MA'. This simple formula stands for and sounds for the entire universe, manifest and non-manifest, what is and that from which it arises. In Buddhist teaching, breath-sound is the subtle energy which shapes and activates consciousness into the universe, literally of name and form. This is (quietly) echoed in the Biblical vision as well. The Biblical passage does not describe the resultant sound, but might we imagine it too came out as *OM*?

> And the Lord God formed man of the dust of the ground and breathed into his nostrils the breath of life; and man became a living being.
>
> (Genesis 2:7)

> All Scripture is God-breathed and is useful for teaching,
> rebuking, correcting and training in righteousness, so that the
> man of God may be thoroughly equipped for every good work.
> (2 Timothy 3:16, NIV)

The use of sound in contemplative practice is as much wound into practices as sitting postures and hand positions. One might even argue that sound practice itself is the source of contemplative practices, like meditation. We'll leave that for others to explore. For our journey, we are curious about the inter-relationship between sound practice and walking. In particular we are exploring sound as it walks, rather than just doing something while we walk. The sound then is integral to the walking practice, rather than simply coincidental, like 'walking and chewing gum', as the saying goes.

Nembutsu as Mantra

We've introduced this practice as a walking *nembutsu*, but it really grows from a larger and more ancient practice known as mantra. Mantra, of which our friend *OM* is but one example, is the large form of sound practice. The *OM* syllable is the sound of all sounds, the 'a to z', as we might put it, or 'the alpha and omega' as the Biblical Greeks use it. All the other sounds have their association with particular cosmic energies. For example in East Asian Buddhist mantra practice, the 'ha' sound is associated with Jizo, the celestial being known as Earth-womb. He is the energy that cares for, protects and awakens the Six Realms of Existence. Because he is characterized as the Cosmic Pilgrim we will spend more time with him later, looking at pilgrimage practices. For now he is represented by this 'root sound' (literally the *bija* or 'seed sound'), as it is called, 'ha'. Other associations tie together other sounds into phrases which similarly represent specific energies or forces or personifications of cosmic power. Many of us know the famous *om mani padme hum* mantra used for practices associated with Kannon / Chenrezig / Avalokitesvara, the personification of compassionate activity. There are hundreds of such phrasings which form the body of mantra practice.

All of this is to tell us that the use of sound in Buddhist contemplative practice has a long, complex and authoritative history. Indeed, schools like the Japanese Shingon have proposed that Truth is unknowable except through three allied practices, *mandala* (the practices of symbolic patterns), *mudra* (the practices of symbolic gestures or hand positions) and mantra.

Another sound practice which informs our walking practice is the practice of sutra recitation. In Buddhist teaching, we have several levels of expressed truth. The first is sutra, those texts attributed to a Buddha or Bodhisattva. These are the most authoritative and potent. The other levels are many different types of prose or poetry which have accumulated and gained authority in different schools and sects over the millennia. The body of sutra is the closest thing to a 'sacred book' for Buddhists. Most sutra begin with the formula "thus have I heard..." reminding us that the Buddha's teaching was oral, the sound of his voice and heard by his students, most notably Ananda, the Buddha's cousin. In yet another way, sound is the medium for experiencing the Buddhadharma. Sutra comes to stand in for the liberative power of the Buddha.

Nembutsu and Recitation

Over the centuries, sutra becomes itself elevated. And with it the recitation, that is the re-presentation of teaching back into sound, comes to take on a special power. Certain texts become designated as particularly powerful. For example, the *Heart Sutra* (The Heart of Perfect Wisdom – *Mahaprajnaparamita Hridaya Sutra*) has been accepted by Buddhists in almost every setting as an especially powerful statement of Buddhist teaching. In many Buddhist countries, the recitation of sutra either by laypeople or clergy releases the power of the word, creating a secondary benefit or merit for both the speaker and listener. It is for this reason, that sutra is the merit provided when monks circulate in the community during alms rounds. That recited sound itself generates merit for the person standing along the alms route. It is this, as noted above, which initiates the exchange of food or money collected by the alms gatherers.

Later in the development of Buddhist teaching, another sutra becomes designated as having special power, the *Lotus Sutra* (The Lotus of the Wonderful Law – *Saddharma Pundarika Sutra*). Its use in chanting services or in alms gathering is similar to other sutras. However, from the 10th to 14th century in Japan, this sutra takes on a symbolic value of its own. Its is said to be the final and conclusive words of the Buddhas, the end of all teaching. Its recitation comes to be seen as sufficient for liberation. The 13th century teacher, Nichiren, defines the sutra's 'name' alone as having liberative value. It is as if our pointing to the sutra orally releases all of its power. Some modern Buddhist (or quasi-Buddhist) sects have continued the recitation of such a symbolic reference to the Lotus Sutra, as *namo moyoho renge kyu* (Glory to the power of the Lotus Sutra) as their primary practice. This *o-daimoku* (honoured phrase) is yet another form of mantra.

This once more, leads us to the *nembutsu*. Almost all of the classic mantra phrases begin with the word *namas*. Anyone who has practiced yoga will recognize *namas-te* as part of the popular greeting and closing used by Indian-inspired instructors. It is what is called an 'honorific', that is a way of giving special status to a person or thing to which it is directed. Combined with palms pressed together and a bow it signifies everything from appreciation, thanks and elevating someone to an intimacy in our hearts. In the word *nem-butsu* (as *namah-butsu*) we focus that honoring act more specifically towards the Buddha (*butsu* in Japanese). Thus the mantra *om namu amida butsu*, at its most simply understood, can be nothing more than a bow and oral acknowledgment of our thanks and indebtedness to Amitabha Buddha, one particular Buddha, the personification of Infinite Light.

In the same way as the *o-daimoku* we met above is emblematic of the Nichiren school, the *nembutsu* is the prime practice and teaching tool of the collection of schools of Buddhism called Pure Land. Many volumes have been written to explain Pure Land and its derivative schools, and we cannot even pretend to do justice to this magnificent doctrine here. For our purposes, we can settle for an understanding of these recitations as the embodiment of devotional practice. The recitation of *nembutsu* establishes the relationship between the humble and imperfect practitioner and Amitabha, the Buddha who has taken a vow to ensure all beings who call out for his aid will be assured of 'being born in the Pure Land'. Although *nembutsu*, as 'the nembutsu', most often refers to the Pure Land practice, we can to similar devotional chanting practice directed at other persona. One might just as devotedly chant *om namu jizo busa* to Jizo, as we do in our Sangha practice, if that were the form of your practice.

How Do We Do Walking Nembutsu?

Bringing this back to our walking practice, we might use our title 'walking nembutsu' as a collection of sound and devotional practices which includes the whole collection of individual mantras, the *o-daimoku*, the general form of devotional chanting (as with *om namu jizo busa*) and its most refined version, the true nembutsu, *om namu amida butsu*. We need to remind ourselves again here that we are not simply talking about doing one practice (mantra, chanting, recitation) *along with* another. The crucial element for us is to integrate the sound practice with the walking practice. We become sound walking, walking sound.

We have stressed that all walking practices are body-mind practices, more specifically, body-mind-in-motion. What will transform the practice of mantra or *nembutsu* into a walking practice is not just that we em-body the sound and its performance, because this is part and parcel of how we do any Buddhist practice. We transform it by making it a moving practice, sound-in-motion.

As we may recall, we learned to incorporate the relationship between breath and step when we began with *kinhin*. We also learned the deepening of that combination through step-counting – that is, relating breath-in-motion to step-in-motion. In performing walking *nembutsu*, we likewise make the recitation float on top of both breath and step; in the same way as we combine our forward step with exhalation, we align the chant. So that the *om* of the mantra arises in the expression of the outbreath. The *om* pushes us forward, launching the step and the rest of the mantra. In the slower, more formal versions, such as we might do around the practice hall, we can actually align step, breath and mantra. Practiced in a line of chanting this becomes a magical experience. The whole group walks, breathes and steps in a harmony that illustrates the Buddhist expression 'just one step'.

It is part of the *nembutsu* tradition to vary the speed of the recitation. The chant-leader will start of with a long slow, even artificially slow chant, typically what would align breath and sound. It is common for the chant to accelerate into a rapid, slurred version, where the clarity dissolves into auditory incoherence. At this stage it will transform into a silent practice and mantra become a mental object, one which stands-in for the phrase. There is great power to this as the flow of the internal, inaudible sound permeates the entire practice experience. As the practice period winds down, the leader will re-introduce coherence and volume as the chant slows to the rhythmic and breath-word alignment returns. This can be the form of our walking practice as well. We will begin with an audible chant and accelerate to a silent symbolic phrase-sound. What begins as sound-step-breath becomes breath-step permeated by a constant sound layer that extends through and between every step. When done for an extended period, this can blossom outwards into the larger space in which the walk takes place.

As I have become familiar with and adopted *nembutsu* practices into my own practice regimen, I have found outdoor walking *nembutsu* to be of extraordinary value. My typical version, and one we use as a Sangha on a regular basis, is from our front gate to the small lake about 1.5 kilometres along an up-and-down dirt road. As I set out I begin an expressed *nembutsu*, aligning the *om* with my left foot-plant (which is also the out-breath). Because this is a walking practice, I prefer the Jizo mantra (*om ha ha ha vis may ye svaha*) to the classic Amitabha one. There is something harmonizing to walk along with the Eternal Pilgrim. He has been my companion for years, and it seems like walking with an old friend to engage this mantra. As the walk progresses, I/we switch into the more rapid and silent recitation. It takes on the quality of a kind of buzz in the head. The whole body becomes that one sound. Sustaining it as the walk progresses suddenly introduces a new mental dimension to the walk. It is as if the walk is floating through an atmosphere of Buddha-presence. The colour of the leaves or the crunch of the snow are never lost or diminished by this. It is more like the transformation that occurs switching from a black-and-white film to a full colour one. The content doesn't change but the experience becomes enriched and more truly contemplative.

I noticed this transformation quite sharply a few years ago while engaged in a walking mantra practice lead by a senior American monk. He announced that the group of us would circle the temple interior. He would then begin the walking chant, and he recited it once. Uncertain that she would remember it properly, someone asked if he would repeat it. His answer? – No! The walk began.

At first the chanting and the steps were incomplete. Some people knew the chant and held its flow. Others, trying to follow it fumbled vocally and in stride to keep up. After about ten circles of the temple everyone had the chant and the flow of the walking settled down. At one clear point, the chant and the walk dropped into sync and there was this clear sense of one voice and one step that continued until the concluding clap of the wooden clappers.

This walking *nembutsu* is a practice which can be done solo or in a Sangha, it can be done as the main practice, or, for a longer walk, say a pilgrimage or *kokorodo*, it can be used for a stage of the walk. In my own clerical training, called a *gyo* in the Tendai tradition, we reserve one full day as walking practice. This is normally about 5-6 hours along a spectacular country road in the rolling Berkshire Mountains of Upstate New York. It is common for it to be punctuated by periods of walking recitation (*nembutsu* or sutra). As with our own lake walk, this combination of the two transforms both practices into something unique and powerful.

CONTEMPORARY PRACTICE: MUNDY'S PRAYER WALKING

> The major difference with prayer-walking (compared to other consecrated activities) is that it intensifies, identifies, memorializes, recognizes, blesses the experience in itself. This is just another way of talking about mindfulness and intentionality – goals well worth our attention.
>
> *Prayer-Walking*, Mundy, p. 158

As we will do from time to time in this study, we will turn to a non-Buddhist walking practice for inspiration and elaboration. The American Christian, Linus Mundy, has been at the front of the line, literally and metaphorically, with his promotion of a practice he calls prayer-walking. In his main guide, *The Complete Guide to Prayer-Walking: A Simple Path to Body-and-Soul Fitness*, he introduces this combination of invigorating exercise and introspective thought with a distinctively Christian flavour.

Mundy's concern is different from the details of technique as we have done here, and that is no flaw. It is his purpose to connect a very ordinary activity with the simplest, but still powerful prayer methods of his faith. In fact, he wants to encourage practitioners to just get out on the paths and roadways as part of their daily spirituality and not be distracted by technique. As he says:

> Prayer-walking is after all like prayer, an expression of a relationship. My chaplain, Dick Gilbert, says it well "When Jesus taught his disciples the 'Our Father', he wasn't teaching words (or technique); he was teaching a relationship. We can teach about prayer and how to pray – but those really are process questions that are secondary to the larger issue of relationship."
>
> (p. 74)

His book describes and recommends an assortment of walking exercises which are in no way exclusive to Christian walkers. Although he clearly situates himself among great Christian walkers like Saint Francis, he is just as much a partner to Thoreau in meeting his God in the midst of His Creation, down lanes, in fields and by lakes.

He connects his walking to several Christian traditions. The first he learned as a young teen when he first entered seminary. He describes regularly seeing senior monks who combined the principle of *ora et labora* (prayer and work), a discipline not unlike walking *nembutsu*. He sees the many processions of his church experience – funerals, weddings, etc. – as embodying walking prayer. Finally, his time on retreat in Kentucky defined for him the connection between walking the 2500 acre monastery grounds and active prayer.

Beyond the expected nature and back-road walks, Mundy describes a number of beautiful variations on walking, such as seasonal walks (Christmas, Lent, Easter); relationship walks (parents, couples, walking with our heroes or enemies); symbolic walks (through scripture) and even walking through your house. In Chapter 7, he outlines for us when you will know you are prayer-walking, not just ordinary walking. He cites:

- when you know you're in love with God and Life;
- when time stops;
- when you're feeling whole;
- when you want to go prayer-walking;
- when you're not afraid of getting lost;
- when you challenge yourself to what you don't know.

CHAPTER EIGHT
JOURNEY 3: THE LONG ROAD BACK

THE ROAD BACK

Once we reach the top of the mountain, or face the shrine or touch the relic, we may say the journey is over. Every subsequent step is nothing but the long arrival home again. Or is it? Whether you have walked into some secluded lake, climbed the steps to a holy space or walked the circuit of a labyrinth, you already know that a large part of the value of your journey arises in that return trip. As we'll see below, we are now entering that returning phase of our journey. It is one which can be seen as, in no particular order or degree:

- a stage of **consolidation**, where we begin to absorb what we have experienced and learned into some new understanding of who we are and our life;
- a stage of **resolution**, where those troubles or questions that unsettled us up to the time of the first crossing the threshold and occupied us for the first half of the walk become resolved, answered or re-shaped;
- a stage of **reconciliation**, where the aspects of our lives which were not shifted or transformed by the approach to the goal can be accepted and any sense of failure is replaced by an acceptance that we must carry them a while longer;
- a stage of **recognizing ourselves anew**, where we come to understand what we have been learning and how this has begun to change us;
- a stage of **re-evaluation**, where we realize what is behind and what is ahead, re-focusing our lives and intentions, perhaps in a small way, with a promise to change some aspect of our daily lives, or in a major, transformative way, where we recognize new intentions, directions, perhaps a new calling or mission for ourselves;
- a stage of **preparation**, where the first glimpses of our new life begin

to take shape, we make decisions about actions that will occur once we re-enter our life off the path; and
- a stage of **appreciation and thankfullness,** where we grow aware of the countless gifts of delights and understanding which have been bestowed on us during our journey, and where we are filled with the desire to express our thanks in some familiar or new way.

In this chapter we will take the long road, as we learn about the practices which deeply transform the contemplative walker over an extended time. The first of these long walks, pilgrimage, has its versions in every religious and cultural tradition in history. The names ring out with mystery, adventure and power to transform. Consider even these few:
- The Hebrew Exodus;
- Bodhidharma's walk from India to China;
- The Muslim's journey to Mecca;
- Christian Crusade journeys to Jerusalem all through the Middle Ages and since;
- The walk to Canterbury, as is the background of Chaucer's masterful *Canterbury Tales*;
- The more modern El Camino di Santiago Campostella and the El Rocio pilgrimages, across Spain;
- The Shikoku pilgrimage of Japan;
- the Bahai 9-day pilgrimage to Haifa;
- the 6-month Walkabout of Australian aboriginals;
- the annual Canadian Aboriginal walk to Lac Ste-Anne in Québec;
- Mao's Long March of 1934-35;
- rock fans visits to Elvis' Graceland or Jim Morrison's grave in France.

It is tempting to see 'from the sublime to the ridiculous' in these, yet each represents some major transformative experience which took (and many which still take) place on foot. Most of us might only dream of such walks, so we'll explore the elements of a personal pilgrimage, and meet Jonny, one Buddhist walker, who created such an experience for himself.

The second long walking practice we'll explore is, without doubt, the ultimate walking practice, and one which should awe and inspire us, but which few of us would even imagine attempting. The *kaihogyo* is a practice developed by and unique to the Tendai Buddhist sect of Japan. It was devised many centuries after the rise of Tendai in Japan. As with most walking practices, it has a variety of forms, from the possible to the nearly impossible. Oddly, in spite of (or perhaps because of) the incredible difficulty, it is one practice which has been thoroughly researched and documented. Learning about the *kaihogyo* can help us to appreciate the potential of all walking practices, and can inform whatever practices we come to explore ourselves.

WALKING PRACTICE # 6
PILGRIMAGE

Types and Purposes of Pilgrimages

Pilgrimage is simply that journey taken by a pilgrim. A pilgrim is any person or group of persons, clergy or lay who devote themselves to some purposeful long walk. The purposes which have driven pilgrimages are numerous and serve to define the many different kinds of pilgrimage. The word, pilgrim, comes from an ancient Franco-Latin expression for someone who travels across fields, a *peregrinus* (*per* = through; *ager* = farmer's field). Our modern word peregrinations, literally wanderings, survives from that origin. The other meaning is telling too: a foreigner. A pilgrim often appears as someone 'from away' (as we say in the Canadian Maritimes). In cultures characterized by birth-life-death within the boundaries of one's village or farm estate, someone who suddenly comes walking across the fields from who knows where, and travelling to some other who knows where, would earn the title of foreigner.

The other broad element which defines a pilgrim is someone who has left something and somewhere behind for their personal purposes. This may be, as noted above, a knight leaving his homeland to visit Jerusalem or a Muslim interrupting his life to visit Mecca as his faith requires. As early as the celebrated *Canterbury Tales*, it is clear that women, lay or clergy, became pilgrims as well, although from the *Tales* each with very stark differences of purpose. Below we'll consider whether Shakyamuni's home-leaving represents a pilgrimage. Pilgrimage is a compression of time, a stepping out of time. This brings us back to our metaphor of crossing/dwelling where this walk represents a rupture in the usual flow of or life-time, not by accident but by design and with purpose. Later we will also learn to view the pilgrimage as an "in-between space", where we travel somewhere between our normal lives and that sought-after space of personal transformation.

Turner and Turner (see *Image and Pilgrimage in Christian Culture*, Turner and Turner, 1978, p. 18) identify four different types of pilgrimage. The first is the *proto-typical*, that is one established by a founder or charismatic leader. The Aboriginal-Australian Walkabout would be such a walk, as would the roads to Jerusalem taken by Jesus and Rome by Saint Paul. These we might call the 'first walks', since they are the trail-making routes, ones set out by the first of those to walk them, and followed by those who come after. A second type is the *archaic*. These emerge from some time later than the proto-typical but historically relatively early devotional activities. The pilgrimages to Glastonbury in England and Pandharpur in India would be examples. The archaic pilgrimage might involve the re-interpretation of an older route by a later religious tradition. For example, there are religious paths in Mexico which have their origins in pre-history but have been re-defined by later Catholics as Christian pilgrimage.

A more modern example occurred in 2001 when a Catholic pilgrimage sponsored by the Oblates to Lac Sainte-Anne in Québec was officially turned over to aboriginal management. The site began as a site of aboriginal healing until the mid-1800's when an Oblate mission was established nearby. It was transformed into a Christian pilgrimage in 1889 through an association with a Sainte-Anne shrine and pilgrimage in Brittany, France. Apparently, the site, a national historic site since 2004, will remain Christian but with an interfaith dimension.

The third type, at least in the Christian-European tradition is the 'mediaeval', which comprises those which emerge from a theologizing of some walk routes. Many of the great pilgrimage routes of Europe, such as the El Camino de Santiago (The Way of Saint James) or Compostella, as it is sometimes called, arose this way. The El Camino was created following the belief that the apostle Saint James, the first of the Christian martyrs, was buried in northwest Spain, (as Iago, he is the patron saint of Spain). The name of Compostela, the town associated with this pilgrimage, comes from the Latin *campus stellae (*field of stars). The view of guiding stars in the Milky Way are part of the long history and legend of this walk.

Outside of the Christian tradition, the Japanese Shikoku might fit with this category. It was a route reputedly established by the Japanese Buddhist saint, Kobo Daishi (or Kukai, the founder of Shingon or Esoteric Buddhism in the 8th century CE). It circles the island of Shikoku and comprises 88 temples. Although its popularity grew at the end of the mediaeval period in Japan, it could also be considered a proto-typical pilgrimage because it was described as a route set by Kobo Daishi himself.

Modern pilgrimages are the last type and are walks introduced in more recent times. In the Christian tradition, the Shrines of Lourdes or Sainte-Anne-de-Beaupré would qualify, since they were identified with modern saints. On the secular side, so-called pilgrimages to cultural heroes or events, Edgar Allen Poe, Jim Morrison, Elvis, European concentration camp sites and hundreds more have sprung up, as a focus for people who share a deep appreciation and some personal connection with these figures or events.

Regardless of how 'sublime' or ridiculous' we may find them, pilgrimages are undertaken for many reasons; we'll focus here on the more spiritual reasons. In most cases, the pilgrim's motives include more than one reason. One simple motive might be the desire *to visit the location of some spiritually or historically significant event*. An associated motive can be the *re-enactment of some central religious or spiritual event*. The Holy Lands or similar sites associated with Biblical history, as with the El Camino described above are good examples for these two reasons. In this case the pilgrim may be seen to be transformed into a version of the involved figure, and their pilgrimage, in a symbolic sense, becomes that same act. Pilgrims often attend *a location that has a sacredness to it*. This might be some sacred ground, as with the aboriginal healing space in Lac Ste-Anne, Uluru (formerly Ayers Rock) in Australia or it might be the location of some relic. The Temple of the Tooth in Kandy, Sri Lanka, is the end point for Buddhist pilgrims who wish to see and be close to what is reputedly an actual tooth from Shakyamuni Buddha. This has trans-historical value of course, but for Buddhists would offer an unmatched opportunity to acquire the merit which is embedded in such a relic.

Many mediaeval pilgrimages represent the motive of *pardon or forgiveness*. The pilgrim undertakes a long difficult and even life-risking journey in the hope that the journey and its goal achieved will relieve some sin or misdeed. In mediaeval times, pilgrimage was, in fact, a common sentence assigned by an ecclesiastical/criminal court. Many modern pilgrimages are set in motion by the *hope for a miraculous cure or event*. We will often see scenes of throngs of pilgrims gathered at the steps of some shrine or the banks of some river. In their company will be the crippled, deaf and blind. Stories will appear demonstrating the 'evidence' that such places are *loci* of rare and miraculous healing powers. One associated reason would be to use the pilgrimage as *a cleansing or to mark the conclusion of a period of unhappiness*. Another associated reason might be to use the period of pilgrimage *to intensify spiritual practice and gain insight.* At the other end of that process, might be a pilgrimage which is *an expression of thanks for beneficial events or spiritual achievement.* The Shikoku pilgrimage has long been used by Buddhists wishing a concrete way to show their appreciation for business success a long life or other gifts.

In his very satisfying travel-biography, *Japanese Pilgrimage*, Statler describes his encounter with a priest at Temple Twenty-Six along the Shikoku which points to a central reason why people undertake pilgrimage. They speculate on the role of the Wisdom Sutras which were brought back to that Japanese island by Kobo Daishi, the founder of the pilgrimage there:

> "You can appreciate the crucial position that the Wisdom Sutra occupied in his [Kobo Dhaishi's] life, in the development of his thought. It is central to his insistence that man can achieve Buddhahood in this life." He [the priest] shoots a look from under white brows, "It is wisdom that impels the *henro* (pilgrim) to make the pilgrimage."
>
> *Japanese Pilgrimage*, Statler, p. 86

For many pilgrims, a pilgrimage is undertaken simply out of *the desire to express one's loving relationship with the Divine.* The faithful will separate themselves from their ordinary lives and designate a block of time to walk with the Lord or with exemplary religious figures, such as the Dalai Lama or the Pope. This may be part of *hearing a call or obeying a religious requirement.* The Muslim pilgrimage to Mecca is well known as such a faith requirement, and may mark the zenith of a person's religious life. Less of a requirement may be *the act of dedication* motive. I recall, a few years ago when the wife and daughter of a well-known fitness figure completed the El Camino in memory of his tragic death in a mountain accident. He died doing what he loved and they used the pilgrimage to mark their respect for him, doing something he wanted to do. The recent Hollywood film, *The Way*, picks up this theme.

If we look at the history of some pilgrimages, there seem to be periods when that pilgrimage was undertaken not as a beginning-end journey after which the pilgrim rejoined their life, but *as a complete change of life*, not unlike going into the monastery or convent. Such pilgrims would, from that point onward, live their lives on the road. Presumably, they could engage with non-pilgrim life, as monks and nuns would do from time to time. Even today, there are such people.

Evidently, there are some individuals who have completed the Shikoku in Japan, who relocate to the island to re-walk the route or, having walked it hundreds of times, dedicate their lives to serving the needs of others who follow that pilgrimage.

Others do a pilgrimage *to see what its all about*. They may or may not have religious intentions, and these may well be enlivened or enhanced by the journey. Finally, and perhaps among pilgrims with the least spiritual motives, may be those who do it as *a challenge or to break up some routine* in their lives as with the weight-obsessed Joost in *The Way*.

It is worth noting point here the difference between walking a pilgrimage route and walking in a pilgrimage ceremony. All the great pilgrimages follow the same route each year. In most cases, you can walk the route anytime. If you do, you may have company and maybe not. I recall our visit to the Basilica of San Francesco d'Assisi in Italy. There were busloads of pilgrims all over the site and services going on in several different locations simultaneously. I expect it was like that most of the time and there may be a special day or days when the crowds are larger. However, other pilgrimages, like the pilgrimage of El Rocío in Southern Spain occurs on Whitsunday (on the feast of Whitsun or Pentecost, after Easter), and thousands of pilgrims from surrounding towns follow the Blessed Virgin to the destination church, the Hermitage of El Rocío in the countryside of Almonte, Spain. Its not clear how much people walk that route at other times. There are benefits to each type of walk.

The Buddhist Pilgrimage

As Buddhists, our most inspiring example is that of Shakyamuni's own flight from his father's palace in Lumbini. This is normally characterized as an abandonment of the lay life and transformation, first as a *sadhu* or wandering religious ascetic and later, a *bhikkhu* or monk. This is in keeping with a Hindu view of the stages of life, where a man is encouraged to depart from his householder life (usually once his family is more settled than Shakyamuni's) and devote himself to the contemplative path. I cannot say if there was any sort of pilgrimage tradition in India at that time (5th c. BCE), and so it is not clear if he was following any contemporary walking model.

For our purposes we may wonder, was his flight a pilgrimage or not? Looking at the motives listed above, he was not seeking any shrine or relic or single sacred place. He had no intention of completing a journey and resuming his pre-walk life. If anything, his pilgrimage would have been taken to mark the conclusion of a period of unhappiness and in the hope for some en-route insight, that is, a walk as a contemplative practice itself.

Buddhist pilgrimage practice was endorsed by Shakyamuni himself as well. Although he discouraged any cult of personality around himself, encouraging his disciples to pursue their own route to Awakening, legend has it that he endorsed a post-Nirvana quasi-pilgrimage system. He instructed his disciples to take his funerary ashes and divide them into 84,000 (a familiar magic number in Buddhist teaching). Each of these was to be covered with earth and marked by a *stupa*, the burial mounds we saw in the previous chapter. Later on, as we noted above, other relics, such as a tooth from the Buddha, the bones of other teachers, whole sutras and more became the cause for reliquary buildings, and the sites for religious pilgrimage in Buddhist countries all over the world.

There are numerous famous subsequent Buddhist pilgrims, including Milarepa, Bodhidharma and Kobo Daishi, for example. It's not much of a stretch to name hundred mores, including Saicho, the founder of Tendai, who travelled to Mt. Tian Tai in China, or Pure Land luminaries Honen and Shinran who passed years in exile, and the travels of Huineng, the sixth Zen patriarch. These may not have been highly structured pilgrimages, as we might describe them. Instead, they reflect more of the strong presence of lengthy walking practices in ancient Buddhadharma.

Becoming a Pilgrim

Not only is the pilgrimage walk a geographical separation from ordinary life, but it represents a separation from the ordinary self and, as we have suggested, a separation from ordinary time. The separation from ordinary self is often demonstrated by a pilgrim costume. If one were to follow the Shikoku, or any Japanese pilgrimage or *henro*, one would immediately stand out by one's costume. Typically, as described in the practice of alms-gathering, itself a proto-type for all Japanese pilgrimage, the pilgrim wears an all-white outfit, unique from head to foot, from the straw sandals to the wicker hat.

For our purposes, should we choose some version of a pilgrimage for our practice, we can reserve specific clothes for that end. If we are members of a Buddhist community, one's practice outfit, be it jacket or robe, might be suitable. If nothing else, one ought begin with freshly cleaned, simple and serviceable clothing, free of advertising or other distractions. White is often the preferred choice, with its suggestion of purity of person, purity of purpose. Needless to say, if the clothing is fresh and clean, we, the pilgrims, ought ensure we begin the walk in a similar state.

Very few things identify the pilgrim more than the staff or *shakujo* described above. This is not unique to Buddhist pilgrimage, and can be seen in countless representations of pilgrims in all traditions. Even in her delightful non-Buddhist walker's diary of the Shikoku, *Neon Pilgrim*, Australian Lisa Dempster tells us the staff was one of the few official pieces of *henro* paraphernalia she chose and, like her, we cannot be too surprised how it gets worn down by inches in the course of her arduous walk. Less obvious, but equally valuable and appropriate might be some religious object, such as a *mala* (prayer beads) to facilitate any chanting en route. Carrying a sacred text, such as a favourite sutra is both handy for recitation and meritorious. There may be emblems, jewelry or other objects whose meaning will impart themselves to the walk. Depending on the formality of the pilgrimage, some booklet may be necessary to collect official stamps at each of the requisite churches, shrines or temples. The full book is both proof of completion and a concrete symbol of the effort.

In addition to the costume and the paraphernalia of the pilgrim, it is common to prepare to either bring something or carry something away or both. Pilgrims might bring a paper version of their vow, they might carry the inscribed prayers or wishes of others unable to make the walk. Some might carry ashes or other relics to deposit in a sacred place. On the Shikoku all *henro* are supposed to carry *osama-fuda*. These are personal name slips which are offered at each temple. They have the added value of being cherished mementoes handed out to those who provide gifts or supplies (*settai*) along the route. Apparently the more times the person has completed the pilgrimage, the more elaborate and valuable their *osama-fuda* become.

Many established pilgrimage sites offer souvenirs, such as figurines or replicas. Less formally, one might collect an object. One of my precious collectibles from a pilgimage-like walk, was a leaf on the ground beneath a tree. This tree, planted at the holy city of Anuradhapura in Sri Lanka is identified as coming from a branch from the original Bodhi tree in Bodh Gaya where Shakyamuni sat. To have made a (perhaps spurious) connection to the central religious experience of the root teacher of all Buddhist teachers, the founder of all lineages and the one who first turned the Wheel of the Dharma, seems miraculous in its own way to me.

As we separate ourselves in geography and appearance, we can consider pilgrimage as a special kind of time as well. Some have described it as a compression of history and historical space and what we might call spirit time/space. Pilgrimage has a whole symbolic level which installs us into the epic dramas of our faiths. There is a saying in the Shikoku pilgrimage, that everyone who walks it also walks along with Kobo Daishi; some, even non-Buddhists like Dempster, report having encountered him. From the perspective of symbolic time, this makes perfect sense. We pilgrims become actors in the sacred drama that unfolds along the pilgrimage route. We walk with Jesus, Paul, Buddha, Kobo Daishi, Moses and all the legends of our traditions.

At times, pilgrimage becomes a metaphor for the whole process and progress of religious practice. On the challenging pilgrimage on the island of Shikoku there are 88 temples. The pilgrim walks through four provinces or prefectures, Tokushima, Ko-chi, Ehime, and Kagawa. The progress is compared to the path to full Awakening. Thus, temples 1-23 represent the idea of awakening, 24-39 austerity and discipline, 40-65 attaining enlightenment, and 66-88 entering nirvana.

Walking and Bowing

Even today in North America, greeting bows are part of a monk's daily routine. The practice of prostrations, a structured sequence of elaborated bowing, is a well-established one in Dharma history, although one which needs coaxing for Westerners. Not only is there little tradition of bowing or prostration in the West, there is overt resistance and hostility to the idea of even bowing to anyone or thing, let alone a full-out prostration. There are various styles from the more elegantly restrained Chinese-Japanese style to the all-out stretching prostration of Tibet. We won't take too much time to discriminate these differences here. We will describe the different styles and consider how to blend that in with a walking practice, be that indoor or outdoor.

The simplest bow is the standing bow. One draws the hands together in front of the heart, palm-to-palm, and bows from the waist. I have been advised that one bows different depths in relation to the status of what or who you bow to. So a fellow practitioner receives a slight bow, a teacher a deeper bow and a *Buddha-rupa* (statue of the Buddha) merits the deepest.

There are three styles of full-prostration bows. These begin with a standing position and take the practitioner to a flat-out horizontal position, belly on the floor or ground. I won't try to detail the full movement in text, only to explain that the three, a Japanese, a Chinese and a Tibetan, have slight variations in performance.

No doubt there are more variations and illustrative videos available online.

Integrating walking and bowing can be done in several ways. In the 2007 film, *Wheel of Time*, we see one version. A remote Tibetan monk takes two years to travel from his temple to the site of the Dalai Lama's construction of a sand *mandala*. The reason it takes him two years is he stops every third step, regardless of what is below him, and does a full prostration. He carries two wooden blocks to bear the wear and tear on his hands. At the conclusion he has a coin-sized callous on his forehead from touching it so often.

Circumabulation may involve bowing-walking as well. A few years ago I participated in a bowing-chanting-walking practice during our annual training period. The practice, called *sansen butsudo*, involved a recitation of the 1000 names of Buddhas of the past, present and future. Each of us would take a position, in a circle, in the temple interior. We would recite a set of names and complete a full prostration (or as full as one's age and physical limitations permitted) for each. We would then move to the next station, rest briefly and continue. It took three hours for each of three days to complete the 3000 prostrations of this practice. Pilgrimage typically invites bowing, in some form, at shrines and temples en route. It is common practice in the Tendai locations I frequent these days that during regular *kinhin*, combined with *nembutsu* or not, one always stops to face the altar at either end of the temple to perform a standing bow.

Whether one performs a series of full prostrations or a simple standing bow, walking and bowing deepens any walking activity with the qualities of determination and humility. We are reminded, in each bow, of the thousands of preceding practitioners whose selfless efforts keep the flame of the Lamp of Dharma burning brightly, through centuries of hardship, persecution and neglect. Those of us who practice in the West, where Dharma texts, Dharma teaching and peace are the norm and in plentiful supply, are well-advised to consider walking and bowing practice to remind us of the lives generously offered so we may practice our chosen paths in relative ease and freedom.

A Pilgrim's Story: Jonny

Jonny is a 30-ish Buddhist man from Ontario. He was immersed in a successful career, marriage and all the enjoyment of his life, including frequent participation in Buddhist study and training. Over a period of time he watched parts of it unravel, culminating in a painful divorce and the recognition that his good life was damaging his physical, mental and spiritual health. To his credit, he recognized the momentum and determined he needed to take decisive action. In his case, he decided to make a pilgrimage, which he defined as travels to important Buddhist sites in Tibet.

His story is good advice for those wishing to follow their own pilgrimage. It begins with him announcing his intentions to those around him, his friends family and co-workers. He made it clear this was something he 'needed to do'. He closed up his work life, handed his key over to his room-mate and packed the simplest of baggage, which included his copy of the *Heart Sutra* which he had decided would accompany him on his journey.

Of note for us modern pilgrims, was his clear decision to disconnect from his electronica. He stopped checking e-mail and gave up all his devices, except a simple cell-phone. He contacted an old friend and cousin whom Jonny knew as a specialist in healthy living – in fact, a man who, with his wife, made their living training others and performing themselves as world-class elite athletes. Once he made the necessary travel and logistical arrangements, Jonny began to prepare with long walks and a simple and healthy diet. Even before he boarded the flight to Tibet, he had lost nearly forty pounds and was walking 15-25 km a day. To help him focus, he made contact with a small Buddhist group where his cousin lived. He attended weekly practice sessions, honing his practice for his journey. As you will perhaps note, Jonny was doing what we pointed to in our earlier chapters, namely beginning his walking practice even before he crossed the threshold to the trail. There is a blurring between the trail itself and both the start and finish. This is an odd state where we are not quite in either world and also actively in both. We will explore this 'in-between space' later.

Here, in his own words, are Jonny's reflections as he prepares to leave Canada.

> **Why walk?** I decided to do this walk about a year ago. At the time, the thing I purposely chose to study was emptiness and ridding myself of the ego. Over the past year I went through some difficult times, and I chose to relieve myself of a lot of material attachments. At the same time, I started to appreciate the day-to-day things I was doing; not looking too much in the past. One of the things which came to mind was that, ever since I was a kid I always loved climbing and adventure; booking any vacations I always paid attention to the culture and history. So, when I

booked this trip, I chose to be engulfed in a culture, to learn more about Tibet and Nepal and Buddhism... Part of the adventure is the actual walking, physical aspect of climbing but also the mindfulness in the quiet walk, to be involved in that walk.

Planning and Preparation. To get into the specific monasteries I wanted to – you can't just walk in – I had to set things up ahead. I had to contact my tour operator to put aside a week here and there. In India and Kathmandu are a number Tibetan *stupas* I want to see. For the most part I'm going to have to figure it out when I'm there.

I've been working on the Heart Sutra, I've been practicing as much as I can; plus some text books and my incense box. The incense is, more than anything, a sense of home.

I don't know the situation I'm going to be in yet, so I don't know how I will apply certain things.

I walk quite a bit now and I go without music, focusing on walking and breath. I know I can apply counting and breath.

I don't know how physically deprived I will be due to the altitude. The guides said we'll be doing about six hours a day, although they said, at that altitude, six hours feels like ten, from the lack of oxygen in the muscles. I'm not doing anything crazy, that's why I booked base-camp one and base camp two which goes to an elevation of 6000 feet.

What's It About? I think its not the end of something, but a beginning. I am starting a new place, in my timeline, I feel I am starting over, the trip will help me provide focus, finish that point in my life and jump-start the next. Hopefully, I can apply what I learned, 'catch the fever'. Right now I'm trying to focus on living day by day, not to get too excited about the future, to miss out on the things I could be happy with right now. The more and more I read, I'm learning the focus shouldn't be on the future.

Jonny boarded his flight to Tibet about a week later.

WALKING PRACTICE # 7
KAIHOGYO

For any walker in search of the ultimate example, the *non pareil* of walking practice, there is the *kaihogyo*. It is not without reason that John Stevens called his definitive study of this practice *The Marathon Monks of Mount Hiei*. In a time of super-marathons, ultra-marathons and the like, no modern running format even comes close to the *kaihogyo*. Dressed in full *henro* costume, these athletes run over unpredictable and ungroomed pathways, up and down steep mountainsides, vulnerable to vagaries of weather, wild animals and limited in their food intake. Since its creation, at the mountain temple complex of Hieizan, only forty-six men have completed the *kaihogyo*. Theirs is not a race-day, their practice requires the daily repetition of a minimum thirty to forty kilometre route for as many as one hundred days in a row. Even fewer have completed the full seven-year practice, which culminates with 84 km per day for 100 days, followed by 30 km per day for 100 days.

I spoke with a Tendai priest who, though a Westerner, trained in Japan and completed a mini-version of the *kaihogyo* as part of his training. Although young and fit at the time, he found it exhausting and hugely challenging. He remarked that he often hears people either marvel at the practice or dismiss it as some kind of lunatic extreme. He tries to set it in some context, by reminding us that we often hear similar reactions when we reveal some aspect of our practice which seems outside the realm of many of our peers' experiences. Be it a day-long silent retreat, an evening of chanting or a six-day *sesshin*, there are those who similarly marvel or dismiss.

Further, my priest-friend notes, when the *kaihogyo* was developed, centuries ago, it was not that unusual for people to take long walks as part of their lives. He points to a non-Buddhist old-timer in his New England region who describes walking dozens of miles daily just to get to his demanding physical labour employment. As my friend notes: "That's just how people lived."

Our journey on these pages remains the accessible and not the extremes, such as the *kaihogyo*. Like the Shikoku or El Camino, it stands as an inspiration for anyone looking to walking practices as a contemplative discipline. That does not mean we should feel inadequate because our walking practice is 'just five kilometres' or whatever distance we can manage. The spirit of the Japanese *kaihogyo* is captured in what is practiced in North American Tendai. They describe it as:

> The (North American) *kaihogyo* is a full-day event, walking meditation through the country-side, for a distance of about 17 miles. *Kaihogyo* practice too, is based upon Chih-i's method of *samadhi* while constantly walking and follows the similar practice held on Mt. Hiei. Meditation in motion out-of-doors offers fertile ground for myriad contemplations and includes esoteric practice, devotion and veneration of nature. It is also a pilgrimage and practitioners discover sacred spots and often stop for the recitation of mantra and the visualization of deities.
> From the Tendai Buddhist Institute website

This practice is nested, as it is in Japan, within a larger multi-form training period called a *gyo*. It is one day of a ten-day intensive training-retreat. I participated in this *kaihogyo* as part of my clerical training.

The walk starts mid-morning, following our usual services in the temple. We form a line in front of the temple and set off down the Upstate New York paved roadway on which the temple complex sits. After about twenty minutes we turn onto a quieter dirt road and progress along some unpaved back-roads which wind through the low hills known as the Berkshires. The line continues at an even and somewhat brisk pace, as set by the senior who leads. After some distance, the lead can be passed along to the next in line, and they are expected to maintain a similarly even and brisk pace themselves. As soon as one receives the *shakujo* staff, and begins to feel and hear its clanking rhythm, one understands something of the centuries of pilgrim walks.

The walk is broken by stops for chants before noteworthy sites, a ancient gnarled tree, a roadside stream, a cemetery and even, on occasion, by the body of some dead animal. This is an especially poignant moment where the words of the recitation hold particular significance:

> Your presence, small friend, is a bell of mindfulness
> Returning me to my breath,
> Reminding me to be careful in my travels and
> Brings us back to the Great Matter of Birth and Death
> Within in which we walk.

Our local version of the Japanese *kaihogyo*, unlike its model, is more humbling than life-challenging. We don't wear straw sandals, we don't repeat it for weeks at a time, we don't forego food. Yet for each of us we recognize it is a substantial physical practice which will call us out of our ordinary lives. We will each have the responsibility to lead and inspire each other. We will briefly dwell in that pilgrim space and walk the path with countless ancestors and others.

This *kaihogyo* is held within the context of a larger and more specialized training, the *gyo*. Outside of that, Tendai does not use the term for lay or mixed walking events, preferring to describe other such long walks as *kokorodo* (the path of the heart). Christopher Titmuss describes this practice as *Dharma yatra*, after his early Thai experience. He leads such events in Southern France and regularly includes two hundred or more walkers on a multi-day journey. I have described elsewhere here our own *kokorodo*, also known as 'walking the way practice', a group walk about 20 minutes down to our neighbouring lake. We and other partner groups, as well as those outside of the Tendai Sangha, commonly use half-to-full day hikes in this way. I am reminded of one Sangha brother, a 65 year old Tendai priest from Vermont, who undertook a 1000 mile *kokorodo* walk over a one hundred day period. One can only admire his determination and persistence, as one can envy his joy at walking the Appalachian woods of his locale. In true *kaihogyo/kokorodo* spirit he captures the 'path with a heart' in his final day blog note:

> Today is the final day of my walking practice. I passed the 1000 mile mark last week and today's walk will be the last.
> ....
> Recently while walking, the faces of my Dharma sisters and brothers have appeared to my mind's eye. I realized the practice was not mine but everyone's. I walked with those who cannot walk. I stood in places of profound beauty with everyone who could not be there with me. And so I thank you for your participation in these special days.
>
> Daichi Curry, from the *Mountain Practice* blog,
> (www.mountainpractice.wordpress.com)

CHAPTER NINE
JOURNEY 4: NEW WALKING

THE END IN SIGHT

Be it rounding a bend in the road, descending a mountain or coming up a set of beach steps to the parking lot, the end of the trail rises up before us like a welcome friend, but also like a sad parting at an airport. Just like a novel, the end is sometimes visible from a distance, and we close in on it, watching it approach, fully able to prepare for and process the conclusion of our journey. Other times, it is suddenly and all-too-often anti-climactically 'there'. "Is that it?" we ask.

Stages of Closing

We also earlier noted, a large part of the value of your journey arises in that return trip. In some walking practices, even where the walk is circular, like the Shikoku or El Camino di Santiago, there is a distinct goal – a shrine, a mountain view, a temple and so on. One's passport has been filled with mementos, the souvenirs are packed, and we have done that walk. Now, the separation between on the walk and off-the-walk grows more clear. The closing of any walk can bring with it different stages:

- a stage of **consolidation**: A contemplative walk is very often initiated out of some sense of discontinuity in one's life, some disturbance to the smooth fabric of our every day. We may initiate our walk to restore wholeness, and the conclusion may bring with it a consolidation.
- a stage of **resolution**: When we use a walk as the framework for addressing some conflict in our lives, the progress to the conclusion may bring with it some resolution. In another sense, resolution may take on the added meaning of making a resolution. It may be sufficiently clear and compelling that we may pause as to silently or aloud speak some new vow or promise for future action.

- a stage of **reconciliation**: Undertaking a contemplative walk is no guarantee that we will restore any discontinuities, nor that we will resolve every conflict. It may very well be, that despite the rigors and sincerity of the practice, we continue to be burdened in some way with our grief, pain or uncertainty. The final stages of our walk may only serve to bring conclusion to that effort, to acknowledge what we have accomplished and to orient ourselves to the future tasks at hand.
- a stage of **recognizing** ourselves anew: It may be that our walk follows the conclusion of some transition or life-stage, and so its completion may mark our cleansing of or purification following those experiences.
- a stage of **re-evaluation**: As with any substantial enterprise, the conclusion of a walking practice, especially a longer one, will bring with it some reconsideration of purpose and intention. The questions which have followed us in our steps will lead us to recognize our lives from a new perspective. This new perspective can often suggest new future directions inspired by an interpretation of past experience.
- a stage of **preparation**: Because contemplative walking practices rarely impose life-threatening circumstances, we will find the closing steps of the walk, and whatever clarity may be arising, will suggest preparations for life after the walk.
- a stage of **appreciation** and **gratitude**: No matter whatever walking practice we may undertake, be it long or short, it will have required personal commitment and effort. Our walk will have presented us with the context of our lives, the effort of innumerable beings who work to support our purposes, the energies and kindness of the Other, no matter how we define that. Therefore, it seems unimaginable that we would reach the conclusion of our walk without some deep sense of appreciation and gratitude. For many, some formal act of gratitude becomes the very final act in any walking practice.

Special Forms of Walking

In this chapter we will examine several less-Buddhist types of walks, practices which have peripheral connections to Buddhist practice compared to mainstream practices like *kinhin* or alms rounds. We start with a collection of symbolic walks, which generally don't involve actual physical walking (but may), relying on the metaphor of a walking. These can stand alone as valued practices and can act as supplements to actual walking. Next we step into the labyrinth, those circling, twisting patterns often associated with Celtic culture but, as we'll see, is also part of East Indian heritage. It has not yet been strongly associated with Buddhist practice; we'll see how it can be a potent a walking practice in itself and one which can be adapted for Buddhist purpose. The American naturalist-philosopher Henry Thoreau has been adopted by the Buddhist mindfulness movement as a kind of mentor-model. His walks in and about the forests of New England and his praise of quiet contemplation has served as a New World template for meditation. In his essay, *Walking*, and other writings, he extols what he dubs 'sauntering', day-long unstructured walking in the natural environment. We'll saunter along with him and consider this practice as we go. Finally, we'll join the march and look into walking for change. This relatively modern phenomenon has brought together the spiritually-minded with those eager for social change. We'll leave aside the placards and speeches to walk somewhat silently through this practice.

Walking In-Between Spaces

We have been accompanied and guided on our journey to this point by the Tweed-inspired metaphor, that of walking practice as the crossing part of religious pursuits as 'crossing and dwelling'. We have used the structure of a journey, with its thresholds, pivot points, setting off and returning. Not all practices fit so smoothly into that image and another image may complement that of crossing. For that we turn to the novel, *The City and The City*, by British speculative fiction author, China Miéville. This 2010 novel continues Miéville's fascinating tales in places that are both familiar and bizarre – the soaring towers of *Perdido Street Station* and the rat-infested sewers and rooftops of London in *King Rat*.

The City and The City introduces the two cities of Beszel and Ul Qoma, located somewhere in Eastern Europe in modern times. We learn that the two cities, each with its own ethnic and cultural characteristics existed for millennia, at first as neighbours. Over time they grew together, but not quite together. To avoid self-destructive wars, they evolved a unique and mind-boggling strategy. From birth, citizens of each city were trained to 'un-see' the other city and its citizens. As adults, the entire populations would carry on their normal lives in what we would describe as full view and interaction with each other. On the other hand, they would simply 'unsee' each other. Eyes would avert, reactions would be muted, conversation denied. It was full separation at a psychological rather than geographical level.

The main character lives in an apartment which exists in the one city, Beszel, but is neighbouring another apartment in Ul Qoma. He can never acknowledge the other building or its inhabitants. He cannot stare at them as they stand in their windows, or they him. To do so would be the criminal act known as 'breach'. Punishment for breach is swift, harsh and without appeal. If he needs to visit the other city for his work, he must pass through a central bureau, be processed through immigration and walk back out the same door into the other city. Once there, he would have to 'unsee' his own familiar city. He would 'unsee' and be 'unseen', even by his own wife.

Within the cities are zones called 'crosshatch', which, for an assortment of reasons must exist in an overlapping form, they are in both cities at the same time. Citizens of both can enter and transit easily. The same unseeing rule applies, and so cars may stop next to each other and the occupants still must 'unsee' each other's vehicle. Again, to violate the separation, even in a crosshatch would be breach.

We won't pursue the plot and its many twists here, although I heartily recommend this as another great journey read. Three main images from the novel form the basis for Miéville's image/idea of in-between space – the idea of 'unseeing' the other, the concept of 'breach', and thirdly, the concept of 'crosshatch'.

This imagery can assist us in understanding walking practice because there are certain aspects of some practices that put us into a shared geographical space while separating us psychologically and spiritually. For example, if we were to undertake a contemplative walk along a public walking path, we might prepare ourselves, as outlined above, with certain preparations, certain symbolic clothing and paraphernalia. As we walk we might be reciting a chant or sutra. Though we are at one level fully exposed to other walkers, we have chosen to 'unsee' them and reside in an in-between space. Not quite in our normal lives, not quite absent from it. We can move back and forth between the two spaces, perhaps a little more easily than the fictional citizens who must immigrate. Nonetheless, we will psychologically mark a leaving and entry, a transition from one space to another.

In a similar sense to Beszel and Ul Qoma, we can reside in the city of our normal life or the city of our religious life. Each life has its own consciousness, concerns and activities. Each has its citizens, streets and avenues. When we walk, I wonder if we are not in those crosshatch zones that lie between the extremes of ordinary life and spiritual. We can be aware of the two spaces but are constrained to choose one over the other. We can be in both simultaneously, but we cannot function in both simultaneously. This would collapse the psychic separation we know between ordinary life and spiritually-infused life.

Returning to the concept of 'breach', we come to understand that breach is an action, the acknowledgment of the other, and is, at the same time, the armed force that patrols the two cities, neither in one city or the other, nor distinct from them. Everyone knows of breach and can recognize the act and the force. We must 'unsee' them as well; to see breach itself constitutes breach. Later in the novel we understand the origins and processes of breach and why someone who breaches can never return to their city.

I see a parallel here to religious or spiritual life. We seek some end, Heaven, the Pure Land or whatever we call it, and we understand that it is the other to our ordinary life. We know it exists and we seek it earnestly. Through our practices, in this case, contemplative walking, we can enter crosshatch zones which allow us to exist in that in-between space for a while, in both spaces and in neither. Were we to shatter the convention and acknowledge that ordinary life and spiritual life are interconnected, we would surely be in breach. The image of the Tenth Ox-Herding Picture that Zen practitioners know and which we will consider next chapter, recognizes that full Awakening unites the spiritual and the ordinary. This is the Zen expression of 'everyday life is the realm of 10,000 Buddhas'. If we breach, there is no going back. We are in breach, the action, and *de facto*, we are *in* breach, the guardian force.

This metaphor contributes to our understanding of some walking practices. When we engage in these walking practices, we do not follow the full journey process, but rather we step into a crosshatch zone, an in-between space. We are in that space where both worlds become visible and we must find some way to negotiate that separation, we can follow the rules and do our best to 'unsee' what we are exposed to at a spiritual level and thereby be free to return to our normal ordinary lives. All the while knowing we have, in fact, seen something. Here are some examples of walking which are more like the in-between spaces of Miéville's crosshatch than journey.

WALKING PRACTICE # 8
WALKING A SYMBOLIC LANDSCAPE

While our primary purpose in this book is to understand and learn walking practices as body-mind practices – that is, ones which engage both our contemplative minds and our full experience of our physical presence – we do have several practices which take walking to a symbolic level. They are primarily but not exclusively symbolic in form; however, we will consider here how they might extend into actual physical walking.

Going to the Pure Land

The Pure Land, The Western Land or *Sukhavati* is described as a realm inhabited by all manner of wondrous life, including countless Buddhas. Entry comes with the pilgrim's surrender to the saving grace of Amitabha, the Buddha of Infinite Light and Life, and full awakening comes through direct instruction and intervention from Him, His Other-power (*tariki*). The simplest and most practiced way to enter this land is through frequent, and even unending, recitation of the phrase, *om namo amida butsu*. The exact meaning of this phrase has produced a number of books and commentaries, so I will direct readers elsewhere for further explanation. Suffice to say, it is a recitative formula which defines the relationship between suffering beings and Amitabha. We touched on this earlier. The faithful practitioner is assured of rebirth in that land.

The associated practice, and more pertinent for our purposes, is meditative contemplation and visualization of Amitabha Buddha, his attendant Bodhisattvas (usually Avalokitesvara and Vajrapani) and the Pure Land. This is taught in the *Amitayurdhyana Sutra* (Amitabha Meditation Sutra), in which the Buddha describes to Queen Vaidehi the practices of thirteen progressive visualization methods, corresponding to the attainment of various levels of rebirth in the Pure Land. The first of these steps is contemplation of the West-setting sun, until the visualization is clear whether the eyes are open or closed. Each progressive step adds complexity to the visualization of Sukhavati, with the final contemplation being an fully formed vision, which includes Amitabha and his attendant Bodhisattvas. In this advanced practice one effectively dwells in the Pure Land.

To assist with this practice, there is a tradition of Pure Land mandalas. Mandalas, which we'll examine more below, are symbolic diagrams or maps whose geometry facilitates meditative exercises. These painted, woven or sculpted objects provided a picture, both literal and symbolic, for the Pure Land, and began appearing around the time that Pure Land teaching emerged in Japanese Buddhism, around 800-900 CE. They supplemented the substantial body of visual teaching devices used by practitioners.

According to Paul Groner in his *Ryogen and Mount Hiei*, the practice of visualization of the Pure Land ought not be confused with the 'constant walking meditation' taught by Tendai master Chi-i. That practice which similarly involved chanting and circumambulation while visualizing Amitabha did not attempt to generate some presence in the Pure Land. It represents more of a synthesis of walking and visualization, but plays down the transformative consequences. Groner believes this walking practice was primarily to build attentive resilience in the practitioner, rather than transform one's life.

In any case, this practice, in either form or with either intent, could be of benefit to the contemplative walker. We all find our places within the broad family of contemplation. The Pure Land may be seen symbolically or literally, as one's faith determines. That Land may be seen as the final stage before full Buddhahood (as Jodo Buddhism teaches) or as a lower level state (as Chih-i suggests). We may view it as a rich symbol for trans-human existence. In any case, combining our walking practice with some form of Pure Land visualization offers many benefits.

Walking the "Stations"

This book approaches walking from a largely Buddhist perspective, but in its most all-encompassing intention, we can also include the religious and practical possibility of the Christian practice called Stations of the Cross. Itself a symbolic pilgrimage walk with 14 stations or points of reflection, it uses the final steps of Jesus as he approaches his crucifixion site and eventual death to symbolize the process of human salvation in the death of the Son of God. The stations proceed from Jesus' trial and condemnation by Pontius Pilate, along the route to Calvary, with his final moments with his mother and friends, his humiliation, his execution and death, and concludes with his entombment.

Any visitor to a Catholic Church will recognize these images which line the walls and provide both reminders of the story of Jesus and a physical meditation for the faithful as the circumambulate the space. There are prescribed recitations and reflections that guide the practitioner through the walk. One may of course complete these as a walk or symbolically as a seated meditation.

The most common version takes place within the aisles of a church. One enters the church by the front entrance and the Stations begin at the front on the left side of the sanctuary and run along the wall towards the back. There, they skip across the central aisle and resume along the right wall back up to the sanctuary.

We might modify this for our contemplative walking purposes in one or both of two ways. First, staying with the Christian format, we can overlay the stations onto a physical route and complete the reflective and recitative recommendations in the course of a longer outdoor walk. Linus Mundy, the 'prayer-walker', who we met in Chapter 7 suggests this. Many Christian festivals in many countries use the stations for an *ex cathedre* event. On the other hand, we can examine the history of the Buddhist story (or any religious history, for that matter) and designate our own 'stations'. These can then become the procession of an outdoor walk.

For Buddhists, there are similar milestones in the Buddha's career which we could use. His birth, his encounter with the four signs, his flight, his wandering, his awakening, his teaching and death. It would not be difficult to pull out sutra text and pertinent reflective activities to accompany this. Christians have evolved a beautiful iconography which represents the stations in plaques, carvings and paintings. An imaginative Buddhist, in this day of Google Images, could easily assemble a parallel visual aid for such a stations walk. One could, as with the Christian stations, perform this practice as an actual walk or as a symbolic meditation.

Mandala

In Buddhist (and Hindu) tradition, we have the contemplative tool of the *mandala*. A *mandala* (Sanskrit for 'circular diagram') is a device used to represent symbolic spaces, typically a map of some sacred geography or location. A *mandala* is usually distinguished from a *yantra* which is defined more as an 'instrument' for meditational practice, a symbol of divine power, more like an abstraction of power. There are hundreds of traditional *mandala*, and in modern times they have evolved into less specific patterns used for meditation, even migrating into other faith traditions. Perhaps the most famous and popular Buddhist example is the occasional construction of a sand *mandala* by Tibetan monks. The construction of such a many-coloured symbol and its final washing away represents the fabrication and transience of the material world.

Elizabeth ten Grotenhuis has interpreted *mandala* (Japanese, *mandara*) in her *Japanese Mandalas: Representations of Sacred Geography*. She explains that these patterns serve a dual purpose. On the one hand, they represent a cosmic landscape, wherein certain Buddhas and Bodhisattvas dwell in fixed relationships to each other and to the cosmos. On the other, the map itself becomes a tool for investigating the structure and nature of the universe and the practitioner's relation to it. *Mandala*, thus are both descriptive and instrumental. *Mandala* are in use in various forms all over the Mahayana world.

Our purpose is not to push too deeply into these figures. Let us use one important paired example to consider the use of *mandala* for walking practice. Within Japanese Buddhism, along with the Pure Land *mandalas* described above, the most common is the Two Worlds *Mandala* set used in Shingon and Tendai sects. The two worlds are the Womb World (*taizokai-mandara*) and the Diamond World (*kongokai-mandara*). A visitor to a Tendai temple will typically see these mounted on either side of the *butsudan* (altar) or hung facing each other. They are central to an assortment of ritual practices which employ these *mandala*, far to complex to explain here. Still, the use of these and other *mandalas* represents a symbolic journey through a cosmic realm, a kind of pilgrimage or circumambulation practice.

WALKING PRACTICE # 9
INTO THE LABYRINTH

Not much can be written about labyrinth walking that hasn't already been covered in the substantial labyrinth literature that followed on Lauren Artress' 1995 milestone books *Walking a Sacred Path: Rediscovering the Labyrinth* (1995) and *The Sacred Path Companion: A Guide to Walking the Labyrinth to Heal and Transform* (2006), and the writings of Jeff Saward in *Magical Paths: Labyrinths & Mazes in the 21st Century* (2003). Artress is widely acknowledged as the person who re-discovered and enthusiastically promoted this unique form of contemplative walking. Her description of the revealing of the gigantic Chartres labyrinth, hidden in plain sight for centuries, seems like a scene from some mystery thriller. Although not specifically connected to any Buddhist practice, it is, like prayer-walking, an immensely valuable practice, not inappropriate for Buddhists or any other faith tradition.

The labyrinths popularized by Artress and others have tended to look to

European pre-Roman civilizations. There are, however, numerous ancient examples in India, Pakistan, Sri Lanka and Nepal, as documented by Saward. He places them as early as the 3rd or 4th century BCE, contemporaneous with the North European examples, but does add the caution that much is yet to be learned about labyrinths in the Asian locations. How, when and why ancients used the labyrinth is less our concern. Our purpose is how we might incorporate this form into our contemplative lives.

First, we must state (perhaps overstate) the distinguishing characteristics of a labyrinth. Labyrinths are two-dimensional unicursal (ie. in a single curved line) patterns, laid out on the ground, typically large enough for one individual to follow a pre-described route from outside-start to inner-pivot and back again on the same route. It may be flat on the ground or three-dimensional, using bushes or stones. A labyrinth is not a maze or puzzle. It is not intended to baffle or confuse. On the contrary, its purpose is to structure the walk, and to do so in a particular way. Unlike circumambulation, where one proceeds around a sacred object or building, circling in prayer, chant or meditation, in identical and repeating circles, the labyrinth is a single journey. One begins at the entry point, follows the route to the centre, pauses for an indeterminate time, and returns. The length of the route, the pace and pause and the en-route activity can be many in form. Individual need, preference and ability make labyrinths infinite in application. Labyrinthologists identify four types of labyrinth, that is:

- **Archetypal** classical labyrinths (and its variants) consisting of a single pathway that loops back and forth to form seven circuits, bounded by eight walls, surrounding the central goal;
- **Roman** labyrinths, usually based on mathematical or geometrical properties, laid out in meander, serpentine, or spiral types;
- **Mediaeval** labyrinths, which are represented by the famous Chartres model, with 11 concentric circuits surrounding the central goal, a number of early examples can be found with anywhere between six and 15 circuits; and
- **Modern** labyrinths, which consciously re-imagine what constitutes a labyrinth, seeking new forms for new purposes.

In some ways, the labyrinth is a micro-example of the religious journey. The stages of walking a labyrinth mirror other walks, especially pilgrimage. It is dwelling and crossing in miniature. As we've adopted in this book, we have stages of preparation, initial threshold, entry, approach, turning point, return, final threshold and re-joining dwelling life. There are many outdoor labyrinths publicly available (several websites can help locate ones near you) as well as permanent indoor ones. These, like the Chartres have been used in the patterning of large public spaces. Materials range from natural ones of grass and gravel, or the one built by my friends, Pete and Lou Bennet, from hundreds of thyme plants (adding an olfactory dimension) to the 3D one created out of blue glass in Chianti Sculpture Park in Italy and many beautiful pavement and stone ones, such as that at the Walter Reed National Military Medical Center Bethesda, Maryland.

A more budget-conscious version came from my first experience with labyrinth construction in our first *zendo* in the group room of a community space we used in rural Ontario. The room was about twenty-five feet square and I decided to incorporate a labyrinth exercise into a day-long meditation retreat. That meant we could only use part of the room for the labyrinth. I decided on a Cretan (one of the Classical forms) pattern and located it in one corner of the space. It took about two hours and two rolls of masking tape, but we ended up with a small and rather rectilinear labyrinth that served us well. For the ambitious and creative builders, there are plans available and even pre-printed canvas ones.

What makes labyrinths so suitable for contemplative walkers is, in part, the structure as described above – a two-dimensional unicursal pattern that sets out a pre-described route from outside-start to inner-pivot and back again on the same route. The suitability lies in the unpredictability of this pattern. A labyrinth is never a simple spiral, but rather includes movement through the circles around the centre in a random manner. Thus, we cannot pre-visualize our way through a labyrinth. The route changes its distance from the centre and the clockwise/counter-clockwise direction of the walk. Because of this unpredictability it is necessary to focus on where one is at all times, ignoring one's moment-by-moment relationship to the central goal or to the extra-labyrinthine environment. Some have suggested that this unpredictability provides an alternating left/right brain stimulation, so that one is obligated to access these different mind activities through the walk.

It is sufficient to simply walk a labyrinth, to bring one's walking attention to that experience. Many times when I've entered into the labyrinth across from one of our local hospitals, only a few feet away from a busy street, I became aware of entering a special space. The traffic fades into the background, the space of the labyrinth rises up and encloses. I don't know any other walking practice that can do this. Beyond just walking it, Artress and her fellow lab-leaders have produced numerous exercises which can be done inside the labyrinth. Before we treat the labyrinth like a crystal ball or magic dice, Artress wisely warns us against imposing an agenda on the walk. Labyrinths liberate our intuitive capacities, free us to gain insight or make connections less available in the straight-line walking world. This does not mean we cannot enter the labyrinth with a task and expect it to reveal an answer, only that we must be willing to accept what emerges rather than what we expect. Sometimes, the experience is inconclusive, and we must be willing to maintain our practice and continue to be patient. Artress' labyrinth tasks include:

- self-healing, grieving, forgiveness and re-connecting with the body and pain;
- 'shadow work', exploring mental patterns, reflecting on inner stories and myths;
- connecting with life stages and decisions, what she calls 'soul-work';
- performing personal rituals; celebration and honouring passage.

From a more specifically Buddhist starting point, there is no reason why we cannot incorporate several of our familiar Dharma practices to the labyrinth. The simplest, as noted above, is bringing our 'attending to body and breath' practice into the labyrinth. The capacity of the labyrinth to enclose and seclude us, even in the midst of a busy urban landscape, makes it ideal for those who may have difficulty finding a quieter or more peaceful environment to practice. As we explained above, the changing flow of the labyrinth supports present-moment attention by keeping us 'on edge', as it were. Recitative practices, such as chanting and *nembutsu* are enriched in a labyrinth. There is a temptation with them and others, like *koan* practice, to drift into a rote-mind, where the chant, mantra or *wado* remains present but becomes flabby, as we drift into shopping lists or recollections. The turning and shifting of the labyrinth space helps to keep mind alert and sharp.

Of special note is the potential of the centre or pivot point of the labyrinth experience. Only a few labyrinths have a simple turning-around space at the centre. More commonly, particularly in modern versions, there is sufficient space, and often an actual bench, located there. The centre is where one brings the issue of a reflection, the decision point of a problem-solving or some personal or other ritual. This contrasts to most contemplative practices, where we engage in a process at the outset and continue it until the end of the elapsed time, or in walking practice, once we complete the walk. This is where the journey structure of a labyrinth is most evident. It builds on the enter-pivot-return cycle, and so our practice can echo that as well. This is especially appropriate for those kinds of practices Artress encourages, ones which have a beginning, climax and ending. Again we must remember that a labyrinth walk which is layered with some mental task offers no guarantee. More like other contemplations, it opens a space of reflection which may produce insight but may simply remind us that the time is not yet ripe for conclusion or decision. Alternately, for more specifically Buddhist practice, we can construct a multi-practice labyrinth session where the entry and exit are of the form of walking mindfulness and the time at the centre becomes recitative, resting on the bench or sitting on a cushion. The reverse would work as well.

The use of labyrinths in the context of Buddhist practice is entirely new. We noted above the use of *mandala* as meditative and contemplative devices, but these are different from labyrinths, primarily because of the quality of structured alternating direction. This does not mean we should erect walls between these practices, only that we should be careful to distinguish the differences. As I discovered with my masking tape indoor labyrinth, performing standard Dharma practices acquires new dimensions from the labyrinth framework. The study and application of labyrinths is still rather new. We have known about them for centuries, yet entering them as contemplative seekers is only a few decades old. We have an opportunity to experiment and discover what the benefits may be for our contemplative practices.

THE MANDA-LABYRINTH

One such possibility, which has yet to be developed, I have christened the 'manda-lab'. We who engage in contemplative walking find ourselves doing so along the crossroads of our ever shrinking world. Those of us who are Buddhists can learn of and draw on a history of *mandala* symbolism and ritual. Those of us familiar with labyrinth practice, within Christian tradition or not, have seen a blossoming of that practice over the past few decades. I imagine a crossroad of those two practices: the manda-lab. We can replace the traditional labyrinth shapes, as described above, with traditional *mandala* patterns, even, as I have discovered, over-lay them. These too have extraordinary symbolic and ritual detail, which can serve to educate us of a Buddhist understanding of the universe. More importantly we can literally walk these patterns as a physical version of the same meditative practices for which they have normally been used.

We might construct such a space where we might have used the Chartres labyrinth, for example. One use would be to simply complete the traditional *mandala* ritual standing in and moving through it. This would require some training in those rituals and I would leave it to my elder Sangha brothers to make that available as they saw fit. An alternate use, might be to describe a physical path through the *mandala* while completing one of the exercises recommended for the labyrinth. (See above.)

I have recently begun construction of a manda-lab, using the *vajra-dhatu* or Diamond World pattern. As I began to lay it out, I recognized opportunities for contemplation on different number sets, different directions and 'realms'. The version I began brought a surprising observation even in the ground-breaking stage. If I lay out the standard 3x3 pattern and add a decorative border, as is often done, it would be a simple matter to identify a certain passage pattern which would duplicate the typical Cretan labyrinth! Even as a bunch of stones laid out on the grass, I can recognize many possibilities for the manda-lab. I don't know that anyone else has experimented with such a practice. It would seem to have all the elements for a meaningful contemplative practice.

The manda-labyrinth

WALKING PRACTICE # 10
'SAUNTERING' WITH THOREAU

Even today Henry David Thoreau (1817-1862) stands out as an odd-ball, a wholly original character. One can only imagine what his neighbours thought of his wandering ways as he trod the paths, fields and forests of his beloved Concord, Mass. As a mix of naturalist and biologist, social critic and hermit, poet and essayist, industrial inventor and backwoods farmer, he was, and still is, a major voice in environmentalism and the contemplative life. Author of a dozen or more books, his titles ranged from *Walden, or Life in the Woods*, his journal of his two year solitary 'experiment' in the woods, to more scientific writing like *Faith in a Seed: The Dispersion of Seeds and Other Late Natural History Writings*. For our purposes, his most interesting title is a small book of essays called *Walking*, written in 1862, at the end of his life.

The modern father of Buddhist-influenced mindfulness practice, Jon Kabat-Zinn, used Thoreau as his reference point for the mindful life. In his own *Full Catastrophe Living* (1990) and in his recorded talks, Kabat-Zinn paints Thoreau as a template for the mindful life. In one of his videos, he himself strolls through the autumn woods around Walden Pond, quoting from Thoreau and encouraging us to slow down and witness our own lives.

I doubt Thoreau would ever have imagined himself in the ranks of Kabat-Zinn or Thich Nhat Hahn (or maybe he would, being the contrarian he was). Certainly, his *Walking* is in no way a guidebook or manual. In fact, most of the text is a rambling commentary on his distaste for 'civilized' life that was the growing urban-industrial Northeast of 19th century America. He stands in the forefront of those who idealized the 'Wild', an imagined Eden-like pristine state of Nature which was being corrupted by settlement and Yankee capitalism.

Walking for Thoreau is defined as 'sauntering', a kind of aimless extended contemplation, naturalist study and silent awe. He describes himself setting off with no purpose in mind. He simply walked out and followed wherever his fancy took him. In *Walking*, he confesses that he finds he usually heads off West. Its hard to know how much of that is chance, design or part of his symbolism for the Wild. I'm sure he didn't know that in Feng Shui, the Asian art of geo-location, West symbolizes creativity and the unspoiled innocence of children. Or that the Buddhist Pure Land is located in the West.

He proposes two explanations for his choice of the term 'saunter'. One he refers to 'sainte-terre', (perhaps sacred ground or holy earth) implying a sacralizing of the ground or traveller's path. He relates this rather romanticized interpretation to the early European pilgrims whose holy missions brought a divine purpose to travel. In some ways he compares his own meandering to the many religious purposes of pilgrimage we discussed above. His second proposed origin for the term relates it to 'sans-terre' (without home-land). Again, he relates this to the Middle Ages where travellers and pilgrims would suddenly appear on the horizon, apparently without any home or connection to that village or community. This reflects his own attitudes towards settlement. In his own writing he explains that he could easily have abandoned the cabin he built on Walden Pond; it held so little value for him, compared to his open wandering in the woods. Without doubt he was by far more 'at home' under the forest skies than under any roof.

One could, as most etymologists have, dismiss Thoreau's explanation for the origin of the term 'saunter' as fanciful. In general, dictionaries refer to its origin as 'obscure'. What is of interest, I think, is how Thoreau surrounds walking with contemplative imagery and quality. One might even add 'father of modern contemplative walking' to his many attributes. He very strongly promotes walking as a reflective practice, even though he avoids any of the instruction or religious connection we have made here. In fact, there is precious little in the way of practical instruction or advice, not that anyone who reads Thoreau should be surprised . He is far more likely to urge us to get on the trail than bother with the details that occupy most of these pages.

In sharp contrast to Thoreau's practice of sauntering, and on the other side of the Atlantic, there was an odd counter-point to Thoreau's abandonment of the civilized town in the Parisan fad called *flaner*. The contrast will help to sharpen our sense of Thoreau. Saunter is one transaltion for the verb, *flaner*. However, the *flaneur*, the person who walks this way, is a far cry from Thoreau, even his polar opposite. If Thoreau wandered the fields, sampling wild herbs and mushrooms, resting for hours at the edge of a pond, the *flaneur* was the urban connoisseur who strolled the boulevards, resting for hours to sample fine food and drink in the pastry shops and taverns. Unlike Thoreau, the *flaneur* belonged to the urban crowd. As Baudelaire described him in *The Painter of Modern Life*, he is "the lover of universal life" for whom the sophisticated urban were "an immense reservoir of electrical energy, a mirror as vast as the crowd itself." If Thoreau aspired to recognize himself in the web of natural life, another creature within the forest panorama, the *flaneur* distinguished himself from the city; he was its observer and taster, flitting along its ever-changing surface.

That said, what does it mean to saunter with Henry Thoreau? First of all, we should avoid much, if any, intention, map or plan. The saunterer does not set a goal or strive towards any end-point. Such a walk would direct us into the wild, natural landscape, as much as possible. Any form of urban parkland, streetscape, structured walking path or civilized beach would have horrified Thoreau, so we avoid them at all costs. From what we read, we must travel alone or, if necessary, with one sympathetic companion, someone who knows the value of silence and solitude. We travel light. Perhaps a shoulder bag or knapsack to carry some refreshments. Thoreau would have relied on streams and wild vegetation. A notebook and pen would be appropriate as well, something to hold plant samples or make notes on our observations, perhaps a poem or reflection. We should be prepared to spend a day, and possibly a warm night in the woods.

Thoreau's 19th century style of walking might not suit many 21st century spiritual walkers, if only for the lack of public or open space within which we might saunter. We may have inherited more of the *flaneur* than the saunterer. The kind of wild that surrounded Thoreau now lies in largely dedicated and protected environments. His much-detested civilization has been the undisputed victor over the Wild, and his spontaneous adventures have given way to organized and pre-planned day-trips. We might consider the recent book, *Between a Rock and a Hard Place,* and *127 Hours,* the subsequent Oscar-nominated film. These document the story of wilderness adventurer or 'canyoneer', Aron Ralston, whose solo and unstructured 'sauntering' in the Utah desert cost him his arm and nearly his life. There is a Thoreau-like quality to this tale and it underlines the unlikelihood of this style of walking for most contemplative walkers. The modern trails which might satisfy Thoreau would be some pilgrimage routes, especially those where a pilgrim eschew inns in favour of outdoor sleeping, in rough huts or even without tents.

Of greater importance may be how we might take inspiration from Thoreau's purpose, or more appropriately his purposelessness, more than his method or context. Here we can find much greater possibility. Above all, Thoreau in his saunters represents the difference between contemplative walking and all the various forms of recreational and sports/competitive walking/hiking. Contemplative walking is solitary, or at least semi-solitary in form. It does not lend itself to large groups or bus-trips (with all due respect and deference to organized pilgrimage tours). It is minimalist and open to surprise. While we may have to assume a route or trail, we should allow for whatever variation or side-trail may appear to us, within the allowances of private property and boundaries of protected areas. Above all, in the spirit of Thoreau, sauntering represents our relation to the natural world. Perhaps not the idealized Wild, but we can at least engage with field and stream, ocean and shore or mountain and sky. The mind-space of sauntering seems to promote the same openness and presence that we have described elsewhere in this book. It is little wonder that Jon Kabat-Zinn draws on Thoreau for inspiration in his mindfulness-based training. Sauntering is more than the wandering of the field naturalist, there is a deep contemplation at its heart. There is a striving to connect with Nature at some spiritual level. Regardless of how we feel about the philosophical worth of Thoreau's idea of 'the Wild' or his libertarian politics, sauntering suggests we lay ourselves open to connecting with and learning from the natural world which our civilization so often denies us.

WALKING PRACTICE # 11
WALKING FOR CHANGE

In April of 1952, a simple and deeply dedicated woman named Mildred Ryder set off on a walk along the Appalachian trail. The 2000 mile Appalachian Trail, which runs all along the eastern coast of North America, from the Deep South to Nova Scotia, is one of the greatest symbols of wilderness preservation and celebrations of walking. She had been contemplating her place in the world and exploring how to live a life of service for most of the first 40 years of her life. That year, Mildred became the first woman to complete the entire Appalachian Trail in one season.

In her recent life, she had given her time to charities and recently joined a hiking group. After several months on the Vermont portion of the Appalachian Trail, living very minimally on the trail, she sat overlooking the valleys of New England. It was here she gained a clear vision of her role in life. She understood she would become Peace Pilgrim, a wanderer who would stand for the way of peace. From 1953 she continued to fulfill what she called her 'mission', crisscrossing the US, side-tripping into Canada, Hawaii and Mexico with her constant message of peace. Her journey came to an end with her death in 1981, at age 73. Peace Pilgrim was not a tourist or an ultra-marathoner. Her walking was nothing but a spiritual practice. She was not walking to get somewhere, nor to log some time or distance goal. She walked for an idea and an ideal – peace. As for all of us who engage in contemplative walking, the path becomes the means to our aspiration. To that we now turn as we consider the final forms of contemplative walking, walking for change.

Expressive or Cause-motivated Walks

Two decades before Peace Pilgrim took to the Appalachian Trail in Vermont, on the other side of the world, a determined lawyer and social activist named Mohandas Gandhi was walking at the head of a different kind of walk. The British colonial government in India had imposed a tax on salt, the most common and ordinary seasoning for the Indian diet. As part of the early challenges to the legitimacy of British rule, Gandhi decided he would defy the salt tax by walking to the source of salt itself, the Indian Ocean, and make salt. The Salt March took place in April of 1930, when Gandhi and thousands of fellow Indians marched 388 kilometres (241 mi.) from Ahmedabad to Dandi in the state of Gujarat to make salt themselves. Once again, a determined person took a walk, not for a view or a stamp in a booklet or for a photograph, but for an idea and an ideal. In an historical echo, thousands of Indians set out in early October, 2012, for a 200 mile protest walk on Delhi to protest the tragic conditions of the modern-day poor. Their target, the government of the very Congress Party Gandhi-ji inspired.

Since then, cause-motivated walks, or more commonly 'a march for...' have become commonplace. How could Martin Luther King have accomplished what he did to end racial discrimination without marches? In 1963, he and his fellow organizers greeted some 2000 buses, 20 dedicated trains, 10 chartered planes, and countless cars in Washington. The March on Washington for Jobs and Freedom was organized by King as the leader of a coalition of the 'Big Six' civil rights, labor and religious organizations. An estimated quarter of a million participants walked from the Washington Monument to the Lincoln Memorial. His legendary motive for the walk is summed up in four simple words: "I have a dream."

I'm sure there have been cause-motivated marches for centuries before these celebrated events. Walking for a cause may have some connection to certain pilgrimage purposes we considered above. However, these examples stand as our models and inspiration for the modern form of the cause-motivated walk. As spiritual people we might connect these walks with those transformative walks which religious leaders like Shakyamuni and Jesus took and lead. We can imagine the scene of these beatific figures strolling and teaching in a North Indian bamboo grove or a Galillean hillside.

We can make a distinction here between two kinds of cause-motivated walks. The first we might call a generative walk. As with the Peace Pilgrim, her walks on the Appalachian Trail formed part of her spiritual awakening, they led her to her mission. Such a walk has the pursuit of insight, vision and clarity as its motivation. They are more likely to be private and solitary. I think these kinds of walks have more in common with pilgrimage than anything. The second, more common cause-motivated walk is the expressive walk, one which speaks from one's conviction and calls out for change and action. It is these which have challenged a salt tax, discriminatory race laws, walls between states and the location of nuclear facilities. The walk is integral with the outcry, the whole body-mind is engaged in expressing *satya-graha*, what Gandhi-ji called 'truth-force'.

As contemplative walkers we can make either or both of these cause-motivated walks our practice. In the first instance, I would guess there are many contemplative walkers who set off on trails because of a concern for the degradation and peril of our natural environment. We may not have a course of action to express, but we walk out of that concern. Solidarity with Nature might be a way of describing it. We walk both to gain strength from the trail and to demonstrate our belonging to the natural world. The word 'witness' comes to mind. As spiritual people, our walking is a silent statement of our concern and solidarity.

Expressive walks, walking or 'marching for...' make that concern even more explicit and focused. This is certainly not to say that every union march or political rally is a contemplative practice. Far from it. Cause-motivated walking belongs in the realm of contemplative practice when we make an inner-outer connection. Writers and commentators of the past few decades in the peace and environment movements have realized this and underlined the importance of tying together personal change and social change. The Buddhist teaching of *paticca-sammupada* or interconnectedness means that the desperate situation of seals and polar bears in the Arctic North has some connection to my life in the South. For us as contemplative walkers, it also means that we are misguided speaking out for peace or environmental respect if we are not simultaneously examining and working on our own inner conflict and self-disrespect. We have, it seems, infinite choice should we wish to set off on some cause-motivated walk. We must be careful that we are not caught up in thinking that the dis-ease of our world is 'out there' and marches and protest will fix that. There needs to be an integrity of our efforts, where our acknowledgment of our troubled and suffering world is but the flip-side of our own troubled and suffering spirit.

Fund-raising Walks or Walks of Alliance

A decade before Martin Luther King arrived in Washington, Puerto Rican, Ramón Rivero initiated what may be the first 'walkathon', that is, a walk designed to raise and direct donations to a social cause. Rivero walked 128 km from San Juan to Ponce, Puerto Rico and raised $85,000 for the Puerto Rican League Against Cancer. I would predict that you too have found yourself scratching around your school, home or office for pledges, and that you have set aside a Saturday or Sunday to join walkers of all ages and abilities to collect funds for one of thousands of charities across North America.

These walks differ from expressive or cause-motivated walks in that they are not acts of protest nor do they call for social change. They recognize real and most often personal awareness of suffering in the form of illness or disadvantage. They align with existing structures of service, usually registered charities with more or less highly visible community profiles. Such charities are already fully engaged in serving some kind of health or community need. Walkathons are *walks of alliance* where we temporarily join those charities in their purposes.

For Buddhists, these walks of alliance are acts of what we call *shila* or ethical behaviour. Buddhists of all stripes ground their lives in the Buddha's teaching called the Noble Eightfold Path. This lists eight steps which he assures will lead us to the end of suffering in our lives and the lives of all beings. These eight are often grouped together in three sets – wisdom, practice and ethical behaviour. The three steps of ethical behaviour include wholesome speech, wholesome action and wholesome livelihood; where 'wholesome' (*samma*) refers to activity which directs one towards the ending of suffering. In this case, participation can be viewed as performing 'wholesome action'. I would venture that those in any other faith tradition could easily see the connection between their moral imperatives and such charity-supporting action.

Therefore it seems an easy and logical conclusion to include charity walkathons as spiritual walking practice. We should, however, bear in mind that such activity is a distinctively modern activity, one that mirrors how our society defines and relates to 'wholesome action'. As we saw above, in our exploration of alms giving, ours is a society that has created an institutional buffer between individual citizens, between those with resources and those in need. Our cities banished begging; until recently we hid the disabled in special housing away from our able-bodied mainstream and for most of the past century we've isolated the sick and dying away from social supports. In some respects charity walkathons have tended to further distance us from the day-to-day lives of suffering. We can set aside a pleasant weekend afternoon to enjoy a leisurely walk, fully organized by others, with rest and refreshment sites and even entertainment along the route. The money raised comes from pledges gathered for the cause and processed as deductions or packets of cash and forwarded to the hosting charity. This is not to disparage the work of charities, nor to minimize the need, only to point to the insulation between those who suffer and ourselves. The Buddha taught that the central truth of our lives was the omnipresence and inescapability of *dukkha*, universal suffering. We need to recognize the ways that the structure of charitable activities, like e-mail solicitation, like media campaigns and even walkathons does erect some level of insulation and isolation between us and the suffering in our world.

Expanding on these observations, journalist Ted Gup wrote an op-ed piece in the New York Times in 2011 called *The Weirdness of Walking to Raise Money*. In summary, he wonders whether the huge energies of both organizers and walkers is worthwhile, why our society values this 'charitable ritual'. He mentally calculates how all the enormous fiscal, organizational and human resource might be applied in alternative ways for the benefit of those in need. He concludes with a statement of his respect for all involved, an acceptance that walkathons are embedded in how we lead our lives and with that question of why we do this still hanging in the air.

I'm brought back again to the scene along a dusty road in rural Sri Lanka in the 1980's when I witnessed my first *shramadana*. This 'sharing the gift of our labour' was and is the backbone of the Sarvodaya Movement started by Ari Ariyaratne in the 1960's (another mid-20th century person turning to walking for social change!). It is not primarily a walking activity, but involves substantial collective walking, because the poor who are the beneficiaries of the Sarvodaya efforts lack much in the way of personal motorized transport. Villagers gathered together along a road, or more precisely where a road would be and spent several days in collective labour to build that road. This is not strictly speaking a walking practice, but I mention it here to contrast two very different approaches to collective service for the poor. One, the walkathon, abstracts or often distances us from the beneficiaries, the other is an active engagement with them. In all fairness, we are seeing more integration in charity walks, with the public walking along with hospice workers or healthcare providers or people who experience conditions like MS, heart disease or cancer. Nonetheless, I am left with confusing, contradictory images of Sri Lankan villagers building their own road and urban North Americans walking for 'The Cure'.

Mindful Walks

In an earlier chapter we considered the educational and mindful 'mall walk' described in Elias Amidon's *Mall Mindfulness*. In his case, he organized a silent, *kinhin*-like experience so his students could relate in a new and more insightful way to the interior environment of a bustling shopping mall. From his reports, the experience was quite effective in shifting how the students understood that space. People use walks as a means for people to relate to their world. We have seen cemetery walks, haunted houses walks, great writers walks and walks through history. We could make some connection with these types of tours, interior or exterior, but not every walk fits our criteria. The crucial dimension which makes any walk a mindful walk is, of course, the mindfulness. That is, we must be attending both to the space of exploration around us and the events and reactions which are occurring within body-mind. The whole purpose of any mindfulness practice is to bring us into contact with the flow of *dukkha*, our sense of lack or existential dissatisfaction, and the presence of compassion.

Sometimes a mindful walk can also have a goal of social intervention. A variation of this was undertaken, as I am told, by a Dharma group in a city near me. The group, a lay and monastic mix, decided they would live on the street for a period of time. Their reasons included developing greater sensitivity to the suffering of homeless people. It fit very well with their own efforts to experience non-attachment. Further, it was a real demonstration of their compassion for those homeless people who 'hosted' them. Finally, it had the powerful effect of drawing media attention to the status of homeless people.

That kind of experiment and practice involves more than walking. Another, somewhat related and more walking-specific mindful walk was inspired by the change-and-info activist Ad-busters, the same intentions that inspired the Occupy movement. Their concern was with the presence of greed and material obsession/consumption in the context of poverty and wealth inequity. They drew a connection to the outrageous, and what some found offensive, promotion of Christmas shopping splurges at area shopping malls. Members of the group wanted to draw attention to this excess and to do so in the spirit of their practice, non-violence, non-confrontation, non-judgement. The group met at one mall, in a busy shopping time one day. They were not dressed in any provocative apparel, nor did they carry signs or any messages. They simply took up places on the mall and, like a flash-mob, began mindful walking within the ranks of shoppers. In a short time this drew the attention of shoppers. As one would expect it drew the attention of mall management and mall security. They were approached and told to stop their walk. They pointed out that they were not inciting anything nor interfering with anyone. They were told their walking was out of place. They pointed to disabled people, moms with toddlers and seniors who were maintaining a similar pace. They were threatened with charges and they accepted that police might be called. In the end, the mall security apparently realized their complaints were unsustainable and left the walkers alone. The walkers did not have any specific objective other than to introduce a different mind-space into what they felt was one of temporary insanity. How shoppers reacted or what they learned, we cannot say. I'll leave it to you to decide if this was a successful spiritual walk for change.

Random Walks

Lawrence Block (under his own name or one of his several pseudonyms) is best known for his series of mystery novels which have added Matt Scudder, Chip Harrison and others to the ranks of modern detective lore. In 1988 he took a genre sidestep with *Random Walk*, a simple almost fairy-tale novel. Some have seen it as tiresome New Age blather, others have cheered it on as a clever send-up, still others (myself included) see it as a speculative fantasy that takes spiritual power as a possibility. Block himself notes that despite this being a very minor piece in his very considerable print output, it seems to have generated more interest and comment than most of his others.

The story of *Random Walk* tells what happens when an occasionally employed bartender in present-day Oregon, a certain Guthrie Wagner, decides to heed an inexplicable voice that recommends he take a walk. He does so, with no apparent goal or destination. And walks and walks, and as he does so, like some kind of magic magnet he begins to attract fellow walkers, people who had no intention of joining him, but quit their jobs, step out of trucks, turn their lives around and fall in with him. This would be a silly story were it not for the parallel story of Mark, an otherwise caricature of American small business triumph, with a penchant for hunting and murdering young women. The two stories tumble towards each other like building storm fronts. The magical resolution, while it might not satisfy the stark realists in the audience, is both ambiguous and satisfying in ways Block's mysteries ought never be.

Apart from recommending one heckuva good read, we should consider the

whole idea of *Random Walk* within our spectrum of contemplative walks, especially in this category of walks for change. In the previous chapter we considered the reasons why people might decide to suspend their lives to undertake a pilgrimage. We mentioned three less religious reasons:
- a cleansing or to mark the conclusion of a period of unhappiness;
- to intensify contemplative practice and gain insight;
- a challenge or to break up some routine.

Many of the modern genre of modern pilgrimage journals, books like Lisa Dempster's *Neon Pilgrim* or Marie-Laure Valandro's *Camino Walk: Where Inner and Outer Paths Meet*, for example, document spiritually-flavoured walks which have very little formal religious dimension. They do, however, have everything to do with reconnecting with personal spirituality. Those three reasons for pilgrimage are the dominant ones in such writing and in such adventures.

Likewise, we may well want to undertake less structured walks than a pilgrimage, what we could qualify as a random walk for similar reasons. This seems to be what underlies a project called Footprint Drumbeats, a project associated with a group called *peacehq*. On their website, (http://peacehq.tripod.com/PHQ_Common/statistics.html) they recommend a kind of random walk variation they call 'Prayer Energized Mother Earth and Humanity Healing Footprint Drumbeats'. They propose that every footstep taken on the planet can be seen as a 'drumbeat cadence'. They call out to all people who walk, dance, run and otherwise caress Mother Earth with their feet to 'hit the highways'. The promoters don't care to justify this proposition. Rather like Guthrie in *Random Walk*, they too have no need to understand what is happening. They leave it as: 'either accept it and join in or leave me alone in my fantasy'.

We have to wonder whether Shakyamuni himself might not have initiated one of the first of such 'random walks'. He certainly walked without a map and without apparent purpose. It may be this is itself a compelling model for contemplative walking. Bhaktimarga Swami would surely agree. He is a Canadian Hare Krishna monk who began a 'random walk' of his own in 2007. Since then, as you can read on his blog (http://thewalkingmonk.blogspot.ca), he has been crisscrossing the continent as the full expression of his religious duty.

CHAPTER TEN
RETURNING HOME

THE NARROW BEACH

The narrow beach at Cayo Santa Clara is one long strip of oatmeal-coloured and textured sand that stretches about 18 kilometres along the Cuban coast. A stone and cement causeway which took ten years to complete joins the 'cayo' or keys to the mainland, near the Villa Clara provincial capitol, Santa Clara. Just after a muted sunrise, masked by off-shore storm clouds, along endless shifting greys, I set off down the beach.

On my one side, the rolling turquoise-blue ocean, punctuated by gentle white-caps as far as my eye can see. The only variation on that horizon is the fading to a gun-metal grey as it blends into the ocean-grey, dissolves into the roiling grey and white of the distant storm. On my other side, a low barrier of yellowy-green tropical shrubs with coconut palms spiking through, like tattered umbrellas after a hurricane. The barrier itself is edged with *bohios*, traditional Cuban palm leaf huts, and white plastic beach chairs. The day is too early and too grey for the throngs of sun-worshippers who will later flood the shore, mimicking the flooding and receding tides. Here and there are empty cocktail bars and ramps that lead back to the main resorts. In the distance are gigantic industrial cranes, marking the neighbouring sugar factory, an odd juxtaposition to these leisure properties. Closer to me is a white-domed cupola, apparently stranded in the dunes and serving no obvious purpose. To these Buddhist eyes, it becomes a *stupa*-mirage, shimmering in the sand. I think back to Anuradhapura and those Sri Lankan *stupas* scattered in similar dunes, part of the landscape of Buddha-rupas, silently telling and re-telling the Dharma story. There are no Buddha-ruins here, only fragments of shattered sea-junk, trash receptacles brimming with pop cans and beer bottles and announcements of the day's *animacion*, the half-hourly amusements of dance or chance.

This Cuban beach-walk is no pilgrimage and I am no *henro*-pilgrim. It would even be a stretch to take my morning promenade as a walking practice. Yet, as I walk this beach at dawn, I recall Unno's *River of Fire, River of Water*, where he explains the well-known Jodo-shu metaphor for the way of devotion. In the image, each of us is a pilgrim walking a narrow path between two eternal rivers. On one side flows the River of Fire, raging banks of flame, like the firewall of a forest fire, hundreds of feet high, unbreachable miles wide and deep. Unquenchable, it blazes as it has since before Time and will forever. On the pilgrim's other side a parallel wall, equally awesome, of endless ocean storms. Lightning and torrents of rain pound onto similarly endless waves and troughs. No ship, no sailor, no creature could find refuge, let alone survive such storms. Between these two, the image affirms a narrow strip of safety and hope. The pilgrim dare not approach either edge and certain destruction, but must balance carefully between. The pilgrim cannot know from whence the walls or path grew nor where they lead. It may be that, like this key-beach walk, it simply curves around to join itself again. It could be an endless samsaric loop that keeps them walking between flame and storm.

What the pilgrim on this narrow path of devotion knows, what is the certainty that he or she may call *shinjin* (faith or 'deep entrusting'), is that escaping the endless path between the rivers can never be the consequence of one's own efforts (*jiriki*, self-power). As samsaric beings, we cannot, out of our own efforts, transcend the predicament of sorrowful birth and death. Our only hope, our true faith, is in Other Power (*tariki*), the promise of Amitabha Buddha. Within this way of devotion, walking the narrow path between storm and flame, must be our expression of faith.

As I walk my cayo-shore, bare feet sloughing into the sand, ankles splashed by surf-waves, I can recognize the pilgrim's dilemma, even on this tourist island. On one side is a beautiful but fatal liquid landscape. I am no creature of the sea and, while I may bounce and bob for a while, I can never dwell there. On the other side, my true samsaric home resides. I can follow the planked walkways to the resort. I can pause at any number of refreshment stands and I can sample the endless *animacion*. I can return to our cool balcony where the roar of the ocean and the beats of salsa music vie for attention. Were I to tire of those distractions, I could move further inland where locals eke out spare lives in coffee and coconut plantations. I could wait out my week and fly back to the comforts of my Northern home.

All these options are there for my choice but all are just variations on the theme of *dukkha*. No matter the level of material wealth, no matter the degree of distraction, *dukkha,* that insatiable sense of lack, remains. All this amid the endless heat of the Caribbean sun, my own version of the river of flame and the storm-cloud-edged ocean, my river of storms. And so, I walk the endless beach, balancing between storm and flame, attending the Voice That Calls.

WHAT HAS BEEN LEARNED

The over-arching point we have made in this journey is the legitimacy and integrity of contemplative walking. There are at least these 10-plus practices that fall into the bowl of contemplative walking practice and together they constitute not just a random collection, but a set and an integrity of practices. I would like to suggest some points of learning, for myself and for you, which we can identify from this excursion.

Buddhist practice and practice instruction always included walking practices.
Buddhists can undertake the Eight-fold Path through walking. Walking practices are not something recent, adapted or borrowed from some other culture or faith. The mythologic stories of the Buddha start with his first three steps; the historical details begin with him stepping down from his horse and walking into the forest. The Sangha, from its earliest times, with a group of wandering monks following the teacher, was a walking community. From that time forward, Buddhist experience has been, to a large part, a walking experience. From the beginning, practice and instruction included some forms of walking practice.

Walking and sitting practices are not alternates, nor is one superior.
Many teachers and teachings have presented walking practice as a minor practice at best, and as nothing more than a break from 'real practice', that is sitting meditation. I believe we can dismiss such 'meditation snobs' who frown on anything other than endless staring at walls as a preliminary practice, something suited only to feeble beginners. Walking practices open up opportunities for sincere and profound contemplation, well within the demands of the most demanding of stationary seated practices. It enriches practice for beginners and mature practitioners.

Walking and sitting are ends of a 'practice continuum'.
Beyond any notion of walking as alternate or relief, we can consider walking at one end of a practice continuum and sitting practices at the other. As surely as one works intensely and inwardly with mind, the other works equally intensely and outwardly with body and space.

We might return to our borrowed metaphor of crossing and dwelling which Tweed uses to define religious activity. Recall that he believes religions involve the making of homes and the crossing of boundaries. In practice terms, we recognize that sitting practice is much more akin to setting up a residence, building a home. The Sanskrit *asana,* usually used to mean a pose or stance, also means to make one's abode. There is a static foundation, there is a fixed geographic location from which one takes and out from which one examines multiple viewpoints. There is the intensity of exploring inner self. Walking practice as crossing boundaries, allows the body to arise in constantly transforming contexts and spaces, it pushes practice towards insight into physical boundaries and into an intuited experience of the body in relation to material and immaterial space. Ultimately, both practices have the identical aim, the end of all suffering. They approach that endeavour from different perspectives, as well as from different locations on the practice continuum.

As end-points on a continuum, both walking and sitting support and enhance each other, they are not exclusionary nor individually adequate to our contemplative ends.

Not only are walking and sitting not alternates, as end-points, there is a complementarity to them. As ends of a continuum, it is never a matter of choosing one over the other, but one of emphasizing a location of balance appropriate to the moment of practice. There will be times when more of one has greater value than another. One is never intrinsically better or preferable. The preference, as we see in most Buddhist decisions, is instrumental and pragmatic – what fits for right now?

Furthermore, I would maintain that while one might (and many have done) cultivate a temporarily exclusive practice of one kind or another, even the preferred means of practice will include elements of both, because each contributes unique insights, less available in the other means. Simply put, our practice is strongest and most flexible when it benefits from moving and stationary practices. Its doubtful that ripping off our eyelids and planting ourselves before a cave wall for several decades, as Bodhidharma's legend tells he did, is other than hyperbolic. Even taken from the long view, his life practice balanced walking and sitting.

No one practice is superior, all have their value and benefit.

This book has presented 10-plus walking practices, primarily from Buddhist practice history, a few from outside but related. I have tried to represent how each practice has benefits to offer to the contemplative walker, within and without the Buddhist Sangha. Some teachers or traditions may say theirs is the fastest, simplest, most powerful, most direct, most authoritative and so on. I believe there is no hierarchy, no 'king of practices'. As the expression goes in East Asian Buddhism, 'there are 84,000 forms of practice'. It is ideal for any aspiring walker to undertake all of these practices (well, maybe not all 84,000!). Each of us should learn and cultivate many practices so we can select the most appropriate for our practice foundation at that time of our development. Only when we have tried and tested the methods will we have the wisdom and capacity to make the best fit.

Walking as a contemplative method is multi-faith and can be an inter-faith phenomenon.

As we have seen in this book, walking has appeared in Buddhism and in other major world religions. For example, at very least, the practice of pilgrimage is effectively a universal practice. People will walk for contempative purposes. People of all faiths have and will do so. Secondarily, like many other contemplative practices, walking allows people to practice their faiths together. Christian prayer-walkers and Buddhist *nembutsu* practitioners and Hindu mantra-reciters can practice walking together, to the benefit of all. In some respects walking practices offer unparalleled opportunities for inter-faith activity.

Many schools and faiths have contributed to the set of walking practices.

The aspiring contemplative walker must acknowledge many faiths have made contributions to the set of practices we have available. Buddhism has made its contribution, and is possibly the leader in such practices. Nonetheless, labyrinth walking, prayer-walking and walking for change, all of which originate outside the Buddhist methods, offer substantial benefits to walkers. Even within Buddhist history, different sects and schools have contributed uniquely. Rinzai's 'racing *kinhin*', the Tendai *kaihogyo* and Pure Land's walking *nembutsu* do not spring from a single source, nor a single insight. Each represents a unique insight and expression of religious methods.

Walking as a contemplative practice is fundamentally different from recreational walking.

We have made this point in several instances. Those who propose 'jogging (or skiing or motorcycle riding or a hundred other claims) is my meditation' really don't understand the defining qualities of contemplative walking. Contemplative walking is primarily a contemplative activity, one which engages body and mind in a reflective and inquisitive process directed at questions of meaning. Walking as we mean it here may produce better health, may be relaxing, may foster friendships and may connect us with our natural world in new ways. These, however, are not its primary purpose. For the recreational walker, such results are foremost, not for the religious walker.

This is not to separate the two kinds of activity, only to distinguish them from each other. For example, it is commonplace in our Tendai practice schedule to have what we call Walking the Way practice. This means that, following a period of sitting practice, we will practice outdoor walking practice. We follow single file and engage in mindful walking and chanting. Typically the walk takes us to a certain point – in one location, it is a bridge over a natural spring, in another it is a nearby lake. The walk leader has the option, usually taken, to end the practice at that point, usually about 30 minutes along. They then announce that the return walk can be formal or informal as walkers prefer. Some will stroll back in conversation with each other, some will walk apart, continuing their formal practice. The distinction between practice walking and social walking has been made clear.

As with sitting practice, proper form reinforces and deepens practice, but form also relates to physical capacity.

I previously mentioned one particularly 'anal' meditation instructor who insisted that if you did not sit in a particular way you were 'wasting your time'. For me, it wasn't until many years later that I realized how much time I was wasting by forcing my body to compose itself according to some model of perfection. I have come to appreciate that most bodies share common structures and that certain patterns of composition and alignment result in greater degrees of strength and focus. Age and accident can change our bodies and their capacities. It is necessary for the practitioner to experiment with their own body, to get to know it well enough that they can allow it to, in a sense, self-compose. My experience has demonstrated that my body, when respected and cultivated with an openness to its idiosyncracies will unfold into its most powerful and dynamic possibility. As in any other lessons, bullying and enforcement are counter-productive.

There are ideals of posture, or form, as it is called. They are like the fine black teak *Buddha-rupa* (statue of Shakyamuni) I often use in setting up a remote training event. That figure demonstrates the ideal, the seated Shakyamuni, to which we ought aspire, to what we can compare ourselves. We can adjust, experiment and relax towards that form without pushing or forcing ourselves. When we realize Buddha, it is as ourselves, not through forcing ourselves to fit a static image or conception.

Likewise, when we are engaged in walking practice we ought be aware of proper form. The roll along the sole of the foot, the backward lean to posture, the extension of the neck, are all forms to explore and aspire towards. Forcing the body will only create blockage and tension. The flow of chi-energy does not come smoothly under pressure.

Conversely, it is unacceptable to pretend that form does not matter, that we can stumble along however we like. Whether it is a theological or practical matter, that 'it just feels right' is hardly a reliable standard. Thousands of years and hundreds of thousands of teachers have undeniable value. Feeling right and doing right are two separate things. My less experienced fellow-practitioners regularly report the difference to their own practice experience when they discover, learn and incorporate some fine point of walking form.

Walking while engaged in other practices is more than simply additive.

I have tried to emphasize that the combination of practices with walking (chanting, mindfulness, visualization) is not simply additive – like walking and chewing gum. I believe that the combination actually creates additional power for the practice. For example, chanting is above all a body practice. Therefore walking and chanting offers a kind of super-charging by bringing deeper and deeper resources from the body through its engagement in walking.

It is unlikely that walking practices constitute a distinct *marga* or *yoga*.

In Asian practices, a set of methods will be defined as a distinct *marga* (path). Often the term yoga was used. In Indian religion the contrast was often made between *jnana marga*, the way or methods of insight wisdom, as contrasted with, say, *bhakti marga*, the way or discipline of devotion or *karma yoga*, the fulfillment of spiritual duty. When I first began this writing journey, I speculated that walking practice might be an as-yet unnamed *marga*. I even hypothesized it as *kara marga* (the way of movement) or *padankan marga*, (the way of the foot). I wondered if it might be possible to construct a set of practices that could represent a fully comprehensive course of training leading to Awakening. I wondered if it might be a parallel to *zen* (meditation) or *jodo* (devotion) or *mikkyo* (esoteric ritual).

As I have outlined in the above points, I prefer not to isolate walking practices as a separate *marga*, but rather to view them as constituting one end on a continuum of practices, relative to sitting meditation.

Walking has yet to be adequately or proportionally represented in Buddhist art, story-telling or practice instruction.

I have been repeatedly surprised at how walking practice has slipped into the background of Buddhism. I do not yet have an adequate explanation why images of walking Buddhas exist only in one artistic aesthetic, the Thai. The three poses of sitting, standing and reclining dominate all other cultures. When we consider the pre-eminence of walking as the lived experience of the Buddha and Buddhists, it defies logic that such images are so rare. Further, I am baffled why the walked experience of the Buddha and Buddhists is so slightly represented in literature and art. Ours is a tradition of instruction with and while on the road. How is it that this shared experience is so little valued and represented? Was this the influence of the residential Sangha wanting to distance itself from the forest renunciant tradition? Were there other artistic and stylistic conventions inherited from Indian art and religion that simply got re-embedded in Buddhism?

I am convinced that, to date, this stands as the first work in English to attempt to gather all walking practices into one coherent set of practices. It strikes me as odd that, in 2500 years, across dozens of interpretations and cultures, this has not been attempted. I am confident that the attempt is not absurd nor forced. I can only hope that others will recognize this gap in both study and teaching and address it vigorously.

The study and advancement of walking as a set of contemplative practices has only begun.

When I first conceived of this book I expected to locate it within the recent and past studies of walking as a practice. To my practitioner's surprise, researcher's dismay and marketer's delight, I found I was walking on barely touched ground. As noted numerous times above, contemplative walkers, except in the practices of pilgrimage and *kaihogyo,* have very had little guidance. Those who want to undertake walking as a contemplative endeavour have a thin library from which to read. Those who want to take a more critical look at walking within the behavioural sciences have an even thinner one. And yet the spiritually-inclined of most faith traditions have turned to the road for their experiences for centuries.

There is now an opportunity for those engaged in research, promotion and development of pilgrimage, labyrinth, *kinhin*, prayer-walking and so on to consider the commonalities of these practices and work collaboratively on this topic and practice. As there are for hundreds of other activities and subjects, we can now associate together in some kind of 'society for the advancement and promotion of walking as a contemplative activity'. We have many models to guide us and only a shared vision to be realized.

RE-ENTERING OUR DWELLING – IMAGINING THE NEXT CROSSING

This book began, was drafted, reflected on, critiqued and re-drafted on the trail. Some of it was up and down Byers Road, my own version of Thoreau's favourite Marlborough Road, some of it on an old reclaimed rail-line bed, the K and P (affectionately known as the 'Kick and Push', which runs from Pembroke to Kingston, Ontario), some of it along the key-beach in Cuba. For me, the road has been my school and my text-book, my companion and my teacher, my friend and my tormentor. It wears uncountable garments, from grey and dusty to green and lush. Like the Dharma itself, when I think I have captured it with my own or my camera's eye, it laughs and shows me a hundred new scenes.

Now, like every pilgrimage or hour of *kinhin* or walk in the labyrinth, the boundary crossing phase of this adventure draws to a close and our former dwelling-place comes into view; we return home. As is frequently the case, that view arises differently with our now-shifted perspectives. The walk changes things, and not surprisingly, for we mostly undertake our walks with that motive. As already listed, we can identify some general lessons we have learned from this book. Equally important, at least for me in these closing pages, is to consider what meaning I may draw from my own page-wandering. I expect, as with any purposeful contemplative walk, the meaning will deepen and shift over time. I came to write this book because in my own practice I found myself much less inclined to sit in a zendo than to walk. Walking began to offer great opportunities for my own awareness and opportunities to share with newer practitioners.

Allow me to borrow an image from one of my favourite Japanese films, *Departures*. This Oscar-winning film is remarkable for many reasons and has been shared and discussed in our Sangha many times. One sub-plot is the separation the main character, Daigo, a frustrated cello player, feels from the father who abandoned him as a child. Several times through the film, Daigo tries to remember him but the father's face is only a blur. At the story's conclusion, there is resolution, in both senses, and there is reunion.

There was a similar resolution for me a few years ago in relation to a past practice experience which brought me insight into walking practice. About twenty years earlier, when I was in the most intense part of my then-Zen Dharma training, I had a recurring visual experience. When I would sit, I would observe a bobbing figure in my visual field. Sometimes, it was just an out-of-focus shape, sometimes it arose as the back of a person. I could never make out any details of its face or identity. I understood then and now that we ought not make such visual images 'mean' anything. That only reinforces the false sense of specialness and egoity of the practitioner. I simply let the figure arise and tried to allow it to be 'in the space', as we say. Like Daigo, my image-figure became familiar, and it remained just out of focus. Besides the shape and size of the figure, the only constant of this experience was that it seemed to be someone walking ahead of me, as if I was following, and staring at the back of the figure's head. It seemed to be leaning on some kind of staff. (What's that you say, Dr. Freud?)

More than a decade later, after I had moved away from the Zen style, and ceased having that experience, I became interested in and familiar with the popular Japanese Bodhisattva, Jizo. His connection to care-giving, protection of the natural world and pilgrimage resonated strongly with me. I can't recall the exact moment, it may have been during my first *kaihogyo* experience. It was definitely in the course of a group walking practice. As I was walking and attending to preserving the space and pace relationship with the person ahead of me, that bobbing figure arose again in my mind's eye. As with Daigo, when the clear vision of his dead father's face restores his memories, my figure's details sharpened and turned to look back at me. It was none other than the Eternal Pilgrim, Jizo. In that moment I allowed a meaning to unfold. (I will not propose that this was what it 'really' was, only that I explain it this way.) I came then to understand that all those past sitting times, when I observed that out-of-focus image, I was behind the walking Jizo and he was leading me/drawing me/calling me to the pilgrim path, to walking practice. Out of that experience, I began to consider walking practice as more than something to do in and around sitting. In Jizo I found inspiration, companionship, authenticity of practice and momentum to explore what walking could be.

Since that time, I have continued to learn about Jizo, especially in his status as Timeless Pilgrim. I have let that image of him walking just ahead of me, occasionally looking back at me with encouragement and care, remain, more in my heart than eye. I have come to understand that notion of *dogyo ninin*, 'a practice of two together', that none of us ever walks alone. That, in turn, has opened the door to a number of visualization and *nembutsu* practices, such as described in this book.

There are moments on the trail when we break through the trees and suddenly stand on the shore of a silent lake. We come over a crest of a hill and a valley breathtakingly sprawls before us. Other times, the trees simply become less dense, or tall trees reduce to shrubs and scraggly bushes. In other landscapes, the sandy flatness acquires more definition with brush and spotty habitation. With much less drama we find ourselves at the end. When I reflect on my appreciation for walking as a practice, it more closely resembles the gradual than the sudden. There was never an 'aha' moment where I knew what walking had to offer. It has been more like that pair of hiking boots that grow more comfortable and broken in with every walk. In much the same manner as this book itself, each chapter of my walking life has shone a new perspective on the humble practice of one foot in front of the other.

Unexpectedly for me, my deepening appreciation for the possibilities of walking has similarly deepened my appreciation for sitting practice. Whereas I began expecting walking to be an undocumented alternative *marga* or set of practices, an exclusive one that would stand alongside sitting or devotion or ritual, I have grown to understand it as part of the sit/walk continuum defined above. As such the two ends of the continuum have grown in my esteem as a consequence. Which is to also say that my new understanding for the width and breadth of walking has re-defined my appreciation for what Buddhist practice or, more generally, any contemplative practice can offer. Because walking is so – dare I say it – pedestrian, so ordinary, it reassures us that the many varieties of contemplative practice begin with unremarkable and ordinary activities. Like breathing or sitting, walking is a plainly human activity which we can use and explore to reveal that which lies within our humanness.

The Ten Ox-herding Pictures are a set of drawings, popularized in 12th century Japan, representing an every-man in one stage or another of looking for a missing or mis-behaving 'ox'. They are a metaphor for our own search for our 'ox', Truth, and the struggle with mind and self that arises within that. The series begins with the herder-seeker thinking something is missing and beginning his search. It moves through the next half-dozen images with the man glimpsing, chasing, tying, riding the ox and so on. The third last is where some people think the search ends, since it is illustrated by an empty space or circle, symbolizing 'a heaven so vast, nothing can stain it'. The ninth is often called 'Reaching the Source'. Finally and how apropos to our journey, the tenth and concluding image is a jolly old man, bulbous pack and bulbous belly, strolling into the marketplace from his wanderings, with ragged clothes and feet covered with road-dust. Sometimes subtitled 'In the World', this final unexpected image teaches us that, at its beginning and end, the Dharma-path is walked right here in this world. And, I emphasize, walked, right here as this world. I do not suggest that I have found and released my 'ox', nor that I have reached the end of this journey. I'll let others evaluate whether my belly is bulbous. My 'ox' evades me still. What I have found, in and through my relationship with walking and its symbolic mentor, Jizo, is the comfort and certainty that my feet are following a well-worn trail. Jizo, the embodiment of the Dharma-message which may be in and out of my sight, will show me the walking trails which bring me to the end as surely as one foot follows the other. I have also learned that the trail has many tangents, many sideroads and shortcuts. I have no Google-view of the whole; I have no laminated guide. The ox appears where he will, the trail unfolds as it will. What matters is the walking-mind we bring to it.

In these pages, we have crossed boundaries and returned to our dwelling place. I sincerely hope, you will continue to feel the call to return to the trail, to once again cross those boundaries of familiarity and routine, to enquire into our shared spiritual questions. I hope the shape and form of your journey will never bore you, that it will tantalize and tempt you to continue. I further hope you have come to understand that neither the crossing nor the dwelling represents any final goal, and that together they offer a complementarity to our spiritual aspirations. Resting and moving contemplative practices, I am sure, need and contribute to each other. Perhaps they will, as the road becomes home, become the other.

As you take to your roadways, wherever that may be and whatever practice you take with you, know that, in the spirit of *dogyo ninin* – the practice of travelling together – you walk in the company of Shakyamuni – the home-leaving Buddha, Jizo the Eternal Pilgrim, Kobo Diashi and St. James, the pilgrimage saints, and one humble and creaky-kneed Tendai priest from Canada. Your every step echoes with those of countless others who are walking somewhere with you. All of these companions urging you onward with a heartfelt 'Gambatte' – Keep strong on your journey, pilgrim!

And remember, as Guthrie notes at the end of *Random Walk*:

> You couldn't take the credit for much because once your feet were on the path, it was no great trick to keep them moving. And you couldn't pride yourself on thinking up the idea, because something outside yourself put the thought in your mind... Either way, he knew what to do. Just take it one step at a time, and remember to alternate feet.

AFTERWORD

Those of us who have spent time on the trail know of the echoes and memories that follow us long after we reach the trail's end. The poles and boots are stored back in the closet, we scan the photos, read over the journal entries, swap tales with our companions. Walkers, as we've asserted in this book, know the cycle of crossing and dwelling, of inhabiting in-between spaces, of setting out and settling back. Every walk completed contains the seed or call for the next. What was over that hill? What would have happened if I took that side-trail. What would it be like in winter? Where might we walk next time? It befits me here to draw together some of the ideas and inspirations which came up over the past pages and suggest what future adventures may offer.

THE SOCIETY

In the closing chapter of *Walk Like a Mountain*, I proposed:

> There is now an opportunity for those engaged in research, promotion and development of pilgrimage, labyrinth, *kinhin*, prayer-walking and so on to consider the commonalities of these practices and work collaboratively on this topic and practice. As there are for hundreds of other activities and subjects, we can now associate together in some kind of 'society for the advancement and promotion of walking as a contemplative activity'.

I am convinced there currently exist sufficient interested academics and practitioners that forming such a 'society' is feasible. I further suspect there is a desire and a will to reach out to each other, to join each other on this trail and see where it might take us. Thanks to those who have encouraged this idea in the pre-print months.

To that end I have established a blog link (http://society4walking.blogspot.ca/). This will provide a focal point for the organizing of such a society whose activities might include:
- creation and sharing of popular and academic writing;

- an inventory/database of related resources and contacts;
- criteria for contemplative trail development;
- sharing of news and initiatives in contemplative walking;
- promotion of trails for contemplative purposes;
- collaboration on trail-related activities for shared purposes;
- workshops directed at skill development and instructor development;
- establishment of a network of interested partners;
- in time, an international conference related to walking as a contemplative activity.

As you've read earlier in this book, no one walks alone. I invite your interest and participation in this endeavour. I welcome your advice, ideas and energies to make this a reality.

THE SCHOLARLY TOME

In my introduction, I referred to a road-not-taken – a *magnum opus*, a wise and scholarly tome that examined images of foot and walk in the most obscure Indian and Chinese texts, that traced the teaching tradition across all schools. This still remains to be written, although I suspect, not as a single definitive volume. I have learned in the writing that there remains a huge unexplored region of Buddhist history, philosophy, and teaching related to walking practices. The vacuum is not confined to the Buddhist tradition either. The same questions can be applied to other traditions as well.

The background question of why walking and foot practices seem so left out in Buddhist literature and art remains a puzzling one. Implied in that question is a broader question which considers the walking experience as an experience shared across religious traditions. We have images of Christ teaching on the mountain, of Moses at the end of a journey across the desert, of Shakyamuni offering sermons at rest points, and dozens more. What role does the journey before and after these religious moments hold in the teaching? Tweed has proposed the image of crossing/dwelling as the definition for religions. How can we understand and integrate the tradition-shaping crossings, what are primarily walking experiences, of world religions?

I will continue to ruminate on these questions and I enthusiastically welcome others to join me on the journey.

WALKER'S SUPPORTS

Walk Like A Mountain was consciously developed as a handbook so as to become a resource for active contemplative walkers. In Buddhadharma we know that the triad of faith-ethics-practice defines our tradition. No matter the depth of Dharma literature, no matter the determination to promulgate the faith, we are always called to exert ourselves through practice. Buddhists are, by definition, practitioners in action, even if that action is staring at walls or chanting the *nembutsu*.

The book was partially developed with the intention of making walking practice, in its many forms, possible, easy and disciplined. What follows on the book then must attend to the needs of practitioners. Here are some of the preliminary possibilities for add-ons to the book currently in development.

The Trail Companion

This is a small accompaniment for walkers which will include:
- selected chants;
- a walk planner and checklist;
- selected quotes form the book;
- samples of trail exercises and reflections;
- This may be in either or both of a portable print format or an electronic 'app'.

Walk Like A Mountain Training Events

These will be facilitated retreat-style events which will provide teaching based on the book's material in abroad multi-faith environment.

National and International Pilgrimage

These would engage contemplative walkers in the creation, development and walking of a substantial walk symbolizing the unity of the North American spiritual community, beyond borders, beyond politics. Such walks would bring together walkers, national communities and border-sharing communities-of-good-will who are willing to prepare a supportive environment for international pilgrims.

The Manda-Lab

In Chapter 9, I proposed the development of what I call the manda-lab:

> I imagine a crossroad of those two practices – the manda-labyrinth. We can replace the traditional labyrinth shapes, as described above, with traditional mandala patterns. These too have extraordinary symbolic and ritual detail, which can serve to educate us of a Buddhist understanding of the universe. More importantly we can literally walk these patterns as a physical version of the same meditative practices for which they have normally been used.

Such a product might be a diagram or an actual walking pattern, permanent or mobile, or simply the means to create one. Exactly what this might look like or how one might acquire one remains for others to ponder. I have begun such an enquiry and hope to write more of my experience in the near future.

All of these possibilities and more will be located and developed through two web-based locations, http://www.tendai.ca and http://www.padakun.com. I invite all readers and walkers to consider how to take this initial journey forward, to join me in this endeavour.

May all your walks be rich and fulfilling, and may we someday share the trail, and as Shakyamuni reminds us – *You cannot travel the path until you have become the path itself.*

Innen Ray Parchelo,
Renfrew, Ontario

A WALKER'S BIBLIOGRAPHY

SUTRAS

Chihmann, Upasika, translator. *The Vows of Samantabhadra*. Singapore: Buddhanet.

Pitt, Chin Hui, translator. *The Original Vows and the Attainment of Merits of Kshitigarbha Bodhisattva*. Singapore: Buddhanet.

Tendai Buddhist Services Manual. Canaan: The Tendai Buddhist Institute.

Reeves, Gene, 2008. *The Lotus Sutra*. Somerville: Wisdom Publications.

ARTICLES

Amidon, Elias, 2000. "Mall Mindfulness," in *Dharma Rain*. Berkeley: Shambhala.

Bell, Teja, 2011. "Qigong for Meditators," in *Tricycle*, Summer issue

Brandon, David, 1986. "Bankei – Seventeenth Century Japanese Social Worker?" in *Beyond Therapy; The Impact of Eastern Religions on Psychological Theory*. London: Prism Press.

Carney, Eido, 1998. "Takahatsu in America," in *Tricycle*.

Cianciosi, John. "Mindful Nature Walking (One Step at a Time)," in *Yoga Journal*, http://www.yogajournal.com/practice/773

Curry Daichi, 2009. "Today is the final day of my walking practice" in *Mountain Practice Blog*, http://mountainpractice.wordpress.com/?s=today+is+the+final+day

Gup, Ted, 2011. "The Weirdness of Walking to Raise Money," in *New York Times*, June 18.

BOOKS

Arnold, Matthew, 1971. *The Light of Asia*. London: Routledge & Kegan Paul PLC.

Artress, Lauren, 2006. *The Sacred Path Companion*. New York: Riverhead.

Basho, Matsuo, author, Nobuyuki Yusua, translator, 2005. *Narrow Road to the North and Other Travel Sketches*. New York: Penguin

Bays, Charlotte Joko, 2002. *Jizo Bodhisattva*. North Clarendon: Tuttle.

Block, Lawrence, 2008. *Random Walk*. New York: Open Road Integrated Media.

Chen-hua, 1992. *In Search of the Dharma*. Albany: SUNY Press.

Chuckrow, Robert, 2002. *Tai Chi Walking*. Wolfeboro: Ymaa Publication Center.

Deadman, Al-Khafaji and Baker, 1998. *A Manual of Acupuncture*, Seattle: Eastland Press.

Coleman, Mark, 2006. *Awake in the Wild: Mindfulness in Nature as a Path of Self-Discovery*. Makawao: Inner Ocean Publishing.

Elftman, Herbert, 1960. *Dynamic Structure of the Foot*. New York: Columbia University Press.

Fletcher, Colin, 2002. *The Complete Walker*. New York: Knopf.

Flickstein, Matthew, 1994. *Journey to the Center: A Meditation Workbook*. Somerville: Wisdom Publications.

Groner, Paul, 2002. *Ryogen and Mount Hiei*. Toronto: Scholarly Book Services.

Hahn, Thich Nhat, 1992. *Peace Is Every Step: The Path of Mindfulness in Everyday Life*. New York: Bantam.

_____, 2005. *The Long Road Turns to Joy*. Berkeley: Parallax Press.

_____, 2006. *Walking Meditation*. Louisville: Sounds True.

Halzer, Josh, 2000. *Warrior Walking*. Dallas: Beckett Media (Unique Publications).

Jacobsen, Knut, 2008. *South Asian religions on display: religious processions in South Asia*. Oxford: Routledge.

Kortge, Carolyn, 1998. *The Spirited Walker*. New York: HarperCollins (HarperOne).

Louv, Richard, 2008. *Last Child in the Woods: Saving Our Children From Nature-Deficit Disorder*. Chapel Hill: Algonquin.

Miéville, China, 2010. *The City and The City*. New York: Random House (Del Rey).

Mundy, Linus, 1996. *The Complete Guide to Prayer-Walking: A Simple Path to Body-and-Soul Fitness*. New York: Crossroad

Pandita, Sayadaw, 2000. "The Five Benefits of Walking Meditation," in *This Very Life*. Walnut Creek: Saddhamma Foundation.

Paranivatana, Senarat, 1971. *The Art of the Ancient Sinhalese*. Colombo: Lakehouse Investments.

Pollan, Michael, 2003. *Second Nature: A Gardener's Education*. New York: Grove Press.

Sato, Koji, 1977. *The Zen Life*. Boston: Shambhala (Weatherhill).

Statler, Oliver, 1983. *Japanese Pilgrimage*. New York: HarperCollins (William Morrow and Company).

Stevens, John, 1988. *The Marathon Monks of Mount Hiei*, Boston: Shambhala.

ten Grotenhuis, Elizabeth, 1999. *Japanese Mandalas: Representations of Sacred Geography*. Honolulu: Univ of Hawaii Press.

Thoreau, Henry David, 1854 (2010 reprint). *Walden or, Life in the Woods*. London: Collector's Library.

_____, 1862 (2008 reprint). *Walking*, Minneapolis: Filiquarian Publishing.

Turner, Victor, and Turner, Edith, 1995. *Image and Pilgrimage in Christian Culture*, New York: Columbia University Press.

Tweed, Thomas, 2008. *Crossing and Dwelling: A Theory of Religions*. Cambridge: Harvard University Press.

Yin Kuang, Master, Smith, Forrest (ed.), Tam, Thich Thien (trans.), 1993. *Pure Land Zen*. New York: Sutra Translation Committee.

ABOUT SUMERU

For further information about books from The Sumeru Press, please visit our website at **www.sumeru-books.com** or use this QR code:

www.ingramcontent.com/pod-product-compliance
Lightning Source LLC
Chambersburg PA
CBHW032253150426
43195CB00008BA/437